COLLABORATIVE
GOVERNANCE

COLLABORATIVE

PRIVATE ROLES FOR PUBLIC GOALS IN TURBULENT TIMES

GOVERNANCE

JOHN D. DONAHUE AND RICHARD J. ZECKHAUSER

WITH A FOREWORD BY STEPHEN BREYER

PRINCETON UNIVERSITY PRESS   PRINCETON AND OXFORD

Published by Princeton University Press, 41 William Street,
Princeton, New Jersey 08540
In the United Kingdom: Princeton University Press, 6 Oxford Street,
Woodstock, Oxfordshire OX20 1TW
press.princeton.edu

Second printing, and first paperback printing, 2012
Paperback ISBN 978-0-691-15630-9

The Library of Congress has cataloged the cloth edition of this book as follows

Donahue, John D.
Collaborative governance : private roles for public goals in turbulent times /
John D. Donahue and Richard J. Zeckhauser.
p. cm.
Includes bibliographical references and index.
ISBN 978-0-691-14979-0 (hbk. : alk. paper)
1. Public-private sector cooperation—United States.
2. Public goods.   I. Zeckhauser, Richard.   II. Title.
JK421.D65 2011
352.3'7—dc22   2010041767

British Library Cataloging-in-Publication Data is available

This book has been composed in Minion Pro and Helvetica Neue
Printed on acid-free paper. ∞
Printed in the United States of America

3 5 7 9 10 8 6 4

To Frank Weil,
with gratitude for his vision and staunch support.

CONTENTS

FOREWORD

Stephen Breyer

Americans are pragmatic. They recognize that the goods and services they seek will likely be supplied (1) by private firms operating in free markets, (2) by firms that are heavily regulated by government, or (3) by government itself. They debate the comparative merits (or the appropriate mix) of these three basic delivery systems—often on ideological grounds. Yet even as they do so, they pragmatically seek systematic ways to improve the performance of each.

Thus, over the course of a century or more, government agencies and the courts have developed and applied rules of antitrust law in order to help free marketplaces function better by keeping them competitive. During most of the twentieth century government agencies developed systematic ways to set prices for, and to control the output of, highly regulated firms, such as electricity producers; and they later found ways to relax (or even sometimes to eliminate) those controls when they believed that doing so would better serve the public. More recently, government regulatory agencies have made conscious efforts to find less restrictive, more effective methods for carrying out health, safety, and environmental regulation, sometimes substituting incentive-based systems or negotiation-based systems for more traditional command-and-control regulatory methods.

In this book the authors, two highly qualified academic experts, seek pragmatically to find and to explore one of the better ways to deliver several different kinds of government goods and services, including some services that now take the form of regulation. In doing so, they draw their subject matter from a vast array of government activities of highly diverse kinds. Governmental entities are responsible for spending more than 30 percent of America's gross national product (see p. 33 below). The federal government alone employs two million civilian employees (see Bureau of Labor Statistics, U.S.

Department of Labor, *Career Guide,* www.bls.gov/oco/cg/home.htm). These government employees help the government obtain, provide, or regulate taxes, welfare, social security, defense, pharmaceutical drugs, education, highways, railroads, electricity, natural gas, stocks and bonds, banking, medical care, public health, safety, a better environment, fair employment practices, consumer protection, and much else. And, in carrying out their tasks, they may write regulations, resolve disputes, investigate private behavior, impose sanctions, license businesses, supply goods or services directly, or enter into contract with private firms to help them secure their public objectives. In a word, governmental programs are large, their subject matter is diverse, and they come in many different shapes and sizes.

From this panoply the authors select a range of actual or potential activities that they call "collaborative." The term refers to instances in which government officials seek to fulfill a public mandate through collaboration with private firms, groups, or individuals. Simply entering into a contract with a private firm to do a job, say, trash collection or prison management, does not necessarily involve collaboration, for the contract may control too many details about what the private firm is to do. But where the government grants to the private entity a significant amount of general "discretion" as to how to get the public job done, then the relationship is "collaborative" (particularly if the government reviews and modifies the delegated authority over time).

In conceptualizing and analyzing the "collaborative" relationship, the authors have performed a major public service. For one thing, governments at all levels ever more frequently enter into collaborative relationships in order to deliver public services of different kinds. The authors, for example, studied the delivery of four kinds of service (park management, emergency medical services, worker training, and preschool education) in six cities. And they found that all the cities but one (Oakland, California) delivered one or more of these services through collaborative arrangements with private entities.

For another thing, the authors help our understanding of the relationship by setting forth a conceptual framework that includes several basic reasons why the government might consider collaboration. The government might seek *productivity,* sensing that the private sector possesses comparatively greater ability to transform limited resources into improved results. Thus government has collaborated with private firms in an effort to make port facilities safe from terrorism (a collaboration that worked well). And it similarly collaborated in its effort to remove enriched uranium from Russia, by selling it to American nuclear power generators (a collaboration that did not work well).

The government might believe that private firms have greater access to *information* that can make the program more effective. Thus the Occupational Safety and Health Administration found it more productive to require employers at individual firms or plants to increase safety by developing and following their own plans rather than simply following detailed OSHA rules.

The government might believe that collaboration with the private sector will give a project greater *legitimacy*, as, for example, when the Agency for International Development collaborated with private non-profit (and other) organizations in order to enhance the credibility of various of its international assistance projects. And the government might believe that collaboration will bring it *greater resources*, as, for example, when the City of New York collaborated with (and received resources from) private firms and individuals in order to rehabilitate its city parks.

Further, the authors provide a general account of potential costs and benefits that arise when government collaborates. On the one hand, the public is likely to benefit insofar as collaboration confers *productivity discretion* upon private entities (say, firms doing business at ports) that are likely to know how to operate or to achieve goals (say, port safety) more effectively. On the other hand, the public may suffer insofar as collaboration confers *payment discretion* on private entities and those entities find ways to enhance their own payments at the expense of the public goal. A private firm helping implement a safety program, for example, might distort its recommendations where doing so will lead to the adoption of systems that later mean extra sales of its own, or related firms', products. Similarly, the public may suffer insofar as collaboration confers *preference discretion* on private actors and those actors then make choices that further their own, perhaps idiosyncratic preferences. (Who will choose the works of art on display in newly refurbished public parks?)

As importantly, the authors provide numerous case studies, rich in detail. They include instances in which collaboration has produced major public benefit, for example, the creation of Millennium Park in Chicago. They include instances where collaboration was a failure, for example, collaboration with private banks in the federal student loan program. They include instances of great importance to the nation, as in education (through the development of charter schools) and health care (through Medicare and drug testing). The discussion, which illustrates their conceptual framework, is useful in helping us understand what went right, what went wrong, when government should enter into collaborative programs, and how these programs might be improved.

Finally, the book emphasizes that any successful collaborative program will evolve over time. It requires continuous monitoring, check-ups, revisions. It requires the government officials to continuously analyze the aspects of their programs that might call for collaboration, of what kind, with what incentives, with what kinds of evaluation. Those officials must subsequently assign roles, design the resulting program, and assess the consequences, which assessment, in turn, should lead to reanalysis. The government manager, say the authors, is something like a circus ringmaster, continuously managing a broad variety of program participants as the program proceeds and then is rewritten. Again, examples give concrete meaning to these general approaches.

Both in the development of its conceptual framework and in its application of that framework to specific examples, the book gives rise to hope. It does so because it shows that collaboration offers a pragmatically sound approach (and a reasonably nonideological approach) for the securing of many public goals. It shows how application of a few simple conceptual tools can help prevent collaboration's failure. And, in doing so, it offers us direct hope for major improvements flowing from collaborative efforts in fields such as education and health care.

The authors' view is nonideological, but I see in their collaborative emphasis a further virtue of an idealistic kind. To encourage those in the private sector, in private firms or in private nonprofits, to strive to achieve public goals collaboratively with civil servants means that those employed primarily in the private sector can spend a portion of their working lives involved in public projects as well. That collaborative effort to achieve public goals inevitably helps to break down barriers between public and private. And that is very much to the good in our constitutional democracy, whose future depends upon the widespread sharing of the view that government is not "us vs. them"; rather, government is "us" *and* "them," working together.

PART I

The Promise and
Problems of Collaboration

Chapter 1

◇◇◇

Private Roles for Public Goals

We live in turbulent times. No doubt it always seems so, but as the twenty-first century hits its stride the gauge of stress and tumult seems well above par. The global economy is wobbling; housing prices have boomed and busted; jobs have evaporated; retirement funds have shriveled; iconic financial institutions stagger from bankruptcy to bailout. And these are just the moment's problems. Looking ahead —and not all that far ahead—we face massive challenges: finding ways to power the economy without fouling the planet, fulfilling the pledge of affordable health care for all, and securing the future of Social Security. Schools fall far short of what parents expect and students require. Roads, bridges, and levees are crumbling from old age and overuse. Big challenges are standard for this restless country, to be sure, but those today beat the norm by a considerable margin.

No one believes, given the complexity and cost of the tasks we confront, that simply scaling up the standard governmental solutions is the answer. Government too often finds that it lacks the skill, the will, and the wallet to figure out a fix and get it done. Corporations— which some hope will be spurred by their sense of social responsibility to save us from the perils that beset us—are often struggling to save themselves, and resist devoting resources to any problem if a profit, direct or indirect, isn't part of the solution. And private charities have too few resources to take up every burden that government shrugs off. A particularly vivid recent trend was the surge in governmental responsibility for shoring up private institutions. That surge both demonstrates that familiar boundaries between sectors have been much in flux, and masks the less dramatic but more durable trend that is this book's focus—the escalation of private-sector involvement in undertakings traditionally considered the province of government.

Yet troubled times can also offer opportunity. We have a tough-minded president with big ideas and the courage to surround himself with some of the nation's best thinkers and doers. The Obama administration came into office with a mandate not only to rescue the country from pressing threats but also to improve the way government works. But such improvement, paradoxically, requires looking beyond the boundaries of the state itself. The magnitude of the problems and the ambition of the goals that mark our era mean that government, on its own, is overmatched.

The Obama administration, its sister administrations at the state and local levels, and governments to follow in the future need what the military calls a "force multiplier," some systematic way to ramp up the impact of government's efforts. We believe that *collaborative governance*—carefully structured arrangements that interweave public and private capabilities on terms of *shared discretion*—can be that force multiplier.

Agencies at all levels face a range of opportunities to collaborate with private actors to achieve public goals more effectively than government can on its own. When well applied, the collaborative approach can be a powerful lever for creating public value. But it is often misunderstood—confused with conventional contracting or charity, or merged with wooly conceptions of public-private partnership—by policy makers and the public alike.

A careful review of the evidence from governments—local, state, and federal—convinces us that the performance of America's government will often hinge on making the best use of collaborative governance. It leverages private expertise, energy, and money by strategically sharing control—over the precise goals to be pursued and the means for pursuing them—between government and private players. That discretion simultaneously motivates private collaborators to enter the public arena and empowers them to play their roles well. The collaborative approach unleashes the unpredictable resourcefulness of an entrepreneurial citizenry to devise fresh and flexible solutions.

Done well, collaboration creates synergies between governments and private participants, allowing them together to produce more than the sum of what their separate efforts would yield.

This approach to getting things done is far from new. Those inclined to view public affairs as, until recently, the state's exclusive domain, might contemplate imperial Roman tax administration, which was delegated to private revenue agents,[1] or the fabled history of the British East India Company, which often acted as a diplomatic and commercial extension of the British government. Lewis and Clark's "Voyage of Discovery," which opened the American West, was a private expedition operating with a loose, flexible mandate from President Jefferson. But those were simpler times. Government and society today are vastly more complex and the whipsaws of change more rapid and pronounced. And while collaboration between governments and other entities can be found in nations across the globe, it is an approach uniquely suited to the market-friendly, bureaucracy-wary culture of the United States.

We are not claiming to have discovered some new species of organizational interaction, nor do we pretend to any startling degree of conceptual novelty. Most of the ideas in this book (or most modern books, for that matter) would not be big news to Adam Smith, Jeremy Bentham, or John Stuart Mill, and some first-rate twentieth-century work on collective action provides us with both inspiration and some direct antecedents for a portion of what you'll encounter here.[2] Our key innovations are, first, to distinguish among frequently confounded forms of public-private interaction; second, to focus with special care on the implications of shared discretion—its rationale, its potential dark side, and the tradecraft required to manage it; and, third, to orient the collaborative approach to some pivotal problems of today and tomorrow.

---

[1] Samuel E. Finer, *History of Government* (Oxford University Press, 1999).

[2] Some of our very favorites in this regard are Mancur Olson, *The Logic of Collective Action: Public Goods and the Theory of Groups* (Harvard University Press, 1965); Robert Axelrod, *The Evolution of Cooperation* (Basic Books, 1984); Oliver Williamson, *Markets and Hierarchies* (Free Press, 1975); and Ronald Coase, "Theory of the Firm," *Economica* 4 (1937). Both Coase and Williamson were awarded Nobel Prizes for their work, respectively in 1991 and 2009.

There is an enormous political science literature on coalitions, social capital, networks, and other relevant concepts.[3] The pitfalls of collaboration—from crony capitalism to political machines—are also well documented.[4] Legal scholars have explored collaboration and related topics at great length, sometimes with impressive insight, and almost always in a language all their own.[5]

[3] Robert Dahl, *Who Governs? Democracy and Power in an American City* (Yale University Press, 1961). Dahl's 1953 book with Lindblom, *Politics, Economics, and Welfare*, draws an interesting distinction between "polyarchy-controlled" institutions and "price-system controlled" institutions. Their treatment of polyarchy-controlled institutions deals with government agencies; collaborative governance imports private institutions into this domain. In the political science tradition we also admire Robert Putnam, *Making Democracy Work: Civic Traditions in Modern Italy* (Princeton University Press, 1993) and *Bowling Alone: The Collapse and Revival of American Community* (Simon and Schuster, 2000), and the work of John Elster, particularly *The Cement of Society: A Study of Social Order* (Cambridge University Press, 1989). A classic in the network literature is David Knoke and James Kuklinski, *Network Analysis* (Sage Publications, 1982); an influential later contribution is Timothy Rowley, "Moving beyond Dyadic Ties: A Network Theory of Stakeholder Influences," *Academy of Management Review* 22, no. 4 (1997). In an example of the network literature with particular relevance to collaborative governance, Kevin McGuire argues that an informal network—originating mostly in elite law schools (nonprofit), seasoned in court clerkships or stints in the solicitor general's office (government), and currently or prospectively belonging to top DC law partnerships (private)—holds special expertise and exercises special influence over the institution at the pinnacle of the judicial branch. "Lawyers and the U.S. Supreme Court: The Washington Community and Legal Elites," *American Journal of Political Science* 37, no. 2 (May 1993). Some interesting ideas about goal congruence—why it's great to have in collaborative arrangements, and a problem when it's impossible to arrange—come up in William G. Ouchi, "Markets, Bureaucracies, and Clans," *Administrative Science Quarterly* 25, no.1 (March 1980). Other noteworthy contributions in the political science literature include Julian LeGrand, *Quasi-Markets and Social Policy* (Palgrave Macmillan, 1990); Barry Bozeman, *All Organizations Are Public: Bridging Public and Private Organizational Theories* (Jossey-Bass, 1987); R.A.W. Rhodes, "The New Governance: Governing without Government," *Political Studies* 44 (1996); and Anne Schneider and Helen Ingram, "The Behavioral Assumptions of Policy Tools," *Journal of Politics* 52, no. 2 (May 1990).

[4] The Carnegie Endowment's Marina Ottaway explicitly characterizes (and critiques) the Global Compact—which stands as the poster child for collaborative governance on the international plane—as a lineal descendant of the European corporatism that, in a bad decade, can morph into fascism. "Corporatism Goes Global: International Organizations, NGO Networks and Transnational Business," *Global Governance: A Review of Multilateralism and International Organizations* 7, no. 3 (2001). A classic commentary on urban collaborative governance gone bad is Lincoln Steffens, *The Shame of the Cities* (McClure, Philips, and Co., 1904). See also Jorg Raab and H. Brinton Milward, "Dark Networks as Problems," *Journal of Public Administration Research and Theory* 13, no. 4 (2003), and Julia Sass Rubin and Gregory M. Stankiewicz, "The Los Angeles Community Development Bank: Possible Pitfalls of Public-Private Partnerships," *Journal of Urban Affairs* 23, no. 2 (2001).

[5] One good example here is Jody Freeman, "Collaborative Governance in the Administrative State," *UCLA Law Review* 45, no. 1 (October 1997). Martha Minow's work mostly deals with contracting, but there is much to learn from her writings that applies to collaboration as well.

There is pertinent wisdom to be harvested in many subfields of economics, including game theory, behavioral economics, institutional economics (especially transactions-cost-based theories of economic structure), and in particular agency theory.[6] The business literature, which addresses many topics closely related to our study of collaborative governance, including corporate alliances and strategic partnerships—areas of inquiry by economists, business scholars, and organizational experts—turns out to be surprisingly rich in material related to collaborative arrangements. This literature has been especially lively since the late 1980s, in parallel with the ferment of real-world experimentation with new models of interaction among firms.[7] And in the literature on public management, approaches related to

---

Her edited volume *Partners, Not Rivals: Privatization and the Public Good* (Beacon Press, 2002) and the book Minow and Freeman coedited, *Government by Contract: Outsourcing and American Democracy* (Harvard University Press, 2009), offer good overviews of how the mainstream (if a bit left-of-center) legal world thinks about these topics. A provocative book from another legal perspective is Jochai Benkler, *The Wealth of Networks: How Social Production Transforms Markets and Freedom* (Yale University Press, 2006).

[6] We have already noted our admiration for *Markets and Hierarchies* but can also recommend a more recent Williamson piece: "The New Institutional Economics: Taking Stock, Looking Ahead," *Journal of Economic Literature* 38 (September 2000). Williamson explored the relative virtues of markets and firms in the organization of economic activity. Our volume, by contrast, looks at the merits of organizing activity across the boundary of the public and private sectors, which is why agency theory is critical for its analysis. While the agency-theory literature is enormous, we confidently recommend John Pratt and Richard Zeckhauser, eds., *Principals and Agents: The Structure of Business* (Harvard Business School Press, 1985). On alliance theory more generally, see Mancur Olson and Richard Zeckhauser, "An Economic Theory of Alliances," *Review of Economics and Statistics* 48, no. 3 (August 1966): 266–279, and Todd Sandler, *Collective Action: Theory and Applications* (University of Michigan Press, 1992). Sociologist Victor Nee has done crossover work in the economics arena that draws upon and complements concepts developed by Williamson (and also Mancur Olson), among others. "Norms and Networks in Economic and Organizational Performance," *American Economic Review* 88, no. 2 (May 1998).

[7] Consider, for example, Farok Contractor and Peter Lorange, eds., *Cooperative Strategies in International Business* (Lexington Books, 1988); Bruce Kogut, "Joint Ventures: Theoretical and Empirical Dimensions," *Strategic Management Journal* 9 (1988); and a special issues of *Organization Science* featuring Mitchell Koza and Arie Lewis, "The Co-Evolution of Strategic Alliances"; Africa Ariño and José de la Torre, "Learning from Failure: Towards an Evolution Model of Collaborative Ventures" (which warns that increasingly popular collaborations "have been characterized by a high level of dissatisfaction with their actual outcomes relative to expectations"); and Anoop Madhok and Stephen B. Tallman, "Resources, Transactions and Rents: Managing Value through Interfirm Collaborative Relationships": *Organization Science* 9, no. 3 (May–June 1998). See also Ken G. Smith, Stephen J. Carroll, and Susan J. Ashford, "Intra- and Interorganizational Cooperation: Toward a Research Agenda," *Academy of Management Journal* 38, no. 1 (February 1995).

what we term collaborative governance are—a tendency toward terminological untidiness notwithstanding—thoroughly mainstream.[8]

The notion of a collaborative effort between government and the private sector sits uncomfortably in many Americans' minds. Our conventional conceptual model has government doing public work, business doing private-sector work, and charitable nonprofits filling the gaps, each sector cultivating its own garden. And for many years this conception of divided realms was a reasonably apt description of the real world. Half a century ago, the standard practice was for governmental action to be carried out by public employees, working in

---

[8] While work in this area varies enormously in quality, one entirely respectable (and relatively early) collection is Harvey Brooks, Lance Liebman, and Corrine Schelling, eds., *Public-Private Partnership: New Opportunities for Meeting Social Needs* (Ballinger, 1984). Eugene Bardach's *Getting Agencies to Work Together: The Practice and Theory of Managerial Craftsmanship* (Brookings Institution Press, 1998) deals with intrasectoral collaboration but is otherwise very much part of the intellectual tradition we aim to advance here. Stephen Rathgeb Smith and Michael Lipsky work related terrain in *Nonprofits for Hire: The Welfare State in the Age of Contracting* (Harvard University Press, 1995), as does John D. Donahue's *The Privatization Decision: Public Ends, Private Means* (Basic Books, 1989) and parts of *The Warping of Government Work* (Harvard University Press, 2008). Other noteworthy public-management texts that contribute to this conversation include Barry Bozeman's *All Organizations Are Public: Bridging Public and Private Organizational* Theories (Jossey-Bass, 1987); David Osborne and Ted Gaebler's *Reinventing Government* (Addison-Wesley, 1992); Donald Kettl, *The Next Government of the United States* (Norton, 2008), and indeed most books by Donald Kettl; Phillip Cooper's *Governing by Contract: Challenges and Opportunities for Public Managers* (Congressional Quarterly Press, 2003); and Lester Salamon's edited *The Tools of Government: A Guide to the New Governance* (Oxford University Press, 2002), especially Salamon and Ruth Hoogland, "Purchase-of-Service Contracting," pp. 319–339; Steven J. Kelman, "Contracting," pp. 282–318; and Paul L. Posner, "Accountability Challenges of Third-Party Government," pp. 523–551. Recent books and articles whose concerns and conclusions comport particularly well with ours, or else contrast with them in productive ways, include: Kettl's *The Transformation of Governance* (Johns Hopkins University Press, 2002); Stephen Goldsmith and William D. Eggers, *Governing by Network: The New Shape of the Public Sector* (Brookings Institution Press, 2004); R. Scott Fosler, *Working Better Together: How Government, Business, and Nonprofit Organizations Can Achieve Public Purposes through Cross-Sector Collaboration, Alliances, and Partnerships* (Independent Sector, 2002); Chris Huxham, "Theorizing Collaboration Practice," *Public Management Review* 5, no. 3, 2003; Ann Marie Thomson et al., "Conceptualizing and Measuring Collaboration," *Journal of Public Administration Research and Theory* 19, no. 1 (2009); David Van Slyke, "Agents or Stewards: Using Theory to Understand the Government-Nonprofit Social Service Contracting Relationship," *Journal of Public Administration Research and Theory* 17, no. 2 (2007); Barbara Crosby and John Bryson, "A Leadership Framework for Cross-Sector Collaboration," *Public Management Review* 7, no. 2 (2005); Keith Provan and H. Brinton Milward, "A Preliminary Theory of Interorganizational Network Effectiveness," *Administrative Sciences Quarterly* 40 (1995); and Rosemary O'Leary and Lisa Blomgren Bingham, eds., *The Collaborative Public Manager: New Ideas for the Twenty-first Century* (Georgetown University Press, 2009).

public organizations and under the direction of public managers. Private players, when they were involved, acted in limited and subordinate roles. As recently as the mid-1970s, America's public sector—federal, state, and local combined—devoted about 40 percent of all outlays to government workers. Today that share has slumped to less than 29 percent,[9] reflecting a shift away from direct production to grants, transfer payments, and contracts. The form and the complexity of interactions with the private sector have also changed. From a short and simple list of the stances a private organization could take in its dealings with government—constituent, contractor, taxpayer, grantee, lobbyist, adviser—the repertoire of potential roles has grown richer, more sophisticated, and, not surprisingly, more confusing. Private roles in producing public value now span a broad spectrum, from suppliers who make a buck meeting the specs of procurement contracts to philanthropists who pursue the common good at their own initiative and on their own terms. The accomplishment of many, and perhaps most, important public missions in the twenty-first century depends on private for-profit and nonprofit organizations.

Yet we—politicians, direct participants, and the public—tend to overlook or misconstrue the nature and implications of the private sector's involvement in public undertakings. There is no broad-based recognition of how extensive collaboration already is, and even less understanding of how it differs from other forms of private involvement with the public's work. And it is too often viewed through the distorting lens of ideology. Debates over the *general* propriety of private involvement in public work, though perhaps entertaining, are mostly a waste of time.[10] The conversation becomes meaningful only when it zeroes in on specific goals, specific settings, specific actors. The conditions that make collaborative governance the right answer to big questions must be understood both more broadly (by the public at large) and more deeply (by scholars and practitioners). This will enable

---

[9] These percentages are calculated from Office of Management and Budget, *Budget of the United States, Fiscal Year 2010*, historical table 15.4, and U.S. Department of Commerce, Bureau of Economic Analysis, National Income and Product Accounts, table 3.10.5, both accessed online in late May 2010.

[10] John D. Donahue, "The Wrong Question about Business and Government," *Governing*, April 28, 2010.

us to choose it selectively for the proper public tasks, avoid it when it is not the right approach, and apply it wisely wherever it is used.

A crucial first step is to recognize that many private roles in public missions are not—and should not be—collaborative, by our definition.[11] Individual charity, corporate philanthropy, and other forms of voluntarism are related to but distinct from the topic at issue here. In these arrangements discretion is not shared but is monopolized, or nearly so, by the private parties. Within very wide parameters, the choices made by private individuals and institutions are presumptively defined as fulfilling "the public good" for tax purposes. There are limits, to be sure. No corporate tax deductions can be claimed for gifts to political parties, or to the CEO's shiftless cousin. But while shareholders might quibble over grants to the chairman's alma mater, or the local polo league, and taxpayers may resent individuals' deductible gifts to arcane artistic collaboratives or exotic religious sects, the government itself has no mechanism to deny such gifts tax-favored status, short of the nuclear option of discrediting the charity itself. The donor has discretion and the government does not, despite the fact that the public sector is a party to the undertaking in that it surrenders revenue it would otherwise have received. No doubt this arrangement promotes occasions of waste or triviality or self-dealing at times, but there are strong reasons for protecting donors' discretion against governmental second-guessing on the merits of the mission. Few among us, for instance, would want government to be in the position of declaring which religions are acceptable and which are not.[12]

A municipal government contracting with a private waste-management company represents the other end of the spectrum. Dis-

---

[11] The murky boundary between "public" and "private" organizations poses a chronic risk of imprecision. A generation ago two scholars observed that a "number of competing approaches have been used to define the public-private distinction, and each has different implications.... To avoid continuing the confusion, provisions for definition must be considered in planning for future research." James L. Perry and Hal G. Rainey, "The Public-Private Distinction in Organization Theory: A Critique and Research Strategy," *Academy of Management Review* 13, no. 2 (1988): 185. This is a sensible plea, often reprised by other authors, and generally ignored.

[12] The comptroller of Texas attempted to strip Unitarianism—one of America's oldest denominations—of its status as a tax-exempt church in 2004, on the grounds of excessive heterodoxy, but reconsidered after mild local protests and louder national ridicule. Ken Herman, "Unitarians Get Religious Status after Intercession," *Austin American-Statesman*, May 25, 2004, p. B-1.

cretion rests entirely with the government. The company's charge—to pick up the garbage and dump it at the landfill—is explicit, complete, and geared to the government's priorities. If town officials want the garbage to be collected on Fridays instead of Wednesdays, starting with Maple Street instead of Elm, or incinerated instead of buried, government is at liberty to alter the mandate so long as it pays up as promised. Such arrangements are common and, when objectives are readily defined and measured, are likely to be entirely appropriate. In collaborative governance, by contrast, each party helps to determine both the means by which a broadly defined goal is achieved, and the specifics of the goal itself.

Collaboration in the Concrete

Chapters to come brim with specific examples of collaboration, but a few quick previews right up front will help to clarify how collaborative governance differs from other ways of getting collective tasks accomplished.

A Park in Chicago

In the mid-1990s Chicago's city government regained control of a choice downtown parcel, long lent to the Illinois Central Railroad. The plan was to build a much-needed underground parking lot, topped with turf and perhaps a few benches and statues. In hopes of lightening the burden on the city's budget, Mayor Richard Daley approached local business leader John Bryan about raising $30 million in private money to help pay for the project. Bryan accepted the mayor's bid for private involvement and raised it—but with a crucial twist. He called for making the acres above the parking lot a cultural showplace, not just a green space, by letting donors put their stamp on a particular piece of the park in exchange for substantial contributions.

It took more time and money than either Daley or Bryan originally expected, but the basic strategy of sharing discretion to motivate private collaborators worked brilliantly. Chicago's wealthiest family, the Pritzkers, commissioned a fabulous Frank Gehry open-air concert hall as the park's centerpiece. Communications giant AT&T led a consortium of donors to provide an elegant plaza surrounding an instantly iconic sculpture by the up-and-coming artist Anish Kapoor. The Crown family hired an edgy Catalan artist to design a fountain for its corner of the park. On occasion the city turned down or insisted on revisions to a private collaborator's proposal. But Chicago's public leaders generally gave running room to families, companies, and individuals who wanted to contribute, reasoning that they had every motive to make sure the projects to which their names were attached would find favor with Chicago's citizens. By the time the undertaking was completed, more than $200 million in private money—its impact intensified by donors' expertise and influence—had poured into the twenty-four-acre plot, dwarfing the public resources devoted to the project. And from the day it opened in mid-2004, Millennium Park has been wildly popular with Chicagoans and visitors alike, a glittering and happily crowded cultural jewel at the heart of downtown. (Millennium Park is discussed in detail on pages 264–271. Another noteworthy venue of collaborative governance, New York's Central Park, figures prominently in chapter 7, where we also discuss the remarkable history of the city's parks system as a whole.)

A School in Massachusetts

On a decommissioned army base forty-five minutes west of Boston, nearly four hundred middle school and high school students absorb an updated model of progressive education at an unusual school. Even the peculiar architecture of the school signals its hybrid status—two-story modular buildings bought secondhand from a nearby college are stitched onto an old redbrick elementary school building. Students at the Francis W. Parker Essential Charter School come from more than twenty cities and towns, drawn to Parker's distinctively intense, stripped-down curriculum and its tradition of close interaction between faculty and students. Advisory groups gather every morning to discuss the day's work, and knit it into the academic year's overall plan. Teachers of English, fine arts, math, and technology plan their lessons together to present students with an opportunity for integrated learning. Rather than giving multiple-choice exams, Parker monitors student progress and readiness for promotion through the exhaustive evaluation of portfolios of student work. These features are common at the pricey, exclusive private schools—Groton, Deerfield, Phillips Andover, Winsor—operating elsewhere in Massachusetts. But Parker is a public school, chartered by state government and funded with government money, some from the state and some diverted, at the state's decree, from the cities and towns where Parker students live. Parker was founded in 1994, in the first wave of Massachusetts charter schools, by a handful of local parents and educational reformers.

The terms of the school's relationship with Massachusetts education officials give Parker a substantial but not unbounded range of discretion. It can create a trademark learning culture and call on all students to embrace "the Parker Way." But it cannot pick and choose its student body; it is required to draw by lottery from a pool open to every school-aged resident of the region. It can follow its leaders' lights in shaping a curriculum very different from that of the conventional public school. But it must subject its students to the same standardized tests as does every other Massachusetts public school, and must submit to consequences should its students' performance fall short. It can raise private grants to supplement the resources that come from government. But it cannot charge any student a dime to attend. Parker is thriving, with the throng of students wanting to attend vastly outnumbering available spots, a growing roster of grateful alumni, and a stellar reputation among Massachusetts parents and educators alike. (The Parker School, and other charter schools, get much fuller treatment on pages 79–103.)

Protecting Ports with the Coast Guard

Bad things can and do happen at American ports. During World War I German agents blew up two million pounds of Europe-bound ammunition in New York's harbor, ravaging the port area and inflicting damage on the Statue of Liberty that weakens its structure to this day. But the passage of many decades without serious incidents lulled Americans into viewing port protection as a second-order issue. That complacency ended abruptly on September 11, 2001. Officials and citizens alike were vividly aware of the vulnerability of ports packed with vessels, cargo, and people from all around the world. An attack on port facilities could cripple commerce. Sabotage at a fuel depot or a dockside natural-gas tanker could obliterate broad swaths of a city. Or a nuclear device could be smuggled quietly through any of the country's hundreds of ports to wreak culture-changing havoc anywhere inland.

It fell to the U.S. Coast Guard to figure out a way to fix the vulnerability. It was easy to imagine any number of clumsy, costly ways to do the job. New laws, or new interpretations of existing laws, could make private parties strictly liable for the consequences of any security breach. If policy truly could impose liability for every eventuality, and if insurance companies could calibrate with precision every portside risk, then the desire of shippers, vessel owners, and port operators to secure liability insurance at less-than-ruinous rates would inspire an effective and entirely private security regime. But not even the most ardent free-market fundamentalist seriously proposed such an arrangement. Too many things had to go right for market-driven port protection to work, and the consequences of failure could be catastrophic. A classically governmental security system was another alternative. The Coast Guard could ring every harbor with a cordon of armed cutters. Vessels would be allowed to pass only after the Guard inspected them from bow to stern light to ensure that neither cargo nor crew nor the ship itself posed any danger. Parallel procedures on the land side would check the identification of all personnel and the provenance of vehicles and shipments arriving at the port by road, subjecting each to the same sort of thorough security scrub. Such arrangements would no doubt lower risks substantially. They would also be stunningly expensive to the government and would cripple waterborne commerce, thus accomplishing aspiring terrorists' objectives without even requiring any effort on their part.

Instead, the Coast Guard created a port-protection system that was thoroughly collaborative. There was a role for insurance-inspired private initiative, to be sure, and a role for armed cutters as well. But the mainstay of the security regime was an intricate skein of provisions specific to each port, each private party, and each type of risk. The Coast Guard defined its role with respect to these provisions as two-fold: first, relentlessly demanding a high level of security for every aspect of every port, and, second, scrupulously reviewing proposed provisions to ensure that they really did deliver the risk reduction that private parties claimed and that the government required. What the Coast Guard did *not* do was insist on any uniform method to be applied across the whole varied spectrum of harbor facilities, shippers, vessels, and other diverse components of hundreds of separate operations. By embracing the collaborative approach, the Coast Guard sought (successfully, by the inevitably partial evidence to date) to square the imperatives of security and smooth commercial operations at America's ports. (The Coast Guard's port protection efforts are discussed in more detail on pp. 64–66.)[13]

The Spectrum of Discretion

There is nothing inevitable or immutable about these examples. Indeed, it was not fated for there to be *any* substantial private role in any of these undertakings. Governments can and generally do manage parks, run schools, and provide security. For present purposes, though, we want to dwell not on the divide between direct and delegated delivery, but rather on the diversity *within* that category of delegated delivery. In so doing, we aim to enrich your sense of what we mean by collaborative governance, and to map the domain it occupies within our repertoire for getting things done. The key, once again, is the allocation of discretion.

What marks Millennium Park as a collaborative enterprise is the conscious decision to let private players exercise influence over what kind of park would be built. This is by no means the only option for a private role in the provision of parks. Roughly 10 percent of the spending on Boston's public parks (as of 2007), for example, went to

---

[13] We discuss port protection in even more detail, invoking a metaphor that we adore, in "The Tummler's Task," a chapter in a forthcoming volume edited by Mark H. Moore.

hire private contractors to provide pruning, turf care, building maintenance, and other services. While some cities, including Oakland and Raleigh, rely almost exclusively on city employees to build and run their parks, in most places some degree of contracting is the unremarkable norm. In contrast to collaboration, however, contractors hew to the government's priorities, exercising little discretion on their own.

Providing another revealing contrast with collaboration, as we use the term, are those parks and aspects of park operations that fall at the other end of the spectrum, with private actors holding most of the discretion. Barely two hundred miles south of Millennium Park, near the center of Indianapolis, a swath of manicured grass, shrubs, benches, and paths winds among redbrick buildings. The terrain is unfenced; neighborhood residents often stroll its greenswards. So who is responsible for this admirable public park? It is actually neither public nor a park. The appealing acreage is part of the headquarters complex of drug giant Eli Lilly. Lilly designed green space into its campus with an eye toward aesthetics and employee morale. Then, to encourage good community relations, it invited residents to share the space.

Voluntary private roles are common, too, in many strictly public parks. Sometimes individuals or institutions donate their time, expertise, or money as their spirits guide them, with government playing a passive role. At other times the relationship moves toward the middle of our spectrum, and public and private capabilities intermingle on terms of shared discretion. Chapter 7 explores some particularly worthy examples in New York City, but such arrangements are sprinkled across many locales. In parks as in other areas, no sharp border exists between collaboration and other forms of private involvement. But the spectrum of discretion provides a meaningful metric of the different ways public and private energies interact to advance collective goals.

So, too, with schools. In Massachusetts, as in every other state, most primary and secondary schools are government run. Our focus, though, is once again on the diversity *within* the broad category of private-sector involvement. Let's start this time with the end of the spectrum featuring mostly private discretion. Here we find famous private prep schools, bound like any other institution to obey state environmental laws and local building codes, but operating with near-complete discretion on specifically educational matters. We also find a much larger number of schools run by religious organizations—more than fifty Roman Catholic secondary schools alone in just this one smallish state. And, exemplifying a different model, we find a welter of voluntary private efforts in and around public schools, from PTAs and endless sign-up lists for volunteer activities, to local educational foundations that fund activities that schools' public budgets can't. To continue the tour, a great deal of private involvement in education comes on terms that leave all or most of the discretion in the government's hands. Most public schools contract with the private sector to provide food services or transportation or maintenance or other services instrumental to but separate from the core educational mission. Many schools also contract for accounting services, teacher training, library management, special education, and other functions that are more complex than running a steam table or school bus, but still amenable to delegation through a well-specified contract. Only some examples of private involvement in education, in short—indeed, only a relatively small fraction—feature the shared discretion that defines them as collaborative governance.

Table 1.1 illustrates how collaborative arrangements in the examples mentioned are situated within the broader terrain of private

TABLE 1.1
The Range of Private Discretion in Public Missions

	Parks	Schools	Port Security
Discretion mostly public	Contracts for maintenance, turf care, etc.	Contracts for food service, transport, etc.	Contracts for security patrols, monitoring technology, etc.
Substantially shared discretion	Millennium Park	Charter schools	Coast Guard–orchestrated security regime
Discretion mostly private	Corporate parks Traditional voluntarism	Secular and religious private schools Education foundations	Security arrangements left to shippers and port operators

involvement in public missions. Our central concern in this book is the range defined by the middle row of substantially shared discretion, though we remain mindful of (and sometimes detour into) the neighboring realms of contract and charity.

The Price of Collaboration

The shared discretion that is the hallmark of collaborative governance can augment government's capacity for accomplishing public missions and increase the flexibility with which such missions are pursued. But shared discretion also extracts a price. Authority becomes ambiguous, strategic complexity grows, and accountability breakdowns proliferate. The critical question for policy is when that price is small and when large relative to the gains achieved from granting discretion. When that price is small, discretion should be shared; when large, held tight.

The sorts of arrangements we describe in this volume have been used to create public value for a very long time and will continue to do so in the future across a broad range of governmental goals. Yet collaborative governance is often an improvised, ad hoc affair, cobbled together by creative practitioners on a trial-and-error basis. Seldom do particular instances of collaboration draw from or add to any common pool of lessons learned. As such it has a mixed record, often working exceedingly well, but sometimes not so well at all. When it succeeds, it produces significant public benefits, as most of our examples will show. But often it is used when it shouldn't be, or ignored when it should be embraced. Even when it is applied in the right situations, the process may be so ineptly designed that it fails to produce much benefit. And when misapplied or bungled in implementation, it can do serious damage.

Given the economic events of the recent past—including the massive governmental rescues of private companies that brought themselves to the brink through their own greed or folly—it is understandable that some readers may instinctively recoil at the notion of granting discretion to government's private collaborators. Some might see our enterprise as representing either a prodigious degree of immunity to evidence, or else cynical cover for more government subsidies and bailouts. Far from it.

The messy financial rescues of late are, we believe, once-in-a-lifetime events that in most instances expose critical failures in past governance. Indeed, while the financial breakdown had many causes, high on the list was confusion over the true nature of the links among public and private actors in the financial system. Key relationships were deeply collaborative, by the standards we develop in this book. But they were not recognized as such. Misunderstanding bred mismanagement. Government doled out discretion to private players on the basis of custom, convenience, or ideology rather than disciplined thinking about how discretion should be used—and how it might be abused. Ensuring that the citizenry understands the prospects and risks of potential investments, for example, is a crucial public mission. But government essentially turned over to the private ratings agencies—such as Moody's and Standard and Poor's—the task of informing the public about the health of financial firms. The government believed, with good reason, that these agencies had the capacity to ferret out and disseminate salient financial facts, but it paid little heed to the raters' incentives when employing their discretion.

Discretion unmonitored is frequently discretion abused, and so it was here. The agencies were paid by the firms they rated. Not surprisingly, they rated generously, and inconsistently. Similarly, the government assumed that it could count on each financial player, such as Lehman Brothers or Goldman Sachs, to investigate the finances and assure itself of the solvency of those whose obligations it stood behind or whose guarantees it accepted. But with each financial firm trading with dozens of others, none had sufficient incentive to intensively monitor its trading partners and raise the alarm in the event of extreme or systemic risks. The government stood by—in some cases under the illusion that its regulations really effectively controlled private behavior, in others counting on private actors to do the right thing of their own volition. With no one rating the raters, no one

monitoring the monitors—in short, no real *governance* in this puta-
tive governance regime—no one recognized how flimsy our financial
sector had become.

That economic debacle may inspire some to insist that government
forswear corrupting entanglements with a tainted private sector and
carry out its work all by itself. Not surprisingly, Americans lost confidence in every single private industry—some dramatically—in the
wake of the financial crisis,[14] while support for conventional governmental programs at least briefly surged.[15] But such a shibboleth against
involving private players in public missions, however understandable, would be both perverse and at war with widely shared values.

The right kind of delegation is, if anything, even more desirable
than it had been before the bubble. The evaporation of so much national wealth, along with the near certainty of straitened public finances for years to come, means we cannot afford to pass up any
chance to create public value more efficiently. If we are smart—and
lucky—a new generation of the right kind of collaboration will
emerge from the wreckage of misbegotten collaboration.

Targeting Collaboration

Not every public goal, to be sure, requires or can benefit from collaboration. Some public functions—imposing taxes, engaging in diplomacy, and conducting military operations—are best left as exclusively governmental activities. Others are so prosaic—paving a road,
running a military mess hall—that government need do no more than
let a contract. Private discretion can't help and may well hurt. And
still other public goals may best be left to corporations or charities
with little or no government involvement at all. But that leaves a vast
middle ground between total government control and pure private
initiative that can benefit—often immensely—from collaboration,
rightly understood and adroitly managed. The challenge is, first, to be

[14] http://www.harrisinteractive.com/harris_poll/index.asp?PID=940.
[15] http://www.harrisinteractive.com/harris_poll/pubs/Harris_Poll_2009_01_13.pdf.

open to collaboration, and, second, to carefully match missions to the right collaborative models. Our aim, simply put, is to improve the odds that analysts will advise and officials will adopt collaboration where collaboration makes the most sense, and that practitioners will implement collaborative arrangements with insight, creativity, caution, and (the ultimate bottom line) success.

Collaboration can be an extraordinarily useful tool. But too often it has fallen far short of its potential. One common reason is that the governmental organizations that need to take the lead in shaping and orchestrating collaborations suffer both a lack of imagination and a characteristic conservatism when it comes to deciding how to get things done. Ideology can also militate against having the public sector grant discretion to a private collaborator. But perhaps the biggest reason why collaborative governance is underemployed and underperforms is that those in charge simply do not know how to do it. Too few people understand the critical importance of matching tasks with delivery models, and then calibrating the proper pattern of shared discretion for accomplishing a particular task. Fewer still appreciate the managerial and analytical requirements to plan and carry out a well-founded collaboration. The result is that we collaborate when we should contract, trust to philanthropy when we should collaborate, shun private engagement where it makes sense to pursue it, and embrace it where government should act alone. And when we do collaborate where we ought to collaborate, we often fail to fine-tune the arrangements in ways that obtain anything approaching all of the achievable benefits.

Even under the best possible circumstances, collaboration poses special challenges. George and Ira Gershwin were loving siblings endowed with astonishingly complementary talents—George for music, Ira for lyrics—and were both by all accounts decent and agreeable men. They still argued for days over the details of meter and rhyme in the chorus of "Fascinating Rhythm."[16] In less ideal circumstances—when affinities between collaborators are weaker, histories shorter,

---

[16] Howard Pollack, *George Gershwin: His Life and Work* (University of California Press, 2007), p. 188.

futures less foreordained, and interests less automatically aligned—
the challenges mount. This is especially so when private actors are
enlisted to advance government's missions. Authority becomes ambiguous, complexity grows, the temptation arises for the players to
work for their own ends rather than for those they are intended to
serve, and performance may be twisted to curry political favor or
serve partisan ends. The results often diverge from what was anticipated or desired. The answer to most questions about how collaborations between the public and private sectors work, or should work,
starts with "It depends ..." This volume will provide some guidelines
for finishing that sentence by helping practitioners figure out systematically what the answer depends upon.

Collaboration from the Government's Perspective

Collaborations necessarily have at least two parties, and any study of
collaborative governance can take at least two points of view, that of
government and that of the private party. We could have simply described how each party views a collaboration, hopping back and forth
from one perspective to another. But we want to go beyond play-by-
play description to offer practical guidelines for making collaborations work better. That ambition leads us to view collaboration from
the government's perspective. One reason is accidental and relatively
trivial: we teach at a school of government, and this is the viewpoint
to which we are accustomed. It is also the usual perspective of the
economics profession, where one of us has his home turf, and where
the other one frequently visits, when public-private interactions are
assessed. A more important reason is that in the rich countries in
general, and the United States in particular, people have gotten quite
good—the occasional spectacular lapse notwithstanding—at coming
up with all kinds of sturdy, sophisticated, flexible, and effective ways
to structure private affairs. Government, however, lags behind in this
regard.

But the most important reason is that we see government as a special sort of actor. Government, at its best, is authorized to define and

act upon broadly shared interests in ways that private organizations cannot. All too often government is *not* at its best, or even close to it. Real-world governments tend to fall far below the ideal sketched in a junior high civics textbook, or even in a jaded university seminar room. The mechanics of democracy can break down and stifle citizens' voices, or can be corrupted so that electoral democracy gives weak or warped signals about what the citizenry values. Flaws of judgment on the voters' part, or deception on the candidates' part, can produce duly elected leaders whose goals are at war with the majority's true interests. And officials and bureaucrats can wall themselves off from public accountability and feather their own nests.

We do not dispute that such things occur. Indeed, we probably have better-than-average familiarity with the flaws of government, both as scholars and as occasional practitioners. As coauthors, we occupy somewhat different positions on the ideological spectrum, so whatever the turn of the electoral tides, there is reliably something going on somewhere in government that appalls at least one of us, and frequently both. But while we long ago shook off romantic illusions about the public sector, we can't join those who characterize government as just another organized interest competing for resources and legitimacy. Sometimes a sneaker company or a garden club really does outdo its public-sector counterparts in defining and creating public value, but not often enough to warrant jettisoning the notion that government has the potential to be a unique category of actor. The ballot box equips government to aggregate interests in ways that other organizations match only occasionally and accidentally. Where government is absent, weak, or undemocratic—a less than clean criterion, we recognize—this generalization collapses. Thus our conception of collaborative governance applies chiefly to inevitably flawed but relatively healthy polities characterized by a decent respect for the preferences of the citizenry.

While we address ourselves most directly to government, however, we modestly aver that we have much to say to the private sector. Readers from the business and nonprofit worlds are cordially urged to join the conversation, and we expect they will find our exploration of collaborative governance both congenial and useful. Aspiring collaborators from the private sector who aim to aid in the creation of public value, after all, need to understand how smart, strategic public officials view the craft of collaboration, so that they can define *their* collaborative roles with a minimum of misunderstanding. The good actors on the private side, moreover—which in our experience describes the vast majority—have an intense interest in making sure that their government *is* smart and strategic when it comes to collaboration, and able to steer clear of the bad actors. The better-equipped government is to pick the right private partners, the safer it will be to share discretion. And the more discretion can be shared without imperiling accountability, the more scope there is for the kinds of flexibility and innovation that can make collaborative governance such a boon. So the lessons laid out here will be valuable to well-meaning readers from the private sector, both to deepen their understanding of their governmental counterparts and to more readily find or fashion their own collaborative niches. On the other hand, if you are a private player hoping to hijack government's agenda while only pretending to create public value, or a cynical official scheming to exploit private idealism ... go read somebody else's book! We don't aim to abet such intentions.

Our Goals for This Book

Collaborative Governance is meant both to provide a conceptual framework for understanding collaborative governance and to serve as a practical guide to the design and implementation of collaborative undertakings. We hope that the lessons of this volume contribute to more successful and visible collaborations, and that the exemplars it presents will prove contagious.

One of the most important lessons we want to convey here is the need to think differently about the responsibilities of government officials. The increasing importance and subtlety of private roles in public ventures mean that orchestrating collaboration, as opposed to managing agencies, will be a core competency for public managers. At one time good government may have merely entailed running bureaucracies efficiently and accountably. Now, to a large and growing extent, it depends on knowing how to capitalize on private capacity. Efficiency and accountability remain bedrock criteria for public missions, but the skills required to reach those goals must mutate with the shift from direct action to collaboration.

In the pages to come, you will encounter governments at various levels relying on collaborative efforts to pursue a wide range of missions, including resurrecting city parks, running schools, certifying hospitals, aiding poor countries, training unskilled workers, and protecting vital infrastructure. Many of these collaborations work exceedingly well. A number are a mixed bag, with some weak points, some strong points, and some question marks. And some collaborations work quite badly indeed. We hope you find the many case studies interesting, illuminating, and maybe even fun. But we seek neither to praise, nor to bury in criticism, any particular attempt at collaborative governance. We also do not seek to produce cut-and-dried recipes for just what practitioners should do when seeking to harness private capacity to public purposes. Instead, we aim to tease out the general principles that span disparate cases, and that can serve as useful guidelines for clear thinking about collaborative governance. We will succeed if our account of Millennium Park in Chicago sparks some insights, not just about parks in San Francisco, but about parks in Seoul, or indeed about health care in Somalia or urban transportation in Spain. The most valuable lessons are the ones that can leap across borders, both political and professional.

This first chapter has introduced collaborative governance and explained the parameters that distinguish it from other ways of getting public work accomplished. Chapter 2 provides the fundamental rationales for engaging in collaboration—to obtain better outcomes, more resources, or both—as well as reservations about when and how to use it. In chapter 3, "The Delegator's Dilemma," we present a detailed discussion of the role of shared discretion, the defining feature of a full-fledged collaboration, distinguishing among three forms of discretion. Production discretion is at the heart of successful collaboration, while both payoff and preference discretion channel self-serving mischief that can undermine the benefits of collaboration.

The four chapters that constitute part 2 delve more deeply into the reasons collaboration can be such an effective form of governance. Chapter 4 explains how collaboration can increase productivity, while chapter 5 examines the importance of information—who has it, whether they can and will share it, how much it matters—in motivating some collaborations. Chapter 6 examines the ways in which using the private sector to produce public value can foster legitimacy, both as a goal to satisfy the public of the worth of an undertaking and as an enabler allowing us to create government programs that depend heavily on the expertise and energy derived from private entities. Chapter 7 presents three case studies in which a major motive for government's opting for collaboration with private parties was the hope of securing more resources for public endeavors.

Part 3 approaches collaborative governance from a practical point of view. Chapter 8, "Tasks and Tools," outlines the skills individuals and groups need to determine whether and how collaboration can be used, and to design, implement, and monitor an effective collaboration. In chapter 9 we examine reasons why collaboration isn't pursued when it should be, and reasons why, when attempted, it sometimes doesn't work as well as it should. The final chapter looks at two collaborations, one of which (Chicago's Millennium Park) has racked up remarkable success even as the other (America's approach to health care) has fared quite badly.

We hope you'll draw on your own experience to make connections to the missions that matter to you. If collaborative governance is the wave of today and tomorrow—as we are persuaded, and as we hope to persuade you as well—let's learn to ride that wave with skill, grace, and a minimum of mishaps.

Chapter 2

◇◇

Rationales and Reservations

Government has a great many things to do (an extra-long list for liberals, but a not-so-short list for candid libertarians too) and lots of ways—including collaboration—of getting those things done. Picking the right delivery model for each public mission is a crucial prerequisite to effective performance. There is little reason to believe that we are systematically selecting the right mix and pattern of delivery models. The public sector in the United States, for example, spends heavily both on primary and secondary education and on medical care. Government directly delivers most of the education it pays for, but only a trivial slice of the medical care. It is conceivable that such huge disparities resulted from careful analysis, but we deeply doubt it. Accidents of history—where capacity happens to exist when an enterprise commences, or the ebb and flow of ideological tides—tend to matter enormously in the processes whereby responsibility is parceled out for public missions. But once bets are placed and stakeholders are entrenched, the status quo, logical or not, is fiercely defended.

A practical approach to collaborative governance begins with three sequential questions: (1) Is government responsible for ensuring that this particular mission is accomplished? (2) Where government *is* involved, should it act on its own or delegate delivery to the private sector? (3) Where government *does* delegate, *how* should it delegate—that is, should it use cut-and-dried contracts and simple financial incentives to motivate private players; or should it rely on private charitable impulses, leaving individuals and institutions to act on their own; or should it turn to the kinds of discretion-sharing arrangements we describe as collaborative governance? Frequently these questions become intertwined and confused. We aim to disentangle the strands, not by offering rigid rules for defining public duties, but by developing guidelines for choosing and using delivery models for the various goals that government pursues.

We set the stage with a (dizzyingly accelerated) overview of the kinds of things that government takes on—the overall agenda within which collaborative governance resides as an important and growing subset. Confusion on this point, and in particular a glaring discrepancy between what economics prescribes and what real-world government produces, threatens no end of mischief and must be addressed up front.

The most obvious objects of any sort of collective action, collaborative or otherwise, are "public goods," defined as those goods and services that, once produced, benefit a whole community.[1] Classic examples include scientific knowledge, national defense, or a lighthouse to warn mariners away from dangerous shoals. There are two defining features to public goods: one person's benefit from them does not diminish anyone else's, and it is not possible to restrict the benefits solely to those who pay. Given those features, free exchange between consumers (who would prefer to pay as little as possible) and producers (who will deliver only what they're paid to deliver) will generate too little production of public goods. Even the most dogmatic free marketeer will concede that government can and should take responsibility for "pure" public goods.

But the elegant concept of public goods doesn't reflect the reality of what governments—egged on by voters—in fact tend to do. Actual patterns of government spending have rather little to do with the principle of the pure public good. Few public goods come close to spreading their benefits equally. A homebody in Nebraska garners much less benefit from a lighthouse than does a sailor, but both are obliged to pay the taxes that keep the beacons shining. Even when citizens *consume* a good equally, they don't necessarily *benefit* equally, since

---

[1] Surprisingly, though governments have been around and providing public goods for thousands of years, the underpinnings of the public goods concept were not understood until 1954, when Paul Samuelson wrote "The Pure Theory of Public Expenditure," *Review of Economics and Statistics* 36, no. 4: 387–389. Samuelson, the first American to win the Nobel Prize in Economic Sciences, died in December 2009 as this book was nearing completion.

individuals' appetites can and do diverge. If I am nervous about possible foreign threats and you are not, I get much more benefit from national-security spending. If you marvel at the mysteries of the cosmos that leave me cold, we don't get the same value from space exploration.

It is thus a helpful concession to reality to consider two other categories of goods and services that government frequently pays for, and for which it must pick a delivery model from a list of options including collaboration: semiprivate goods and directed goods. *Semiprivate goods* are ostensible public goods that provide greatly disproportionate benefit to some individuals or groups. The public playground tucked away in a distant corner of town, for example—even if the swing sets are in principle open to all—offers extra benefit to people residing in that neighborhood. *Directed goods* are paid for publicly but are delivered to specific individuals with no pretext of equally shared benefits. While public goods occupy center stage in theory, directed goods—education, health care, Social Security checks —constitute a huge portion of actual public spending.

If we think about these three categories of government-funded goods as falling along a spectrum, we find that at one end are those whose benefits are shared, to equal degree, by all citizens. At the other end are goods that benefit only specific individuals. On a scale of 1 to 100, a true public good, such as a tornado-warning siren in a twister-prone Oklahoma town, might score close to 100. A semiprivate good, such as a neighborhood park, might be ranked 50. And a publicly funded college education for Jenny Jones would have a value below 10.

Just as with public goods, our special categories of directed and semiprivate goods rarely appear in pure form but come in a nearly infinite variety of alloys. When government delivers higher education at a state college, or pays for it through Pell Grants, part of the justification is that an educated citizenry confers broad social benefits. But few would disagree that Jenny and her family reap many times more than a pro rata share of the benefits from Jenny's college degree. A new state highway from Springfield to Oakdale might be a genuine boon to the nation's motorists, but it especially benefits people living in Springfield, Oakdale, and points in between. A single service often has both directed and semiprivate aspects. A summer-job program steers employment opportunities toward disadvantaged youth (directed good), who are put to work beautifying road medians in some parts of town (semiprivate good). Two congressmen might concur on the merits of assimilation assistance directed to political refugees, but a representative from California might prefer a program focused on Afghans clustered in the Bay Area, while one from Michigan might focus on help for Iraqis concentrated near Detroit.

Government's direct role in the delivery of public, semiprivate, and directed goods can range from heavy to light (see table 2.1). But the potential for virtually any collectively financed good to feature large directed and semiprivate elements has crucial implications for collaborative governance. The good news is that government can recruit and motivate private actors through the careful identification and judicious manipulation of directed and semiprivate features. The bad news is that private actors may themselves be better equipped to manipulate the public services with which they are involved, often in hard-to-monitor ways, maximizing directed or semiprivate elements and draining away the broad public benefits that provide much of the rationale for collective financing. Directed and semiprivate aspects of publicly funded goods both shape, and are shaped by, the actions of private players involved in their delivery.

The Agency Relationship

Collaborative governance is actually a special form of a general arrangement that scholars refer to as an "agency relationship." Such relationships, at their simplest, feature two players: the "principal," whose interests are to be served, and the "agent," who is tasked with serving those interests. Civilized life features an intricate network of such relationships. Thus a taxi driver and his fare represent an agent and a principal, as do a lawyer and her client, a doctor and his patient, a senator and her constituent, the executive director of a nonprofit and the organization's board, a corporation's CEO and its stockholders.

In an agency relationship, the principal's interests are supposed to take precedence. But her interests and the agent's interests tend to diverge, sometimes subtly, sometimes profoundly. You would like to have a careful, unhurried office visit with your doctor, but he is eager to get on to the next patient. The CEO would like to maximize value for his shareholders, but he also likes to collect a large annual bonus whether or not shareholder wealth rises. The passenger would like to take the quickest, cheapest route between her hotel and the airport; the cab driver would like to run up the meter on the outlying perimeter road.

Even when interests diverge, agency relationships would present no problems if the principal could monitor and control the actions of the agent. A principal who is solidly in the driver's seat with a clear view of what is happening can simply require the agent to serve her goals. But such control is frequently impossible because the principal does not know what the agent knows and often cannot see what the agent sees. A traveler in an unfamiliar town can't tell whether the cab driver's route to the airport is really the shortest. If the doctor recommends a high-profit procedure, the patient may not be aware of the relative risks and benefits. Even when she does have a clear view of what the agent is actually doing, the principal will not always be able to determine whether it is in fact the best course of action for advancing her own interests. Few heart patients seeing test results would know whether a bypass operation is indicated.

Collaborative governance can be thought of as a form of agency relationship between government as principal and private players as agent.[2] The same is true of simple contracting, but in those sorts of arrangements the governmental principal aims to impose firm control. In collaborative governance, as we have noted, the governmental principal willingly grants its agent a certain amount of discretion. This is not to do the agent any favors but comes as a consequence of

[2] It is actually always more complex, in that government itself is the agent of the citizenry. In some of our examples we assume that *this* agency relationship is working reasonably well; in others we explore the implications of potential lapses in government's fidelity to citizens' interests for the relationship between government and *its* private agents.

reasoned judgment that sharing discretion will pay off in terms of performance. There are also potential losses engendered by the granting of discretion, as we will explain in theory and illustrate in practice throughout this book. For any number of reasons the agent may deviate from the assigned mission. The principal incurs costs when these deviations occur, and from the efforts it undertakes to prevent them. Perhaps counterintuitively, finding effective ways to limit such losses is good news for both parties. The tighter the link between the relationship's likely outcomes and the principal's desires, the more the principal can loosen the leash constraining the agent. In short, principal and agent have an aligned purpose on one critical matter: to align their purposes.

The rationale for involving private players in public work, again, is to amplify government's ability to accomplish its missions. Why and when government should (or should not) engage private capacity to get its work done—and on what terms, whether contracting or charity or collaboration—will be the result of a bundle of conflicting arguments. A major private role can provide superior productive efficiency. But it can also invite the private provider to distort the mission to meet its own preference rather than those of the broad public, or to siphon off benefits at the public's expense. Once the *general* pros and cons are well understood, it is then possible to examine specific public missions, and to decide what kinds and what degrees of private involvement are justified.

Our special concern is collaboration, where government relies on private actors whom it motivates, influences, and constrains, but does not fully *control*. This incomplete control, moreover, is deliberate, acknowledged, and (for reasons we will shortly explain) a prerequisite to high performance. Yet that same lack of full control gives rise to reservations about delegating public duties, since private actors can exploit their share of control to advance their own ends. In short, collaborative governance can offer real advantages but no free lunch. Fundamental trade-offs in values and objectives are always involved when the private sector acts on behalf of the public sector.

A diverse bundle of factors, driven by decisions made (or not made) by multiple actors over a long time, has shaped the status quo of private involvement and made it what it is. To undo all that has gone before in the name of some theoretical ideal is often quite costly. Shaking up stale arrangements, conversely, can sometimes yield major advantages, quite apart from their theoretical merits. Whether the more promising watchword is "If it ain't broke, don't fix it" or "Throw the rascals out!" generally depends on a careful assessment of the net costs and benefits, not just of reaching our destination, but of undertaking the journey itself.

An Appropriate Level of Collaboration

The broad policy debate between liberals and conservatives is often framed in terms of the proper size of government. That argument tends to be somewhat sterile. Each side points to the other's weakest areas—the woefully inefficient government operation, the private firm doing expensively and badly what governments elsewhere do cheaply and well—to make its case. Minds are rarely changed.

We can generate more useful results if we recognize that the American government's share of the economy—whatever hooting or cheering we hear from partisans, pundits, or demonstrators—is unlikely to depart wildly from the 30-something percent of GNP it has occupied for decades.[3] We can then set out to identify the areas in which government should act directly, and where it should defer or delegate. Shifting the focus away from the size of government, and instead toward how government gets its work accomplished, will generate less ideological heat and more analytic light.

Government spending across the spectrum of public, semiprivate, and directed goods, over time and between sectors, displays great variation in the use of collaboration. Table 2.1 shows how delivery

---

[3] From 1970 to 2008 the average was around 31 percent, ranging rather narrowly from 29 percent (in 1973, 1974, 1999, and 2000) to 33 percent (in 1983, 1991, and 1992). The governmental share bolted its historical range as the overall economy shrank and emergency measures swelled public spending, reaching 36.1 percent in 2009. But we expect this spike to last only a few years. Office of Management and Budget, *Budget of the United States Government, Fiscal Year 2011*, historical table 15.3.

TABLE 2.1
Reliance on the Private Sector

	Light Private Involvement	Heavy Private Involvement
Public goods	Logistics for defense, 1970	Logistics for defense, today
Semiprivate goods	New York City parks, 1950	New York City parks, today
Directed goods	K-12 education Social Security	Higher education Medicare

models can vary dramatically within a single category of spending, with no obvious differences in the underlying rationale.

Again, the political mood when policies were introduced and subsequent inertia frequently explain the assignment of a particular delivery model to a particular task better than does any objective assessment of its appropriateness. Medicare's pharmacy coverage program (Part D) was enacted in 2005 under the conservative administration of George W. Bush, whose party controlled both houses of Congress. Not surprisingly, private providers are the ones offering insurance. Social Security was passed in 1935 under FDR, when liberals were in charge. It features no major role for the private sector. Significant changes for either program seem unlikely in the near future, barring an improbable shift in America's political center of gravity.

Other arenas, though, offer better prospects for reconsideration. The budget for defense logistics, for example, ebbs and flows as history unrolls, as this mission has no powerful domestic constituency to anchor the status quo. This makes it more likely to be reconsidered in the light of new evidence or arguments. The dramatic shift for New York City parks, addressed in some detail in chapter 7, was the product of a funding crisis that made the prior delivery model untenable. As demographic currents bring new floods of students and parents into underperforming schools, the prospects grow for reform.

We lament the tendency for initial arrangements to become petrified policy, and encourage aspiring reformers to seize every opportunity to consider delivery models on their merits. A fresh perspective and a skeptical eye conduce toward a more logical pattern of delivery models for the things that government does—and on balance, we believe, a larger role for collaboration.

The Motives for Collaboration

There are many reasons to pursue a collaborative approach to government's missions, but most of them can be summarized as the search for *better outcomes,* or *more resources,* or both.

Better Outcomes

This justification applies when the government has a well-founded expectation that engaging private collaborators will produce more public value, relative to the resources used, than the public sector could deliver on its own. The explanation might be the primal advantages in productive efficiency that are conventionally, and for the most part correctly, attributed to the private form of organization. Two further factors, beyond an Economics 101 productivity edge, may enable private organizations to produce more output from the same resources. They may have better *information* about what should be produced. A private corporation, for example, may be better equipped than any public entity to offer a well-targeted job-training program for the hard-to-employ. Similarly, private production may offer *legitimacy* advantages. If the citizenry prefers private to governmental delivery, for whatever reason, the legitimacy thus bestowed becomes an advantage that can render results produced through collaboration better than those produced by government, quite apart from productivity itself.

There are thus three reasons government may secure better outcomes if it collaborates with the private sector. These three—productivity, information, and legitimacy—are the subjects, respectively, of chapters 4, 5, and 6. The decision diagram presented in figure 2.1 summarizes the logic of pursuing better outcomes through collaboration.

We present this, for simplicity, as a choice between outcomes that are known with certainty. The success of real-world collaboration will

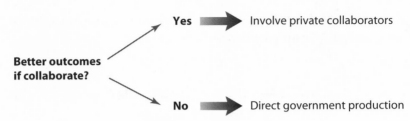

Fig. 2.1 The Decision to Collaborate: Outcomes

always be partially, and sometimes profoundly, uncertain. (We intro-duce some ideas for dealing with uncertainty in chapter 8.) But the basic notion is fairly clear: the reasonable prospect of better outcomes motivates collaboration.[4]

More Resources

The second major justification for a collaborative approach—beyond its potential to generate more public value from any given level of resources—is that engaging private collaborators may yield *more re-sources* for public purposes. This is not simply taxation by another name—requisitioning resources from private sources, willing or not, to serve a public goal. Rather, well-structured collaborations can in-duce private players to contribute willingly to a shared endeavor, ben-efiting both themselves and the public at large.

Under the right circumstances private entities—citizens, corpora-tions, or nonprofit organizations—are willing to contribute their own resources to boost the total expenditure on some goods that create public value. Boston's Greenway offers an instructive example. When Boston's Big Dig—a fifteen-year, $15 billion project to shift the city's central traffic artery into underground tunnels—was finally completed, a great swath of vacant land became available where previously there had been highways and access ramps. Citizens and officials were nearly

[4]The right decision rule is actually more nuanced. It is worth undertaking a collaboration even if the chance of a substantially better outcome is small, so long as the cost and risk are similarly small. More important, if a successful collaboration can be replicated, with the payoff multiplied, even risky experiments become desirable.

unanimous that the space should be turned into an urban park. But city and state governments were in no position to put up the resources required to build and equip the new Greenway. The Greenway's governance model embodied a gamble that significant donations would be forthcoming if private entities participated on terms that gave them some control over the details of how the Greenway would take shape. (The upshot of this episode, as discussed in detail in chapter 6, was a failure to garner the expected private resources or creativity.)

Donors who are willing to supplement the tax dollars flowing to some public purpose sometimes exemplify self-interest in the broad sense that encompasses an altruistic element. Or they collect a disproportionate share of the benefit from the public purpose. Or they value their share disproportionately highly. We see examples of each scenario in the pages to come. By any combination of these rationales, they collect enough benefit from the incremental spending to justify paying the incremental cost themselves.

But even if government is seeking more resources than it can raise through taxation, why collaborate? Why does government not simply solicit arm's-length private donations for the project, rather than establishing a complicated, collaborative relationship? The answer comes in two parts. First, arm's-length donors might rightly worry that without some structure to clarify roles and obligations government will ratchet back its own spending as an enterprise receives more voluntary contributions. Second, donors are likely to be much more generous in support of a project if they can influence or put their stamp on its destiny. There are certainly instances of donors contributing to government-run endeavors over which they have little or no control. But private funding for public purposes usually rises in line with private donors' ability to influence the mission.[5] Even in the

---

[5] State-run colleges and universities would seem to be a salient exception. Despite the fact that they collect most of their funding from the government, they still receive substantial contributions from their alumni. The largest endowments for state universities are those of the University of Texas system ($11.6 billion) and the University of California ($5.2 billion). One possible explanation is that they are in a sector (higher education) where they have private-sector counterparts that routinely solicit significant alumni donations. Thus contributing to one's alma mater seems to be standard practice. Interestingly, and consistent with our theory that generosity comes only with control, major portions of most of the largest endowments have

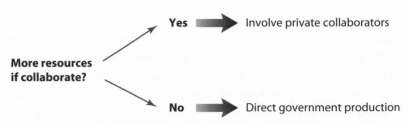

Fig. 2.2 The Decision to Collaborate: Resources

absence of a "better outcomes" rationale for collaboration, then, there may be a "more resources" motive, as figure 2.2 depicts. (As with figure 2.1, there may be substantial uncertainty on the returns to collaboration, in this instance about the amount of additional resources private collaborators will provide.)

Multiple mechanisms, some straightforward and some quite sophisticated, permit the public and private sectors to share responsibilities and control. Chapter 7 explores the use of collaboration to secure private support and addresses the range of mechanisms by which governments can benefit from offering a share of influence in exchange for resources.[6]

Illustrations of Collaboration

The chapters to come present a wealth of detailed cases in which government pursues its missions by engaging private players, through varying means and with varying effects. A few brief examples of collaboration in action, most of them explored at length in later chapters, will help to make the logic a bit more concrete at this stage of the story.

---

actually been privatized. That is, private foundations own and have responsibility for these funds. They award them to special purposes, such as athletics or scholarships, as opposed to putting the money into some general fund.

[6] These two broad rationales for collaboration—better outcomes and more resources—frequently work in tandem. Individuals and institutions may predict that their involvement will produce better outcomes—and thus a superior return on resources—which will amplify their willingness to contribute resources to the enterprise.

New York City's Department of Parks & Recreation

By the early 1980s, New York City was losing the struggle to maintain its public parks. The Department of Parks & Recreation—while not particularly dysfunctional—was simply overwhelmed by its mission. As New York's mid-1970s fiscal crisis cut into the department's resources, squalid and often dangerous parks became a highly visible symbol of a city in decline.

Improvisation under pressure eventually produced a strategy of recruiting the private sector to help with park investment, maintenance, and management. Such involvement came in a wide variety of forms, ranging from the familiar extremes of conventional voluntarism ("friends of the park" groups clearing litter or supervising playgrounds in a neighborhood park) to conventional outsourcing (contracting out vehicle maintenance, construction, and other well-defined tasks). More complex arrangements that typify collaborative governance, featuring some sharing of decision-making authority, also emerged.

In New York's most famous park, informal groups of concerned citizens coalesced, with the active encouragement of department officials, into the Central Park Conservancy. After years of escalating involvement this private nonprofit was given formal responsibility for managing the park. Downtown in Bryant Park, restoration and management were delegated to a "business improvement district" authorized under New York State law to collect and spend resources from surrounding businesses. Adrian Benepe, the parks commissioner under Mayor Michael Bloomberg, declared such "partnerships" to be the linchpin of his management strategy. He and his senior staff often spent more time orchestrating the contributions of various nongovernmental actors than they did managing the department's workforce. While New York City did not cede formal ownership of any park, it delegated much of the operational responsibility to private players.[7]

---

[7] See John D. Donahue, "Parks and Partnership in New York City A: Adrian Benepe's Challenge" (Harvard University, Kennedy School of Government Case Program, 2004), and also *Rebuilding Central Park: A Management and Restoration Plan* (MIT Press, 1986).

The use of collaboration by the parks department was motivated by both of the major rationales we have discussed. Structuring roles for private players enabled *better outcomes* as well as *more resources*. The collaboration worked admirably, amplifying the parks department's own efforts in the service of its public mission.

Smallpox Vaccinations for "First Responders"

The specter of biological terrorism surged to the forefront of American anxieties in the wake of the September 2001 terror attacks, and a deliberate release of the smallpox virus was a grim, suddenly imaginable scenario. Smallpox had been eradicated worldwide two decades earlier, with the exception of two known virus samples in government labs, but the possibility of *unknown* caches could not be ruled out. Routine vaccinations had ceased, rendering most Americans vulnerable to this devastating and highly contagious disease. Late in 2002, the Bush administration announced a plan to immunize select groups to reduce the devastation should a smallpox attack occur. General immunization was rejected, since smallpox vaccination involves a high risk of some discomfort plus a low risk of grave complications. Instead, the administration planned to vaccinate military personnel bound for overseas conflicts and, domestically, about ten million "first responders." These responders are physicians, nurses, firefighters, police officers, and others who were likely to be exposed early in a bioterrorism attack, and whose services would be critical in limiting any smallpox outbreak. The short-term goal was to vaccinate one million critical Americans by the end of the summer of 2003.

The federal government took a simple approach to immunizing the military: service members were identified and ordered to report for vaccination. The direct approach, when government is able to accomplish a goal unaided, has undeniable advantages. The civilian side of the effort proved considerably more complex. Rather than delivering vaccinations through the Public Health Service, the Centers for Disease Control, or some other federal entity, the Bush administration chose to rely on hospitals and other mostly private medical organizations for two tasks: first to nominate half a million doctors, nurses, and emergency medical technicians as first responders to be vaccinated; and then to administer the vaccine. In delegating the first task, Washington was relying on the *information* justification for collaboration; hospitals knew much better than did the federal government which personnel would be most urgently needed in a crisis. In delegating the second, it was capitalizing on the *productivity* and *legitimacy* rationales. Medical institutions were expert in the technical task of targeting vaccines; moreover, they were perceived by the public as the right institutions for the job.

Within weeks of the immunization initiative's launch, half a million military personnel had rolled up their sleeves to be vaccinated. The civilian campaign, by contrast, started slowly and stalled quickly. Hospital directors and medical professionals weighed the aggregate and abstract benefits of readiness to respond to a possible attack, against the more specific and concrete risks of inoculation. These risks were far from hypothetical and would be borne disproportionately by medical staffs, their patients, and their families. A doctor or nurse receiving the vaccine faced the near certainty of some discomfort and malaise, a modestly high probability of missing some days of work, and an unknown but real risk of serious health complications. There was the small, but far from negligible, chance that recently vaccinated health workers could pass on the vaccinia virus (the mild but not innocuous relative of smallpox used to confer immunity) to their family members or vulnerable patients, who could suffer severe, even fatal, infections. As private players balanced the costs of vaccination to themselves, their families, and their patients, against the public benefits of preparedness against terrorism, many opted against the vaccination. Some hospitals explicitly, and publicly, declared that they would not participate in the government's campaign. Many more private institutions and individuals simply opted out quietly. By midsummer of 2003, fewer than 40,000 civilians had been vaccinated, versus a short-term goal of 500,000 and an ultimate goal of 10 million. Within a few months, the inoculation campaign was quietly halted.

The vaccination program for civilian first responders—in contrast to the parallel military campaign—fell far short of its goals because those charged to carry it out had interests, concerns, and loyalties that diverged too sharply from those of the policy makers. These private entities exercised their discretion to shape the outcome into something quite different from what government officials had in mind. In this case, the collaborators balked, and the project failed.

Federal Programs for Worker Training

The Workforce Investment Act governs the use of federal funds for a range of job-training efforts, including programs for young people, workers displaced by technological change or foreign competition, and currently employed workers seeking additional skills.[8] This law continues a long-standing American preference for private involvement in workforce development. But even more than its predecessor legislation, it mandates a collaborative approach to human-capital investment. It is founded on the presumption that while the public at large has a strong interest in worker training, government is poorly positioned to carry out the training itself.

The *better outcomes* motivation for engaging the private sector applies strongly and in several ways to job training. There is a strong presumption that private organizations will be more productive, on average, at structuring and running training programs. Even if governmental agencies were organized and motivated to deliver the highest-quality and lowest-cost training, they would be handicapped, relative to private actors, by their shortage of pertinent *information*. Effective workforce development requires fine-grained knowledge of current and future skill requirements, and about the potential of particular workers—knowledge that government generally lacks. Recognizing this, the act mandates the extensive involvement of private entities, both for-profit and nonprofit. Each state and locality is required to establish a governing body, with a majority of business representatives, to oversee federally funded training activities.[9] Private-sector involvement comes not merely in governance, but in delivery. Community colleges and other nonprofit educational institutions are

---

[8] Public Law 105-220, *112 Stat. 936.*
[9] Chap. 1, sec. 111, (b) 3; chap. 2, sec. 117.

eligible to deliver training; so, too, are for-profit training providers. Private firms are explicitly allowed to deliver government-supported on-the-job training to eligible workers.[10]

This general mandate to engage the private sector plays out in wildly different ways across America's cities and states, with widely varying results. In some cases the mix of public money and private discretion works just as envisioned, and the right workers are trained the right way in the right skills. In other cases training is flatly ineffective, or focused on workers who don't need it, or delivered to benefit firms rather than workers. And often the outcome is somewhere in between. Where government knows how to work it well, collaboration lifts skill-short citizens to a new level of earning power. In other jurisdictions, the collaboration is unevenly effective or flatly fails.[11] (This arena for collaboration is discussed in more detail in chapter 5.)

Where Have We Been? Where Are We Going?

These three brief illustrations of collaboration represent a very small sample from a very large population. We will encounter the accomplishments and challenges these cases exemplify in chapters to come in the context of many more examples, developed at considerably greater length. The goal, for now, is to provide a little concreteness amid the parade of concepts of this first part of the book, and to set the stage for the detailed case studies that await in part 2.

This chapter introduced the broad rationales that motivate reliance on collaboration—sometimes explicitly, usually implicitly—as a strategy for accomplishing government's work. Asserting the rationales, of course, is very different from ensuring that they produce the desired results. We have not yet discussed in any detail the potential downsides of collaboration. When private actors are engaged in public

---

[10] Chap. 5, sec. 134.

[11] For one perspective, see John D. Donahue, Lisa Lynch, and Ralph W. Whitehead, Jr., *Opportunity Knocks: Training the Commonwealth's Workers for the New Economy* (Massachusetts Institute for a New Commonwealth, 2000). For a more detailed assessment of an earlier but closely related legislative approach, see Larry L. Orr et al., "Does Training for the Disadvantaged Work? Evidence from the National JTPA Study" (Apt Associates, Bethesda, MD, 1994).

missions, on terms that give them a significant measure of influence over public resources and public purposes, they may exercise that discretion to pursue their own goals, not those of the public. We now turn to the intricate challenge of balancing the benefits and costs of private discretion.

Chapter 3

<><><><><><><><><><><><><><><><><><><><><><><><><><><><><>

The Delegator's Dilemma

Shared discretion is the defining feature of collaborative governance. If one side makes all the decisions, a public-private relationship is a contract, not a collaboration. The crucial question concerns just *how* discretion is shared. How this question is answered shapes the effectiveness, the legitimacy, and the managerial difficulty of establishing and maintaining a collaborative effort. Creating public value by capitalizing on private capacity requires the careful balancing of the benefits and costs of discretion in order to maximize the net advantage of collaborating relative to what government could achieve on its own. Neither the theory behind such balancing nor the actual implementation is easy. Dealing out discretion is rather like riding a unicycle: there are multiple ways to fail. You can fall forward, backward, or to either side. But the feat of finding the elusive balance point can be a marvel to behold and a satisfaction to accomplish.

There is not a fixed amount of discretion in any situation. What is granted to the private sector is not necessarily lost to the public sector. Collaboration at its best evokes the biblical tale of the loaves and fishes—the more discretion is shared, the more discretion is available for sharing. The right allocation of discretion gives each party authority where its information, expertise, and interests are greater. The smarter they are in sharing discretion, the more value their collaboration can create and the greater the opportunities to enhance the well-being of both parties.

The Three P's of Discretion

Discretion shows up in three discrete domains: production, payoffs, and preferences. Production discretion lies at the heart of collaboration. If private players have no leeway over how to play their roles, there's no reason to choose the collaborative approach instead of simpler options for pursuing public missions. But payoff and preference discretion open occasions for opportunism that can undermine the benefits of collaboration.

Production Discretion

One fundamental motive for collaboration is the belief that by engaging private actors the public sector can accomplish its mission more effectively than it could if it acted alone. But this motive, by itself, does not call for collaboration. It is often possible—and, when possible, generally desirable—for government to harness private efficiency advantages without encountering the complexities that arise with shared discretion. Simple government procurement contracts represent a familiar example.

Suppose a public agency requires a truck to be delivered, a garbage route to be served, or a software program to be created. The government's requirements are entirely clear. Officials in charge have good reason to believe that it will be cheaper or better or both to acquire the goods or services from the private sector rather than to produce them internally. The sensible course in such cases is to specify and publish its requirements, invite competing bids, and choose the provider who agrees to deliver on the best terms.[1] Depending on how finely the requirements are written, the contractor, once selected, may have a good deal of latitude over how to meet the terms of the deal. But setting goals, ranking priorities, assessing performance, approv-

---

[1] The basic terms of the choice between internal production and contracting-out are described in John D. Donahue, *The Privatization Decision: Public Ends, Private Means* (Basic Books, 1989), chap. 5.

ing revisions, and other authoritative functions remain government's exclusive prerogative.[2]

Frequently, however, it is impossible, impractical, or unwise for government to specify in advance what actions it expects of its private agents. The Department of Homeland Security can hardly spell out what combination of ambulance drivers, nurses, and emergency room technicians would be most valuable to blunt a smallpox outbreak in Muncie, Indiana, so it lets administrators at Ball Memorial Hospital set priorities for vaccinating first responders. Even if the Occupational Safety and Health Administration concentrates on trash compactors as the greatest danger in grocery stores, the manager of the local Safeway may know that reducing the risk that loading-dock workers will slip on spilled produce would deliver far greater safety gains at the same cost. No government agency is likely to match an automaker's judgment over the relative promise of innumerable changes in fuel, engines, design, and materials to boost mileage and hold down the costs of new-generation vehicles. Legislators and government inspectors likely know far less than do a port facility's managers about how to reduce the port's vulnerability to a terrorist attack. Accordingly, these more intricate and difficult-to-specify public goals often can be advanced more efficiently if private players are given significant discretion, not just over the technology of production, but also over the specific goals to be achieved. When government yields such discretion, it has departed from the domain of contracting and moved to the realm of collaboration.

In almost any moderately complex undertaking, having collaborators participate in specifying the mission and the methods greatly enhances the potential for creating value.[3] If the only way in which

---

[2] Effective contracting is a challenging task. The government encounters a range of risks: erring in determining its requirements, mishandling the translation of these requirements into contractual terms, choosing poorly among competitors, and inadequately monitoring the provider's performance. With security, or any protective measure, a distinctive contracting challenge is that it protects against low-likelihood events. Little is learned when such events do not occur. Thus absent effective monitoring of, say, private airline security firms in 2001, deficient performance may make itself known only after a disaster, as the United States saw on 9/11.

[3] This general theme appears in the literature of regulation as relating to the preference for performance standards over specification standards. Performance standards give the regulated firm the ability to determine how best to meet the requirements of the regulation.

private players exercised discretion had to do with production choices, collaboration would be a colloquy between those fabled optimists Pangloss and Pollyanna, with private efficiency advancing the public interest in the best of all possible ways. Alas, production discretion is often accompanied by payoff discretion and preference discretion, both of which hobble a collaboration's capacity to meet public goals. These two features of discretion's dark side are our next subjects.

Payoff Discretion

Suppose that for some public mission it is clear that private collaborators will be able to create more total value than could the government, either acting alone or issuing a tightly defined contract to a private firm. The question then becomes how that extra value will be divvied up. A private party with discretion over production often acquires some control over the distribution of the extra value. When it can get away with it, it may grab the lion's share for itself.[4]

Justice Louis Brandeis famously observed that "sunlight is the best disinfectant." We endorse the sentiment when it comes to collaboration, and add that active measurement operates as a scrub brush to intensify the effect. Thus payoff discretion would pose no problem if both the nature and the scale of the benefits produced by a collaboration were readily visible and easily measured. The entire extra value would wind up distributed in a transparent way between government and its private collaborator.

Outside of textbooks in economics, alas, such ideal conditions rarely exist. Some payoff discretion is inevitable and should be thought of as a normal concomitant of collaboration, a cost to be weighed against the benefits. But payoff discretion can be subtle, raising the risk that the toll can greatly exceed the inevitable minimum. It is often difficult to monitor precisely the amount of the payoff and who receives what portion of it. A private collaborator might collect some

---

[4] In Aesop's original fable, there are four animals, and the lion takes everything. We deal primarily with a two-animal case—government and its private collaborator—and use "lion's share" in its currently accepted meaning, albeit one faithless to Aesop, namely, the largest portion.

of its benefits in the form of an improved competitive position, favorable legal precedents, future political influence, or other currencies that the government would have trouble counting, let alone controlling. When benefits flow covertly to the private collaborator, someone bears that cost, though it is frequently unclear where, when, and even in what form the cost burdens fall. The victims may be consumers confronted with higher prices, or the collaborator's competitors who reap less profit.[5] And since "the government" is a convenient abstraction covering a multitude of different institutions at various levels, the collaborating government agency might not be adequately anxious about costs to the public in areas outside its bailiwick, even if those costs are perfectly observable.

Costs are just one part of the equation. The government might also have trouble tallying the benefits the public receives. How long will a boathouse built by a friends-of-the-park group last? How much will a trainee's earning power increase as a result of her participation in a nonprofit's skill-building program? Have security upgrades reduced the risk of a terror attack on some particular chemical plant from very low to very, very low, or has the risk stayed pretty much the same?

Government often lacks the technological expertise required to produce a critical product or service. It may not even know what capabilities might be available or created. So even simple procurement contracts must often grant *some* discretion. So it was in 1986 when the U.S. Navy wanted a handheld water desalinator so that shipwrecked sailors could make enough fresh water to survive for several days on a life raft. The navy solicited competitive bids to develop a prototype. All parties expected a follow-on production contract, also subject to competitive bidding.

Recovery Engineering, a Minneapolis-based start-up company, won the R&D contract at a price that would at best let it break even.[6] The real return would come later. Despite having to provide technical specifications to the U.S Navy, and consequently to all other bidders on

[5] The sum total of gains and losses by different parties needn't be zero. Indeed, if a firm utilizes its discretion to gain market power, others will lose more than it gains.

[6] We thank Brian Sullivan, the CEO of Recovery Engineering over its entire career, for information. Zeckhauser, his thesis adviser, served on the board of the company.

the future production contracts, Recovery Engineering would secure proprietary knowledge about costs, technological know-how, and manufacturing processes that would give it an extraordinary three-pronged advantage in bidding for the subsequent, much larger, production contracts.[7] Not surprisingly, Recovery Engineering won the production contract at a price that offered significant profits. These long-term profits, in turn, provided the financial footing for substantial investment in the development of the market for similar products while also funding additional R&D projects.[8]

What are the lessons from this experience? One might argue that the taxpayers would have been better off had the U.S. Navy performed the R&D itself at the outset, or had it barred the development contractor from bidding on the production job. But either approach would have brought big disadvantages—an inferior design or barring the most effective producer—and almost certainly would have led to a less satisfactory product. This problem is common whenever government seeks to procure innovative products that must be designed before they are produced in quantity.

The central lesson is that to enjoy the production discretion that comes with collaboration, government must accept some payoff discretion as well. It should be sensitive to this trade-off, should seek to strike a favorable balance, but should not abandon collaboration at the slightest hint of payoff discretion. If the toll incurred owing to

[7] Other firms tempted to bid on the production contract would need to include a factor in their bid to cover any costs that they didn't know enough about to estimate correctly. Recovery Engineering's information advantage almost certainly deterred some competitors and led less-informed firms to set their production-phase bids far too high. The firm's competitors were consciously seeking to avoid what game theorists label the "winner's curse," a misfortune often experienced by individuals who win the bidding at a traditional "high-price wins" auction, say, for a piece of furniture. The cursed fail to draw the appropriate inference that their win implies that everyone else had a lower valuation than they did, implying that they should have curbed their estimate about the quality and value of an item.

[8] Our desalinator story has a very happy ending for Recovery Engineering, for consumers, and hence for the government. Building on its initial success with specialized purifiers for military applications, it moved into the much larger market of water filters for home use, developing the PŪR brand. This fostered competition in that market, where Brita then had an exceptional market share, leading to lowered prices and improved quality for consumers. The firm eventually grew to seven hundred employees, went public, and in 1999 was sold to Procter & Gamble.

payoff discretion is irremediably expensive relative to the benefits derived from production discretion, to be sure, collaboration is simply
the wrong model. But government is too often timid about turning
to private collaborators with clear-cut information advantages, both
from the fear of payoff discretion (even when relatively mild) and
from a reluctance to concede that it suffers any information deficit.

A sobering illustration comes from the spring of 2010 when an
explosion on a BP drilling platform unleashed a cataclysmic oil leak
into the Gulf of Mexico. As days turned into weeks and the costs—
environmental, economic, and political—mounted, the Obama administration's impulse was to assure an anxious public that "we're in
control." Even though BP demonstrated a commendable willingness
to take responsibility for the spill and its consequences, its relationship with the federal government morphed from collaborator to mis-
creant, and a recently retired Coast Guard admiral was named as the
point person for dealing with the disaster. The instinct to hold discretion close was understandable, but unfortunate. Understandable,
because it was politically infeasible to simply trust BP to do the right
thing, and because there was no Yellow Pages roster of mile-deep
blowout repair firms to which the government could issue a cut-and-
dried contract. Unfortunate, because the federal government utterly
lacked the requisite expertise. The Coast Guard is expert at many
things—rescuing boaters, orchestrating port protection (as discussed
elsewhere in this book), and, if need be, confronting aggressors with
armed force—but responding to a breakdown in sophisticated oil-
production equipment on the seabed is not among them.[9]

The right approach—easy to stipulate in retrospect, of course—
would have been to recruit experts from the private sector, where the
relevant expertise inevitably resided, and grant them discretion to
figure out the best way to oversee and guide BP's efforts—including
helping to craft the most promising sequence of options to try for
stanching the flow. The experts might have come from a single firm.
But more likely they would have constituted an ad hoc task force

[9] To be fair, Admiral Thad Allen, the federal point person on the BP spill, had extensive experience responding to catastrophe as the temporary deputy to the head of the Federal Emergency Management Agency in the recovery after Katrina.

assembled from firms specialized in drilling services, deep-sea operations, remote sensing, oil skimming, the logistics of arranging a massive exercise, and so on. And they would have come from many nations, in contrast to the all-American approach that characterized the initial period of the cleanup. In this unprecedented situation, the federal government would have had to cooperate to permit unfamiliar experts and unforeseen methods to stanch the flow and cleanse the Gulf. No doubt the private collaborators would have found ways to assimilate some surplus in the process, and it is equally clear that some of them would have been rather embarrassing associates for the government. But the benefits of accelerating or improving the eventual fix even modestly would have swamped these costs of collaboration.

A public agency seldom enlists private collaborators simply to do (a little bit more effectively or less expensively) the exact same thing the agency would do itself. To justify the risks and complexity of collaboration, the potential losses from payoff discretion, and the unease within its own staff that collaboration might inspire, government must have a well-founded belief that private players command a different, and generally superior, set of production possibilities. But having a different production model often shapes not merely the amount but also the distribution of value.

Consider a collaborative approach to a new generation of passenger vehicles and the wide range of payoffs that could result. The Clinton administration developed such a program, and, given today's fervent concerns about oil prices and carbon emissions, a collaborative approach to advancing auto technology is likely to be in our future as well as our past. Government is poorly equipped to understand the details of such an enterprise well enough to issue the right marching orders on its own. Unfortunately, this tends to make it exceedingly hard for the government to be confident that its collaborator's recommendation of a particular approach is driven by its expertise, rather than by its interests. An auto company is likely to favor a new-generation car campaign relying heavily on reformulated fuel that imposes most costs on the oil industry rather than on redesigned engines. If new kinds of engines must be developed, the firm would like to maximize the government's share of the research and development investment required. Similarly, a company that has already made progress on diesel-electric hybrids would like the campaign to anchor on that technology rather than on alternatives that might play to the strengths of rivals.

Collaborators are likely to tilt payoffs toward themselves whenever they can. Any private organization, whether for-profit or nonprofit, has stakeholders with their own particular interests, and government would be foolish not to anticipate that its private collaborators will tend to serve such interests, even at the expense of the government's priorities, to the extent that they are able. Such tilts are particularly likely when detection is difficult or when the relationship is one-time or short term.

Government can generally anticipate such self-interested behavior, and can reduce the risks of payoff discretion by following one of two paths. The first is simply to squeeze discretion out of the relationship, transforming it from collaboration to simple outsourcing. That path knowingly surrenders the benefits that come from granting discretion to private partners, rather than suffer the downside. The alternative route accepts that private discretion entails both gains and losses for the public, and manages the relationship with an eye to maximizing gains and minimizing losses.

This second approach generally calls for sophisticated skills in crafting the terms of a collaborative relationship. Suppose, for example, that officials at some local school district want to hire a for-profit education management company to run a troubled school. The officials are reluctant to write a voluminous contract spelling out in detail just how the company should go about improving performance, since this would be both costly and clumsy, would tax the capability of the officials, and, most important, would undercut the prime justification for enlisting the outside organization. So the officials try to find ways to make private discretion more productive, and less risky, in terms of the educational mission that the district wishes to advance. (Chapter 4's discussion of charter schools takes up this class of issues in greater detail.)

In some circumstances it is a simple matter to structure arrangements that liberate private collaborators to make the most of their special capabilities while protecting the government's interest. If both the *scale* and the *value* of outcomes are clearly and unambiguously visible, private production discretion can be given free rein. Imagine that the district officials possessed a set of standardized tests that precisely measured any student's stock of skills and knowledge. This fabulous test battery can calibrate not only the student's progress in reading and writing and arithmetic, but every other attribute that officials prize—study habits, civic-mindedness, character—so that it serves as an all-purpose indicator of public value. Each student in the troubled school could be tested at the start and at the end of the school year. (While we're indulging in fantasy, imagine that the tests take only half an hour or so to administer, imposing no weighty burden on student or teacher schedules.) District officials could then pay the management company on the basis of this educational value added, leaving it up to the company's expert judgment to determine how best to go about adding that value. The payment schedule could be fine-tuned to reflect virtually any set of public priorities—for example, requiring all students to reach some minimum level in various subjects, or paying extra for gains made by particular groups. When production can be precisely measured and evaluated, officials can allow their management company, acting as their agent, almost complete production discretion. Concerns about payoff discretion are eliminated. Viewed one way, such an arrangement gives private collaborators complete freedom. Viewed another way, it gives them no choice but to do what the government wants them to do. Using our terms, such a happy (but improbable) arrangement features complete production discretion untouched by any payoff discretion. Since their governmental counterparts see all, private collaborators have no choice but to focus on the public's agenda.

Such perfect measuring rods, though, are somewhere between the coelacanth (in existence, but vanishingly rare) and the unicorn (a happy fantasy). Even tolerably good measurement schemes are hard to find in education, and in many other public arenas. Tests can measure some things quite well (basic arithmetic and spelling skills), some with reasonable accuracy (reading comprehension, mathematical problem-solving), some rather badly (writing skills), and some hardly at all (character development). Most tests capture only snapshots at one point in time, rather than the ideal before-and-after that would permit reasonable inferences about value added. Students move, drop out, or get sick on test days. And test results can be fuzzy. Students may or may not take the test seriously, and their chance guesses will produce statistical randomness.[10] Even in the best of circumstances, tests measure value added in some relevant areas but not others, almost always with a modest amount of bias and a certain level of random error. The less precise the measure, the more room there is for collaborators to abuse their discretion in what they produce to serve their own purposes.

Matters are graver still when the measure of value is subject not just to error, or omitted concerns, but to manipulation. The school-management company may select, or influence the selection of, the tests by which its performance will be measured. And even if the tests are conducted independently, perhaps on some statewide basis, the company may be able to rack up good scores by doing cheap things that offer merely fleeting benefits (drilling students in the subset of material expected to feature on the test), instead of doing hard but valuable things (expanding students' general knowledge and bolstering their capacity to learn). The company also may be able to influence who gets tested, say by arranging for students who would pull down the average to be disproportionately absent at test time. If the school district expects or suspects such shenanigans, it can respond by asserting tighter control over the who, what, and when of testing. To the extent that it brings the picture of value added into clear focus, it reduces the risk posed by private production discretion.

Government could alternatively seek to avoid short-term efforts to game the system by basing rewards on long-term results. Some or most of the management company's compensation could depend on students' educational and economic success ten, twenty, or forty years out. In principle, it would be possible to overcome most impediments to results-based accountability systems. Practically, however, matters

---

[10] In the charter school one of us was involved in launching, the statewide standardized tests were generally viewed with contempt by the students, and it was considered a point of honor among the brightest to refuse to take them seriously.

are rather different, for two reasons. First, the ideal monitoring and payment system may be too costly or impossible to operate: no private contractor will allow payments, even moderate incentive payments, to be tied up for twenty years. Second, it is rarely feasible in practice to make such systems sufficiently precise to prevent public value from leaking away.

Mere vulnerability to payoff discretion does not, on its own, make collaboration a bad idea. A collaboration can generate more public value than leakage drains away. But at their worst, ill-informed or poorly structured efforts at collaboration can generate results that are inferior, from the public's perspective, to what could have been obtained through either direct governmental production or tightly specified contracts.

The prudent school district may simply accept the leakage associated with private production if it judges that the gains from production discretion outweigh the losses from payoff discretion. Alternatively, it may narrow the scope of the management company's discretion. The challenge for district officials, as they whittle down the company's operational leeway, is to preserve areas of discretion that primarily operate to create, rather than divert, value, while curbing discretion where the ratio tends to go the other way. The district might require the adoption of approaches that it believes are especially conducive to good performance, or induce such approaches through an incentive scheme. For example, it could set a floor under hours of instruction per day or days of instruction per year, set a ceiling on the number of students in each classroom, or mandate that teachers be required to have particular educational qualifications, or offer extra compensation if such standards were met.

Selectively slicing away discretion may prevent abuse but often entails the sacrifice of some productivity. Constraints on discretion may also distort the management company's behavior in wasteful ways. Requirements that teachers possess advanced degrees, for example, could lead the company to fire a talented teacher who lacks formal training, and replace her with a more expensive, better-credentialed, but less effective alternative. (Elite private schools often flourish by hiring great teachers who lack the credentials required by nearby public schools.) As always, the central concern is to balance what is gained against what is lost with each alteration in the allocation of discretion. As the cases in part 2 will demonstrate, cut-and-dried guidelines like "avoid payoff discretion in area X" are much too crude.

Alternatively, a school district might adopt a quite different strategy: seeking out a partner whose own interests are reasonably well aligned with those of the district. That is, it could recruit collaborators who are likely to use their discretion in the public interest even when unobserved and uncompelled. (When one author's spouse ran Harvard's real-estate operations, she discovered the advantages of hiring varsity athletes for summer landscaping jobs, since these employees, committed to staying in top condition, worked themselves hard even though the limited work-site monitoring made slacking off an option.)

A conventional and often sensible prescription is to select nonprofit rather than for-profit collaborators when it is impossible or ill-advised to either channel or constrain agents' payoff discretion. The rationale for this is twofold. First, nonprofit organizations have much weaker motives to claim material payoffs since (more or less by definition) they lack owners who are entitled to benefit from, and thus motivated to push hard to accumulate, financial surpluses. Extra money, of course, tends to be seen as a good thing no matter what the organizational form. But for-profits are engineered to be systematically more avid for financial payoffs than are their nonprofit counterparts. Second, nonprofits sometimes share some or most of government's agenda, and (like those happily ditch-digging student athletes) work to advance it for their own intrinsic reasons. Thus nonprofits not only lack the fierce financial appetites that can squeeze out other goals, but they also tend to be founded upon and organized around missions analogous to, and overlapping with, those of the government.

Unfortunately the plusses of nonprofit production must be weighed against its two major minuses. First, for-profits tend to be more productive than their nonprofit cousins precisely because hunger for net revenue and aversion to loss inspire an intense focus on productivity gains and cost reductions. Second, although relying on nonprofits reduces the public's vulnerability to payoff discretion, it tends to amplify a related but different category of conflict between collaborators' core agendas, the challenge we label preference discretion.

Preference Discretion

Preference discretion comes from the same source as payoff discretion, a share of control in the hands of a collaborator whose interests diverge from those of the government. Payoff discretion merely involves money. Preference discretion is a much broader concept.

Only in rare cases will a private collaborator's preferences align neatly with those of the government. There are almost always some dimensions on which preferences diverge. Even in a fond marriage, you may prefer a Mexican restaurant tonight while your spouse would rather have sushi. Similarly, as coauthors, we may find ourselves in rock-solid agreement on the fundamental message yet tug in different directions on the details. Indeed, one author knows that colleagues esteem the sorts of novel ideas he has served up in previous writings, and wants to include plenty of conceptual innovation. The other puts more emphasis on accessible writing and meat-and-potatoes applicability. While both of us cherish both novelty *and* usefulness, we weight them a little differently.[11]

Divergence of preferences complicates the use of collaboration to achieve public goals. If interests divide only at the margins, it matters little. But the divergence may lie at the core, since a diversity of views about the public good is mostly healthy and in any case inevitable. Consider some different ways preference discretion can manifest itself.

Focused philanthropy. A community organization may be zealous about offering effective, low-cost training to those who need it most, but only if they belong to the neighborhood or the ethnic group that stirs the founder's loyalties. A park volunteer may be willing to devote endless hours to nature programs for preschoolers, while athletic

---

[11] If we had merely assigned chapters to the individual better able to write them, the book's style would have wobbled back and forth. In fact, we collaborated heavily on every component to ensure that both sets of preferences were well served—a more costly approach than government can pursue in most collaborations.

programs for teenagers leave her cold. And whatever their goals, few philanthropists are indifferent to personal credit, a matter of little concern to the general public beyond its strategic benefits in promoting generosity.

Semiprivate and directed goods. When benefits from a public good go disproportionately to some individuals or groups, as we observed in chapter 2, we refer to them as semiprivate or directed goods. Managers in charge of producing public goods, be their organization public or private, will produce those that disproportionately benefit them or their favored constituencies. Thus a plant manager crafting a pollution-reduction plan will probably do more to curb the soot that befouls his town and his company's image than to reduce carbon emissions that invisibly alter the climate of the whole planet. A benefactor of Central Park might esteem flower beds in general, but value most highly those visible from her terrace, and may give with restrictions intended to favor her local flowers. And given that climate change will afflict today's kindergarteners more than today's elderly, senior citizens with flocks of grandchildren are more likely to favor measures to control carbon emissions than would their heirless contemporaries.

Divergent values. It may be integral to a training provider's mission for trainees to absorb religious tenets along with workplace skills, even if government funders insist on separating church and state. Because a recent recipient of a smallpox inoculation risks transmitting a dangerous or even fatal vaccinia infection to immunocompromised patients, such as transplant recipients or HIV sufferers, many medical personnel judged their government-mandated duty to get vaccinated to prepare for a hypothetical smallpox attack to conflict directly with their core value of protecting their most vulnerable patients.

Whatever form it takes, preference discretion arises more commonly with nonprofit than for-profit collaborators. Nonprofits tend to have strong interests in particular goals or causes, quite apart from revenue or profit maximization. But preference discretion is not unique to nonprofits, since for-profit entities may have objectives beyond mere profit maximization. As with payoff discretion, preference discretion presents a challenge to efficient and accountable collaboration. Government cannot be sure whether a collaborator is guided by its expertise or its interests, as it seeks to shape the outputs from a collaboration. But as with payoff discretion, the presence of preference discretion is not a game-ending foul. It simply presents one consideration practitioners must weigh against others—particularly the crucial upside of production discretion—in deciding whether to pursue a collaborative relationship.

Conclusion

The outcomes of a collaboration can range from spectacular to calamitous, though the more usual range is from reasonably beneficial to modestly perverse. The quality of results depends enormously on government's ability to fine-tune the terms of the collaboration to maximize the net benefits it yields. (Later chapters, particularly 8 and 9, develop this theme in considerable detail.) Production discretion can be a true boon for the public at large, but to get the net tally right we must subtract the inevitable losses from payoff and preference discretion. The central lesson of this chapter—and indeed the whole book— is that while collaboration doesn't promise a free lunch, it can often beat the items on the standard menu: stand-alone government, simple contracting, or conventional philanthropy. The imperatives for effective collaboration are easy to state but difficult to accomplish. The examples we shall meet in part 2 show how public and private collaborators across a wide variety of arenas have dealt with these challenges, frequently for better, occasionally for worse.

PART II

Rationales—More,
Better, or Both

Chapter 4

Collaboration for Productivity

Private organizations, as a group, tend to outclass public organizations in operational efficiency. This observation implies neither contempt for government nor infatuation with the private sector. The two sectors simply have different strengths. Most private organizations have to compete to survive, whether they are nonprofits seeking contributions or for-profits seeking net revenue. A key dimension of that competition is usually prowess at transforming resources into results. In a robustly competitive market, inefficiency invites extinction. Government agencies have their own pressures, to be sure, but these include imperatives for transparency, due process, and even-handedness, frequently at the expense of maximum productivity.[1] Sometimes narrow productive efficiency is a second-order goal for government. Sometimes when productivity *does* matter greatly, government can tap private-sector advantages through simple contracting. And sometimes—the subject of this book, and in particular this chapter—public-private collaboration is the most promising way for government to arrange for the productive pursuit of its missions.

We start this chapter with four relatively brief accounts of collaborative governance at the federal level inspired, to a significant degree, by productivity concerns—two of them success stories, the others less happy. We then segue to the state and local level for a more detailed inquiry into an ambitious, consequential, and so far quite inconclusive

---

[1] One of us has framed this as a distinction between the *intensive* accountability that characterizes the market economy and the *extensive* accountability that characterizes government. See John D. Donahue, *The Warping of Government Work* (Harvard University Press, 2008), chap. 5, and also "The Right Kind of Accountability," *Governing*, April 16, 2008.

campaign to pursue public goals more productively through collaboration with private players.

Collaborating Productively for Port Protection and a Nuclear Cleanup

Port Protection

Almost instantly after the terror attacks of September 2001, the minds of officials and citizens at large turned to other vulnerabilities that—like tall buildings and fuel-filled airplanes on September 10—had not theretofore occasioned major concern. Atop any knowledgeable observer's list had to be maritime ports. More than 360 ports open to international commerce dotted America's vast coastal reaches. They ranged from small harbor facilities catering mostly to local commerce, to enormous complexes that included factories and refineries, truck and rail hubs, and even airports, as well as loading, unloading, repair and maintenance, and other facilities for seagoing vessels and their cargo. All told, around 95 percent of American imports arrived by sea.[2] It was not hard to imagine all manner of evils slipping into the country unnoticed amid the daily surge tide of oil and sneakers and oranges and televisions and toys.

Congress quickly passed the Marine Transportation Security Act, which incorporated the provisions of the International Ship and Port Facility Security Code that had been negotiated, in record time, after the 2001 attacks. The U.S. Coast Guard—still adjusting to its recent relocation from the Department of Transportation to the newly created Department of Homeland Security—was tasked with putting the new legislation into effect.

The most straightforward way to respond to this mission—especially, one might think, for a military organization—would be for Coast Guard experts to huddle with a handful of other security specialists and issue stepped-up new security rules to which shippers, operators,

---

[2] Katherine McIntire Peters, "U.S. Port Security Measures Cover the Waterfront," *Government Executive*, September 10, 2004.

and other port denizens would be expected to submit. But to predict this path would be to miss both the essence of the security task and the culture of the Coast Guard. No uniform, top-down port-security regime could actually work—at least not without strangling port operations, stifling trade, and triggering a rising tide of bankruptcies. American ports were so wildly diverse in size, layout, function—and hence security considerations—that no single approach could work for more than a tiny minority. Tens of thousands of private parties—port operators, shipping firms, ship owners and insurers, trucking and transshipment firms, and many others—each occupying its own economic niche, were involved in and dependent on the functioning of the ports. These private players had expertise, stakes, and vulnerabilities that the Coast Guard could not hope to incorporate into port security plans unless the players themselves were brought into the security system.

Fortunately, a one-size-fits-all security plan imposed by government fiat was also antithetical to the Coast Guard's culture. For a range of reasons—some well understood, others mysterious—the Coast Guard had long been known for flexibility, innovation, and a collaborative mind-set. Its distinctive orientation would prove a perfect match with the towering challenge of rapidly building the right kind of security system for 360-plus diverse American ports.

A cross-continental series of marathon meetings was orchestrated by Captain Suzanne Englebert. The meetings—partly the standard review-and-comment sessions required by the Administrative Procedures Act, partly negotiated rule making, partly encounter sessions, with, on occasion, a bit of slumber party thrown into the mix—yielded thousands of proposals, warnings, complaints, and brainstorms. Once the products of stakeholder meetings and internal deliberations had been distilled into a final plan, what emerged was a security regime in which the Coast Guard took a hard line on the *what* of port security—the performance levels that had to be met—but left its private collaborators lots of discretion on the *how*. An operating company, portside factory, or trucking depot linked to a container port faced a nonnegotiable mandate from the Coast Guard to control access to its facilities to ensure that only screened personnel could enter. But the private parties had almost unlimited freedom to develop their own ways to control access, so long as they could convince the Coast Guard that their plan, if faithfully implemented, would do the job—and that they would indeed faithfully implement the plan.

There is no single port-security regime for the nation, in other words, but an enormous array of interrelated plans customized to each port, each private party within the port, and often each season, time of day, and type of shipment. Can such a convoluted system work? So far, so good. There have been no noteworthy terror incidents at American ports. Terror attacks are—fortunately—rare events, of course, so a few years or even a few decades without a disaster doesn't definitely prove the soundness of a security regime. The Coast Guard does not, to our knowledge, stress-test the system by staging fake incursions analogous to the bogus guns and bombs that government inspectors try to sneak past airport screeners, which might offer some gauge of effectiveness. Yet neutral observers, including the hard-to-impress Government Accountability Office, give the Coast Guard and its network of collaborators generally good marks for progress—while noting that the range of choice left to private players makes the enterprise highly, and inevitably, complex.[3]

Cleaning Up Rocky Flats

As the Coast Guard was gearing up to face the shadowy new threat of terrorism, other government agencies were still cleaning up from the Cold War. Among the worst of the messes were a number of redundant nuclear-weapons factories. More than eighty facilities that made bombs or parts of bombs had to be decommissioned. Most of the sites were contaminated with both noxious chemicals and radioactivity. Federal organizations—chiefly the Defense Department, the Department of Energy, and the Environmental Protection Agency— were responsible for ensuring that the weapons sites were decommissioned safely, but had limited internal resources for cleaning up con-

---

[3] U.S. Government Accountability Organization report GAO-04-838, "Maritime Security: Substantial Work Remains to Translate New Planning Requirements into Effective Port Security" (June 30, 2004), p. 4.

taminated equipment, buildings, or soil. Most of the cleanup work was contracted out to private firms, though the terms differed dramatically from site to site.

Every site presented its own set of complex and unpredictable technical requirements. This made it tough for government agencies to predict in advance and incorporate into a site cleanup contract the specific challenges that would arise. There was often a gap between what a contractor was supposed to do, according to the terms of its agreement with the government, and the most efficient action given the way circumstances had turned out. Sometimes the agreed-upon plan would be followed even though it did not quite fit the changed conditions, resulting in inefficiency ranging from moderate to egregious. Sometimes the original contract was so obviously out of line with current requirements that it had to be reopened and renegotiated. This process was expensive. Work was held up during redrafting and costs ballooned, particularly since the incumbent contractor held all the cards when the government needed to revise the mandate but had no alternative providers up to speed on the status of the job. Of the ten large nuclear-cleanup projects underway in 2008, nine suffered, some grievously, from schedule slippage and cost overruns. One project fell fifteen years behind schedule. Another went $9 billion over budget.[4] Conventional contracts were proving to be blunt instruments for dealing with such intricate and unpredictable endeavors.

There was an exception to the generally dreary pattern, though. The Rocky Flats complex was located not far from Denver—some citizens thought not nearly far enough. The city skyline was clearly visible from a factory whose main product line was nuclear explosives.[5] Rocky Flats had produced a range of doomsday devices during the Cold War. Its specialty was plutonium "pits," the Hiroshima-scale fission devices that triggered a fusion reaction in hydrogen bombs. Environmental and safety concerns gradually grew in importance

[4] U.S. Government Accountability Office, "Nuclear Waste: Action Needed to Improve Accountability and Management of DOE's Major Cleanup Projects," GAO-08-1051 (September 2008).

[5] An alarming photo showing the bomb factory's proximity to Denver is on p. 47 of Kim Cameron and Marc Lavine, *Making the Impossible Possible: Lessons from the Cleanup of America's Most Dangerous Nuclear Weapons Plant* (Berrett-Koehler Publishers, 2006).

relative to military priorities in the final third of the twentieth century. In 1989, a few months before the Berlin Wall fell, a joint force from the Justice Department, the EPA, and the FBI raided Rocky Flats to investigate what turned out to be well-founded suspicions of environmental crimes. Rockwell International, which had been running Rocky Flats under contract to the Energy Department, was fired and fined.

Rival contractor EG&G was brought in, though its mandate was not to resume production, but rather to shut down Rocky Flats and clean up the site.[6] The Energy Department structured its arrangement with EG&G along fairly conventional lines: the contractor was basically reimbursed its reasonable costs for whatever the department directed it to do. The parties settled down for a process that was expected to take seventy years or so. As one governmental manager put it himself, the department issued orders covering "what to do and how to do it, so all they had to do was whatever DOE said.... They got paid for showing up, not necessarily for accomplishing anything."[7] This was not far from the norm in nuclear-cleanup contracting, alas, at Rocky Flats and elsewhere.

As the routine five-year contract renewal date approached in 1995, the Energy Department decided to experiment with more sophisticated relationships with its private agents. Contractor Kaiser-Hill proved ready to participate and won the chance to show what it could do. When EG&G turned over the complex's keys to Kaiser-Hill, Rocky Flats was a 385-acre wasteland, dotted with two hundred contaminated buildings and storage tanks, vast caches of radioactive equipment, and hundreds of tons of poisoned earth.[8] Along with enriched uranium and toxic chemicals, Rocky Flats was riddled with deadly plutonium. Virtually every man-made artifact would have to be carefully packed up and shipped away, as well as much of the soil itself.

---

[6] Ibid., p. 55.

[7] Ibid., pp. 69–70.

[8] U.S. Government Accountability Office, "Nuclear Cleanup of Rocky Flats: DOE Can Use Lessons Learned to Improve Oversight of Other Sites' Cleanup Activities," GAO-06-352 (June 2006), p. 8.

Not quite "mission impossible," perhaps, but given what counted as par in nuke-plant cleanup, it seemed sure to be a very long, very costly process.

Yet a mere decade later, a year ahead of the contractual schedule—and more than half a century ahead of the Energy Department's original projections—the site was clean and empty, purged of chemical and radioactive contamination, and poised to open as a wildlife refuge. And it had all been accomplished at a cost half a billion dollars below the allowed budget.

How did the outcome so spectacularly beat expectations? Simple good luck helped, to be sure. Details of geology and climate that became clear as the project developed meant that the contamination was mostly confined to the plant itself and the immediate vicinity. Several of the managers on both the public and private sides were, by all accounts, unusually creative and determined leaders.[9] But the main explanation seems to be a recognition on the part of both federal officials and Kaiser-Hill managers that cleaning up a massive radioactive site was too complex and uncertain a task to be handled by conventional contracting. Though they didn't use the term, the model they adopted was a classic example of collaborative governance. (The Rocky Flats story is one more illustration that a teeming diversity of arrangements, including those we term collaborations, are bundled within the term "contracting.") The government granted a wide range of discretion to Kaiser-Hill in order to unleash its productive potential, and carefully arranged to minimize the damage wrought by payoff discretion along the way.

Kaiser-Hill's mandate was cast in terms of outcomes—basically to shut down Rocky Flats and leave behind an expanse of safe, usable land—with minimal process requirements and potent incentives to save time and money. The goals, the right and expectation to employ discretion in finding the best ways to advance them, and the rewards

---

[9] Chap. 3 of Cameron and Lavine, *Making the Impossible Possible* (pp. 75–99), deals with this in depth, though its hagiography is both a little shallow and rather tilted toward the private players in the collaboration.

for success were diffused throughout Kaiser-Hill, so that frontline workers were empowered and motivated to innovate.[10]

At Rocky Flats, as at other nuclear facilities, there were hundreds of bulky "glove boxes," sealed enclosures for working with radioactive materials. Standard cleanup practice had been to (very carefully, very slowly, and very expensively) break the glove boxes into pieces small enough to fit into hazardous-waste containers for shipment. But Kaiser-Hill workers dreamed up a novel process for using chemical decontaminants to dial down the radioactivity of the glove boxes enough that they could be shipped out whole, saving many years and vast sums of money.[11] Incentives to reduce costs and save time—and the discretion to choose the best means to do so—led Kaiser-Hill to simply blow up a few of the large, uncontaminated buildings on the site. The previous practice of dismantling all structures, radioactive or not, was gladly abandoned.

The search for productivity gains from collaboration went both ways. The special secure containers required for shipping radioactive waste were in short supply nationwide, and the Energy Department could not commit to meeting its responsibility for providing them to Kaiser-Hill on the schedule required. Delay loomed. But DOE officials knew that other cleanup sites would often reserve containers that they ended up not needing. Rather than letting the guaranteed availability of containers constrain the pace, the contractor accepted that the government would do everything it could to keep the containers shuttling to the site.[12] Energy Department managers were always available on-site for consultation, so that legally required approvals for the hundreds of adjustments to the cleanup plan became minor formalities rather than clock-stopping ordeals.[13]

Kaiser-Hill's successful cleanup effort involved no element of charity. The firm was paid around $8 billion for its efforts, including over half a billion dollars in incentive fees. And some payoff discretion no

---

[10] U.S. Government Accountability Office, "Nuclear Cleanup of Rocky Flats," pp. 4–5, 17, 20–22, 56 and Cameron and Lavine, *Making the Impossible Possible*, chaps. 6 and 7.

[11] U.S. Government Accountability Office, "Nuclear Cleanup of Rocky Flats," p. 4.

[12] Ibid., p. 26.

[13] Ibid., pp. 20–22.

doubt slipped in. While most observers, including the stern Government Accountability Office, have found much to admire in the Rocky Flats story, the GAO laments the potential for mischief introduced when the Energy Department took Kaiser-Hill's word for it that sites were no longer radioactive, instead of conducting its own audit.[14] But overall the GAO commended the Energy Department and Kaiser-Hill for showing how to do a better job on complicated contracts. And we concur, though we'd incorporate the friendly amendment that this sort of enterprise differs enough in degree from conventional contracts that it warrants the label of collaboration.

Productivity-Based Collaboration Gone Awry

Space Shuttle Flight Operations

When it was developed in the 1970s as a replacement for primitive single-use rockets, the Space Shuttle was intended to transform space travel into a commodity. The orbiter itself and its solid-rocket boosters —the most costly parts of the system—could be reused for one mission after another. Only the massive, but relatively inexpensive, fuel tanks would be jettisoned to burn up in the atmosphere. The National Aeronautics and Space Administration expected that orbital launches would become cheap and routine, and that the private sector would eventually take over the mundane work of shuttling corporate and government payloads into space.

The shuttle's glide path from cutting-edge experiment to cut-and-dried routine turned out to be much slower and bumpier than expected. Blasting people and equipment skyward on a column of flame, then bringing them home safely through the incandescent heat of reentry, involved thousands of technical challenges; and as each was surmounted, new ones emerged. The explosion of the *Challenger* in 1986 dramatized how very far from routine shuttle flight remained. Safety upgrades ordered in the wake of the disaster frustrated predictions of steadily declining costs. The three-year grounding of the

[14] Ibid., pp. 7, 39–40.

shuttle fleet required to implement these changes led military and commercial launch customers to abandon the shuttle and return to expendable rockets, shattering hopes for the scale economies that underlay the shuttle strategy.

By the mid-1990s, the shuttle program was in deep trouble. Its costs were straining the patience of Congress, and its operational demands were draining resources and management attention from other NASA missions. The Clinton administration's NASA chief seized upon a bold strategy of delegation to shrink both the cost and the management burden of running the shuttle. NASA's tangled skein of separate shuttle contracts, and most NASA personnel involved with the shuttle, were folded into a single Space Flight Operations Contract. A company called United Space Alliance (USA) won what turned out to be an eight-year, nearly $10 billion contract to handle virtually every aspect of the shuttle missions, from astronaut training to system assembly to launch and reentry management. A dozen major contracts were consolidated into the deal with USA, which also accepted oversight responsibility for the subcontractors that remained independent. Most NASA technicians and other workers with direct shuttle duties switched their badges to USA; a small remnant stayed behind to oversee the contract.

Despite heroic efforts to codify every element of shuttle operations, the contract was not and could not be fully specified; the shuttle system was simply too complex and volatile. Periodic upgrades, altered missions, process improvements, and continuous technological tinkering made every launch unique. Even after it built a sophisticated set of incentives into the contract, NASA could not unambiguously evaluate USA's performance. The operations model continued to evolve following the handoff, and the remnant of NASA personnel involved was too small—and, increasingly, too unfamiliar with the details of the enterprise—to exercise full oversight.[15]

---

[15] NASA eventually shifted its aspirations from oversight to what it called "insight"—a less intensive form of monitoring that left much to the contractor's discretion. Some shuttle managers, intensely concerned that the growing knowledge gap between NASA and United Space Alliance imperiled flight safety, called for efforts to reunite decision-making authority with flight

The paucity of competition undercut the government's prospects for cost savings through simple contracting. Very few private firms had the scale, experience, and technical know-how to contend for the shuttle operations contract. The short list was limited to two companies: Lockheed-Martin and Boeing. USA was a joint venture formed by Lockheed and Boeing to bid for the contract, and United Space Alliance's corporate bylaws specified that neither of its parents would compete against it.

NASA should not be faulted for seeking to leverage private productivity advantages. The agency's stumble—one seen all too often—was a failure to recognize the *kind* of delegation strategy it was actually pursuing. The illusion that any up-front contract could specify USA's mission across a vast range of functions and a long period of time led NASA to neglect alternative strategies for aligning public and private interests. Most seriously, NASA failed to face up to the near certainty that the relationship would need to be continuously adjusted as circumstances changed and new information surfaced. A collaborative delivery model was misconstrued as contractual outsourcing, and thus undermanaged.

Safeguarding Enriched Uranium

For an item of such grim significance, an atom bomb is not very difficult to make. An entry-level fission weapon, of the sort that obliterated Hiroshima, is basically a device for slamming two pieces of enriched uranium together to achieve critical mass and unleash a chain reaction. (In "enriched" uranium, the proportion of the unstable isotope U-235 has been artificially, and drastically, increased.) Making such a device requires only modest technical skills and readily available equipment. Only about fifty kilograms of highly enriched uranium—roughly the volume of six one-liter soda bottles—would be enough for a fission bomb that, if detonated in an urban center,

---

operations, either by unwinding the delegation or by making shuttle operations more conventionally private.

could kill hundreds of thousands of people and cause hundreds of billions of dollars in property damage.[16] Its fuel is relatively easy and safe to work with in quantities and configurations short of critical mass. For an aspiring terrorist with ambitions to incinerate a city, the main challenge is obtaining those fifty kilograms of enriched uranium. Enrichment requires expensive, sophisticated technology that only a few countries, and no known terror organizations, possess. A reasonable strategy for the bad guys, then, hinges on stealing the fuel from some laxly defended depot or buying it from some rogue supplier.

Ensuring that highly enriched uranium is secure from theft or clandestine sale is thus a first-order policy goal for the United States and any other country that could be a target of nuclear terrorism. Pursuit of this goal since the end of the Cold War has involved—not exclusively, but importantly—worrying a lot about Russia. Russia had vast stockpiles of weapons-grade uranium left over. Some experts estimate one thousand tons, others fifteen hundred, but no one knows for sure. It was certainly enough for thousands of bombs.[17] A single ton of this uranium, even crudely and wastefully processed, would be enough to obliterate a score of cities.

Concerned about Russia's stability, the United States began taking steps in the 1990s to reduce or secure Russia's stores of the fuel. One such initiative involved subsidies and technical advice for security measures at weapons depots. But the most significant initiative aimed to get rid of the warheads, and in an economically elegant way.

Early in 1993, Russia and the United States sealed an agreement to recycle nuclear warheads into fuel for power plants. This deal, informally called "Megatons to Megawatts," was designed to give Russia as a whole—and, more specifically, key scientists, technicians, and military personnel—a strong and enduring financial stake in countering the twin hazards of black-market sales and careless storage. Nuclear personnel became gainfully employed in dismantling warheads and

---

[16] This paragraph draws on technical material summarized in Gunnar Arbman et al., "Eliminating Stockpiles of Highly Enriched Uranium" (Swedish Nuclear Power Directorate, April 2004), accessed April 2006 at Pugwash Conference Web site, http://www.pugwash.org/reports/nw/heu-200415.pdf, pp. 13–14.

[17] Ibid., pp. 5 and 8.

transforming the highly enriched uranium cores into a mix potent enough for power plants but not for bomb making. This uranium was then shipped to the United States for sale to power utilities. The arrangement was expected to last until 2013, net $12 billion in hard currency for Russia, and get rid of five hundred tons (or about twenty thousand warheads' worth) of highly enriched uranium.[18] A prominent defense expert has termed this deal "one of the most intelligent national security initiatives in U.S. history."[19]

The organization assigned to implement this arrangement—to take possession of the Russian uranium and give the Russians cash in return—was and is the United States Enrichment Corporation. USEC's roots date back to the weapons programs of World War II and immediately afterward, when the government established a network of processing plants to make fuel for America's growing nuclear arsenal. In the 1960s, revisions to the Atomic Energy Act authorized the production of less potent fuel blends for commercial sales to power utilities, as a sideline to bomb making. The unit responsible for the commercial work, the United States Uranium Enrichment Enterprise, was one of many organizations assembled into the Department of Energy in 1977. The Energy Policy Act of 1992 then transformed this operation into the United States Enrichment Corporation, a stand-alone corporation, wholly owned by the federal government.[20]

Just as USEC was taking on a major antiterrorism role, however, a long-simmering debate was coming to a boil: is making reactor fuel more like producing warheads, and thus a proper job for government, or more like processing coal or oil or natural gas, and thus rightly left to private enterprise?

---

[18] This paragraph draws on data published by the Nunn-Turner Initiative, at http://www.nunnturnerinitiative.org/db/nisprofs/russia/fissmat/heudeal/heudeal.htm, accessed February 2006.

[19] Richard A. Falkenrath, "The HEU Deal and the U.S. Enrichment Corporation," *Nonproliferation Review*, Winter 1996, p. 62.

[20] Statistics and historical facts in this paragraph are from Marc Humphries, "Privatizing the United States Enrichment Corporation," CRS Issue Brief 95111 (Congressional Research Service, December 4, 1996). At the time it was spun off, USEC (like many Energy Department units) was heavily outsourced, with a nucleus of around 160 government employees supervising several thousand Lockheed-Martin contract employees who actually ran the enrichment facilities.

Objections arose almost from the moment USEC's predecessor branched out into processing uranium for commercial uses. Critics warned that public ownership was inconsistent with the efficient manufacturing and marketing of commercial nuclear fuel. As early as 1969 President Nixon had pledged to get government out of the enrichment business "at such a time as various national interests will best be served, including a reasonable return to the Treasury."[21]

Generic discomfort with public ownership of a production operation grew more specific when foreign suppliers began displacing U.S. exports of nuclear fuel and even making inroads into the domestic market. By the mid-1990s the U.S. share of the world reactor-fuel supply market had slipped from that of monopoly to control of barely a third.[22] Many members of Congress worried that unless America's uranium enrichment capacity was placed where it belonged—in the private sector—it would be operating at an inherent competitive disadvantage and would continue losing ground to overseas rivals. They believed a private USEC would be both enabled and motivated to improve efficiency by tapping capital markets to upgrade technology, by streamlining operations, and by taking a more rational approach to workforce management than government rules permitted. Concerned about the federal budget deficit, many also appreciated the prospect that the sale of USEC would generate cash.

Thus, in the mid-1990s, USEC's managers were grooming their agency for sale just as they were assigned to drain bomb-grade uranium from an insecure Russia under the Megatons to Megawatts program. The Energy Policy Act of 1992 had explicitly specified the ultimate full privatization of USEC, with these criteria, among others: maximize the proceeds for the government, keep USEC in American hands, and preserve a domestic source of nuclear fuel.[23] The Megatons to Megawatts program was not yet then in existence. In 1995 USEC managers submitted a report to the Clinton administration and Congress, outlining two different paths to privatization. One option was to seek a merger with some other enterprise to provide diversification.

[21] Quoted in Eric Moses, "Uranium, Inc.," *Government Executive*, April 1, 1997.
[22] Ibid.
[23] Ibid.

The other was to turn USEC into a stand-alone, single-business firm through an initial stock offering (IPO). The USEC Privatization Act of 1996 allowed for either approach.

Many observers felt the merger approach was more logical, since a merger would embed USEC within a larger enterprise featuring deep pockets and diversified risks. But the IPO was greatly in the interests of USEC managers and the eight investment banking firms advising them.[24] With a shove from payoff discretion, USEC took the path of the IPO. In 1998 a stock sale effectuated the shift from public to private ownership. The Megatons to Megawatts program was no longer a matter of public management, but a complex collaboration with an independent entity that had its own goals, constraints, and constituencies. A consequential constituency was the former management team, now substantial shareholders in USEC.

At the time of the stock sale, most observers expected USEC's pivotal role in Megatons to Megawatts to harmonize with, and even ease, its shift to independent, for-profit status. As one investment banker put it, "this was a company that possessed a vital link with government, which would certainly limit the downside risk."[25] A monopoly on a service unlikely to go out of fashion—mopping up Russian uranium that might otherwise fuel a terrorist bomb—was seen as ensuring steady work and a reliable cash flow for USEC, and thus justifying a high stock price. The stock sale, however, brought less than the Clinton administration's supposedly cautious prediction of $2 billion and much less than what the GAO had predicted USEC might be worth when privatization was first proposed.[26]

Subsequent events proved the market's prescience. The stand-alone USEC had a single line of business, aging equipment, and a precarious financial structure with very little working capital. Conflicts emerged between the company's institutional imperatives and its mission. In order to raise much-needed cash and almost immediately after going

---

[24] Terry Langeland, "Megatons to Mega-problems," *Bulletin of the Atomic Scientists* 58, no. 3 (2002): 54.

[25] David M. Schanzer of Janney Montgomery Scott, quoted in Daniel Gross, "Turning Arms into Energy, If Not Much Cash," *New York Times*, January 13, 2002, sec. 3, p. 4.

[26] Sale price from Langeland, "Megatons to Mega-problems," p. 54; GAO reference from Humphries, "Privatizing the United States Enrichment Corporation."

private, USEC started selling off stockpiles of uranium it had inherited from the Energy Department. But USEC was such a dominant player in the market that these sales drove down uranium prices. At the new price levels, USEC found that Megatons to Megawatts (MTM) transactions were suddenly not profitable.[27]

Responding to its commercial needs, precisely as would any independent for-profit company, USEC next sought to negotiate a better deal with its supplier. It altered the terms of the transactions and reduced the Russians' cash inflow. The Russians, in turn, threatened to pull out of the program until new legislation led to a $325 million subsidy from the U.S. Treasury that softened the blow of the forced repricing.[28]

But the first round of pressuring the Russians failed to shore up USEC's profitability, in part because of increasing import competition. In 2000 its stock plummeted and the company laid off a substantial fraction of its workforce. While some in Congress expressed second thoughts about the wisdom of privatizing the company, scattered proposals to bring it back into government gained no traction. Instead, USEC sought restored profitability in part through trade protection and in part by once again taking an aggressive negotiating stance with the Russians.

Purchases slowed and at times halted altogether as USEC pressed to improve on the terms of the preprivatization Megatons to Megawatts agreement. By early 2002, USEC's Russian counterpart agreed in principle to reopen the pricing scheme, and by the middle of the year formal contractual and treaty revisions cut the price USEC paid for Russian uranium by one-quarter, with a longer-term agreement to adjust the provisions to reflect market conditions.[29] The revised deal sharply improved USEC's financial prospects, as profits from Russian uranium balanced out the company's losses at its domestic enrichment operation. Layoffs ceased, as did threats from USEC to pull out of the Megatons to Megawatts deal. The sweeter terms for USEC, of

[27] Langeland, "Megatons to Mega-problems," p. 55.

[28] Ibid.

[29] Details are presented in Nancy Dunne, "U.S., Russia Set for Uranium Deal," *Financial Times*, February 26, 2006, p. 6, and in Kenneth Bredemeier, "A Nuclear Power Fissure," *Washington Post*, August 19, 2002, p. E-1.

course, came at the expense of its Russian counterpart, but once the G. W. Bush administration reaffirmed USEC's monopoly, the Russians had little leverage to use in protesting.[30]

"The most common form of stupidity," wrote Nietzsche, "is forgetting what we were trying to accomplish."[31] The cascade of events shifting the deal in USEC's favor was fairly predictable, once the organization was transformed into a for-profit corporation. But the goal of Megatons to Megawatts was not to ensure the fuel supply for U.S. commercial reactors, nor to solidify USEC's finances. It was to lower the odds that enriched uranium would fall into the wrong hands by giving the Russians a financially attractive alternative to illicit trafficking. The leaner the terms of this deal for the Russians, the greater their temptation to divert fuel to alternative channels. Failure to recognize and structure incentives to rectify the conflict between the purpose of the program and USEC's motives has very likely weakened a bulwark against nuclear terrorism. This collaborative model required an analysis of incentives, and an organizational architecture to align public and private goals, that simply did not occur. Payoff discretion was ignored; the collaboration's perils grew, and we are still living in their shadow.

The Charter-School Movement

Charter schools represent a well-developed example of productivity-motivated collaborative governance—and a prominent strategy for shoring up American education. A charter school is funded by government but run privately.[32] Its defining feature, the charter, is an incompletely specified contract that codifies the educational mission,

---

[30] Langeland, "Megatons to Mega-problems," p. 56. See also Falkenrath, "The HEU Deal and the U.S. Enrichment Corporation," p. 63.

[31] Friedrich Nietzsche, "The Wanderer and His Shadows," in *Human, All Too Human: A Book for Free Spirits*, trans. R. J. Hollingdale (Cambridge University Press, 1996), p. 360.

[32] The U.S. Department of Education defines charter schools as institutions that "provide free public elementary/secondary education under a charter granted by the state legislature or other appropriate authority." National Center for Education Statistics Statistical Analysis Report, *Overview of Public Elementary and Secondary Schools and Districts: School Year 2001–02* (U.S. Department of Education, May 2003), Glossary of Key Terms.

in most cases rather broadly, and that circumscribes, but does not eliminate, the freedom of teachers, administrators, and trustees to run the school as they see fit.

Education has been a particularly fertile area for innovations in governance for at least two reasons. First, authority for education policy has long been decentralized, with fifty states and tens of thousands of localities holding licenses to experiment. Second, for several decades public education, both elementary and secondary, has been seen as suffering from chronic performance deficits. The consensus that public education is broken motivates the search for new approaches. This consensus is somewhat overblown, to be sure; American public schools range from abominable to superb, and performance trends have been moderately positive, on average, since the 1970s. The conventional wisdom is certainly correct with respect to many poor urban schools, which badly lag behind their counterparts in richer suburbs.[33]

Public-school reforms can be roughly divided into three categories. The first includes campaigns to improve the performance of traditional schools without fundamentally altering their form. The second includes efforts to engage private organizations through conventional contracts either to perform particular functions (such as special education, tutoring, or library management) or to manage entire schools or even districts. Charter schools are the third branch of the broad reform movement, with a different—in our terms, collaborative— model for applying private energies to public missions. (The school-choice movement, another proposed response to performance deficits, aims less to improve public schools than to replace them.)

First, we look at a number of specific charter schools—with an emphasis on successful models—examining not just performance outcomes, but the nature of the educational process in each. Then we summarize what more systematic data tell us about the charter-school movement as a whole. The story is mixed—but in a way that solidly supports our theme that effective public-private collaboration

[33] Data from U.S. Department of Education, National Center for Education Statistics, National Assessment of Educational Progress, Long-Term Trend Assessment, at http://nces.ed .gov/nationsreportcard/ltt/results2004/, accessed December 2005.

hinges, perhaps paradoxically, on key capabilities within government itself.

A Sampling of Schools

Let's start in Buffalo. The old industrial city on the country's northern rim is strewn with shuttered factories, patterned by broad streets of once-grand, now badly faded houses, with here and there redevelopment projects struggling like new plantings in a blasted field. Many of Buffalo's people, those with the best prospects, left long ago. Those who remain—descendants of the Slavs and the Italians and the African Americans who flocked to the factories in the days when the buildings rang with the sounds of production—eke out economically modest and sometimes precarious existences.

Buffalo's public schools, for the most part, are the sorts of schools that you expect to find, and generally do, in a city in decline. Most of the city's people have sorted themselves out into distinctive neighborhoods—whites here, blacks there—so that most neighborhood schools are starkly segregated. The most talented teachers decamp for other cities, and the best that remain tend to shun as bad bets the troubled schools in poorer parts of town. The mix of money from federal, state, and local sources never seems enough to make the schools work as they should. Buffalo schools are far from the nation's worst, but most are very far from the best.

There are exceptions, predictable ones in Buffalo's prosperous areas and a certain school that is far from predictable. Well to the east of downtown, away from the Lake Erie waterfront, a school stands just off a dreary main road lined with pawnshops, check-cashing operations, and liquor stores with barred windows. On the outside the school is dull redbrick, a century old. Inside, though, is all color and order and focused energy. Student artwork covers almost every inch of the walls. The ancient linoleum gleams as if it had been laid down yesterday. Open one of the doors lining the broad corridors and there are children, quietly reading in some rooms, listening to a teacher in others, sketching designs or working at computers in yet others. They range from kindergarteners to eighth graders.

Every child wears a neat uniform—plaid skirts for the girls, black pants for the boys, white shirts for all. Every child is African American. When a visitor enters with the principal, they leap to their feet with a greeting. The principal invites them to sit, then calls on child after child by name to explain the day's lesson. As a child rattles off what she has just learned about Magna Carta or photosynthesis or exponents, the cynical eye looks in vain for signs of rehearsal or intimidation or rebellion against the rigor of uniforms and schedules and ritual greetings. The children seem as happy and lively and latently mischievous as children should be. It's just that this is school, and they have learned and accept how one behaves at school.

The former Public School 68 was renamed the Westminster Community Charter School in 1995. It is still a public school, required to admit all local children—to admit them, at least, to the lottery, since there is much more demand for a Westminster education than the school can meet. Westminster is in a rough neighborhood, with a poor and transient population. Most nearby schools score predictably low on standardized tests. Westminster's students outperform all but three of the forty-some schools in the Buffalo area.

Some five hundred miles to the east another charter school operates on a decommissioned army base slowly being shifted to civilian uses. The children at the Francis W. Parker Essential Charter School are older, on average, than those at Westminster—middle and high school, instead of elementary and middle school—and a notch or two up on the socioeconomic scale. They come from cities and towns across a fifty-mile swath ranging from Boston's western suburbs out to Worcester. While Parker—which we encountered briefly in chapter 1—draws more students from humbler towns like Leominster and Fitchburg than from Concord, Sudbury, and other tony locales in its domain, few Parker students are truly disadvantaged. The local schools they would attend in Parker's absence range from adequate to excellent.

Parker students aren't fleeing mediocrity, but are instead drawn to a special sort of education that suits a special sort of student. Parker attracts the smart kids who march to their own drummer. The sort who learn to play the lute instead of the guitar, prefer fencing to football, can't bring themselves to finish a science test but can build a robot that has local high-tech firms inquiring into licensing deals. Most would probably not fail at their hometown schools, but neither would they thrive as they do at Parker.

Parker's curriculum is an updated version of classic progressive education. Students do the work of learning; teachers act as coaches. Rather than the scatter of separate classes that most schools offer, two broad domains (Arts and Humanities, and Math, Science, and Technology) claim between them most of the curriculum. The conversation switches seamlessly from the aesthetics of a Michelangelo sculpture to the economic and cultural setting in which it was produced, or from the rules of calculus to the programming of a rocket's trajectory. Students meet with faculty advisers not yearly or monthly but every morning, in small groups that gather to focus the efforts of the day and connect them to the work of the days before and to come. While Parker's culture is genially contemptuous of standardized tests, and students and teachers rigorously avoid anything that could be construed as test preparation, its scores are routinely among the best in the state.

Parker was launched the same year as Buffalo's P.S. 68 became Westminster, both as early instances of the charter-school movement. Parker was the product of an alliance between a group of parents dissatisfied with their local schools—however good by objective metrics —and a celebrated pair of educational reformers, Theodore and Nancy Faust Sizer, who were living in the area in semiretirement. The Sizers had developed the model they called "essential" education over the decades when Ted served as headmaster of a legendary private school and as dean of Harvard's Graduate School of Education. The Sizers knew that the model could work spectacularly in an elite private school, with ample funding and the ability to choose its students. What the Sizers and a group of allies were eager to learn, though, was whether they could make the model work in a public school, with government funding—roughly ten thousand dollars per student, instead of double or triple that sum—and with open admission. The passage of a charter-school law in Massachusetts gave them a chance to find out.

The Sizer motto "Less is more" gained extra urgency as the founders ruthlessly economized on everything else to be able to hire excellent teachers and plenty of them. Parker's first building was an old army-intelligence headquarters, windowless and grim but cheap (and bomb proof.) Much of the battered furniture came from yard sales and looked it. Parent volunteers handled much of the administrative work. Every dollar saved went into teacher salaries, or into a reserve fund for eventually acquiring a decent building. (Massachusetts, like most states, left charters on their own to find the facilities that their public competitors received for free.)

Within little more than a decade the Sizers' experiment showed persuasive results. Parker could turn ten thousand dollars into a superb year of "essential" learning. Alumni were triumphing at elite universities and moving into successful—if still, often, slightly eccentric—careers. Parker was to become famous as a vital option for a certain kind of student, a kind of student that showed up in virtually every town from Boston to Worcester, and the annual lottery for joining Parker's entering class was an avidly awaited event.

One may be forgiven for assuming that the Academy of the Pacific Rim (APR) is located in Asia, given its intense eleven-month curriculum, or perhaps in California, given the mandatory study of Mandarin, or at least that the school's faculty and student body are predominantly of Asian origin. Instead the academy is housed in an old Westinghouse Corporation warehouse in the Hyde Park neighborhood of Boston, and its student body is nearly 60 percent African American. Asians constitute just 3 percent of the roughly 475 pupils enrolled in grades five through twelve. Half of the student body lives at or below poverty level.

The academy was founded in 1997 on the principle of "East Meets West," emphasizing the standards, discipline, and character education drawn from Japanese, Chinese, and other Asian societies together with the individualism, creativity, and diversity characteristic of Western society. APR's pedagogical approach is heavily skewed toward character development through the Japanese principles of *kaizen*, or continual improvement, and *gambatta*, persistence, as well as five more "Central Character Virtues": purpose, responsibility, integrity, daring, and excellence. Together these produce the acronym for the school's character development program: KG-PRIDE. Teachers periodically rate their classes, as well as individual students, on their adherence to the character principles based on such indicators as the use of respectful language, consistency in turning in homework, and the students' effectiveness in maintaining tidy classrooms, as well as a clean lunch area, where students prepare and serve food. (The school, intent on devoting as many resources as possible to hiring the best teachers, has no janitor.)

Character development complements carefully constructed academic instruction, which begins with a disciplined approach to math, science, and the arts and humanities at lower grade levels and gradually morphs into more student-directed free-form explorations of those subjects in higher grades. One inviolable principle: no social promotion. Instead, students who are weak in a subject are given tutoring, individualized instruction, and even summer courses to correct the deficit before moving up. When even those efforts fail to bring the student's knowledge or skills up to par, he or she is simply held back rather than promoted to the next grade. Yet that tough promotion policy does not discourage the vast majority of parents whose child is held back. Roughly 85 percent of held-back students stay at APR.

A central goal of APR's rigorous academic and character development program is to prepare students for college and careers. Uniforms are the usual attire, but, on the first Wednesday of each month, students can "dress for success," donning ties and sport coats or business-appropriate dresses to attend a lunch seminar with a business or professional person who explains the nature and requirements of a particular career. APR's Pacific Rim Enrichment Program requires high school students to spend more than two hundred hours over three summers in internships with local law firms, hospitals, or other businesses, or in organized summer programs at Harvard College or Boston University.

APR's board sets high standards for faculty. They are expected to use a wide variety of pedagogical approaches, from lectures to group discussions to individual tutoring. Each teacher designs his or her own curriculum, and many work late into the night or over weekends preparing lessons. Individual instruction and tutoring add to the workload, with the result that APR middle school students receive anywhere from twenty to sixty-four more instructional days than their public school district peers, and high school students get ten to fifty more instructional days than district peers. Principals and deans monitor and evaluate classrooms frequently, and teachers do regular peer reviews. Effective teamwork among the faculty, including sharing information about how individual students are progressing and what needs to be done to remedy problems, as well as coordinating the curriculum for each grade year, is a criterion in each teacher's formal biannual evaluation.

The result of APR's unique approach to education is only partly shown by statistics, but those statistics are very impressive. Every tenth grader passed the Massachusetts Comprehensive Assessment System test on the first try in 2007, and 92 percent of alumni enroll in college. Character development has few metrics, but if outside observers— whether academics or researchers preparing reports or parents visiting the school with the hopes of winning the lottery for a slot at APR—are right, APR is succeeding in its mission to instill the principles of KG-PRIDE in its students.

The charter-school movement is by some measures the largest and most consequential contemporary experiment in collaborative governance. As such, we give it pride of place as the centerpiece of this chapter. The movement is built on the bet that in at least some ways—ways that matter—private actors can be more productive than government in turning resources into educational value added. In 1991, Minnesota became the first state to authorize charter schools. Since then, the movement has grown to encompass schools in 40 states, the District of Columbia (now a major testing ground), and Puerto Rico. By the fall of 2009 there were about 5,000 charter schools enrolling about 1.5 million students. Charters are primarily funded by their claim on the funding that follows a student who opts for a charter instead of a conventional public school, although many also benefit from private donations and various public and private grants.[34]

The charter approach has attracted a remarkably broad range of political support, finding champions from all but the distant left and right fringes of the political spectrum. Presidents Bill Clinton, George W. Bush, and Barack Obama have each led aggressive and high-profile efforts to promote charter schools. The movement has also gained support from the philanthropic elite, performers, and other celebrities. The Andre Agassi College Preparatory Academy, for example, was launched a decade ago by the tennis star—himself a ninth-grade dropout—primarily to serve underprivileged minority students in his hometown of Las Vegas. Its goal is to send all its students—who are selected by lottery from an oversubscribed pool of applicants—to college. The academy is both a high-performing school and a favorite cause within Agassi's circle of A-list athletes, who have helped the academy raise prodigious amounts of private funding to supplement the resources it receives from government.[35] Westminster, Parker, and APR are exemplars of successful charter schools, and we could point to a great many more, including networks of schools like the Knowledge Is Power Program (KIPP) with eighty schools as of 2010, and Achievement First with seventeen. Other charter schools are disappointing— and some, alas, are dreadful.

The Case for Charters

In principle, the charter movement should promote the replication of successful models and the suppression of bad ideas. This could happen in any combination of three ways: supply decisions, demand decisions, and effective orchestration by the state and local governmental

[34] Charter schools typically face a financial handicap in that state and local payments cover current spending only, leaving them in the lurch for capital costs. Countering this, to a degree, charters tend to have better access to grants and donations than do conventional public schools.

[35] The school's Web site is http://www.agassiprep.org/. In his autobiography Agassi writes with pride and passion of the school, and reports that on any given day Shaquille O'Neal, Lance Armstrong, or Muhammad Ali might drop by. *Open: An Autobiography* (Alfred A. Knopf, 2009), p. 381.

managers overseeing charters. On the supply side, those creating or extending charters could imitate the practices that worked best, much as we see in markets for private goods. Demand side forces could work if parents enrolled their children in effective charter schools and pulled them out of poorly performing charters. Astute orchestration by government could include everything from providing information to parents on the performance of various schools, to tough decisions about granting and renewing charters.

With restaurants, the magic of the market builds on the best and gets rid of the worst. With charters, the evidence suggests, the process is much less automatic. Some locales do well at winnowing out the inferior models and replicating the better ones.[36] Others do poorly, thus indicating that details of policy, regulation, and institutional structure are critical. Charter legislation varies widely from state to state in many of its provisions, such as which entities can issue charters, what kinds of organizations are eligible to operate such schools, the length of the charter, and limits on numbers. Most states exempt charter schools from some or most of the collective-bargaining, teacher certification, and other requirements that bind conventional public schools. But charter schools' discretion is controlled in many domains, including some that the schools might feel most important. In most cases they cannot choose which students they will accept but must admit among applicants by lottery. They must adhere to state norms on student assessment, financial management, and some curricular requirements, and are bound by the terms of their charter.

Charter schools were invented to improve the performance of primary and secondary public education. This goal includes increasing efficiency by reducing the resources required to deliver each increment of educational value, increasing effectiveness by boosting the overall educational value delivered, supporting diverse learning styles, giving parents some control over the style of education their children

---

[36] The recent large-scale study that is most negative on charter schools, the CREDO (2009) study from Stanford University, looks at evidence from sixteen states. In five, charters outperformed traditional public schools; in six they underperformed. See http://credo.stanford .edu/reports/MULTIPLE_CHOICE_CREDO.pdf, and, for our online appendix to this chapter, http://press.princeton.edu/titles/9401.html.

receive, and giving less-affluent students access to innovative educational approaches usually found only in private schools. The mission also has dimensions that go beyond serving current students, including experimenting with new pedagogical ideas to expand the repertoire of methods available to all educators.

It is not initially obvious why the comparatively complex, collaborative charter-school model should form so prominent a part of the educational reform portfolio. Given the managerial burdens and risks of collaborative governance, and the vast investments already made in existing schools, one might have thought that reformers would have focused on improving the performance of conventional public schools. Some scholars and practitioners ply this route, of course. But many are ideologically disinclined to place their bets on government-run schools, or discouraged by the evidence of failed past efforts. They proclaim that the basic structure of public education is too rigid to change to meet today's needs. The case for charters starts with the presumption that the private sector can offer greater flexibility and hence greater efficiency. Charter advocates view private organizations as more prone to good performance—more responsive, more efficient, more attentive to both costs and new opportunities—than public schools, either inherently or because of the incrustations of rules, regulations, and dependent constituencies that have built up within existing school systems.

But even if we are confident that the private sector has a large and reliable efficiency edge, why not tap that advantage by the straightforward approach of contracting? Why have reformers invested so much energy in the charter movement instead of pushing to expand service contracting for particular functions within schools or, more ambitiously, for the management of schools or whole districts?

There are many reasons, actually. Charter operators are usually nonprofit, while contractors are often for-profit, and there are both cultural shibboleths and entirely reasonable causes for caution about mixing the profit motive with education. Charters may also represent an acceptable middle ground both for those whose first choice is getting government out of education, and for those whose first choice is some improved version of the classic public school.

There is ample room for skepticism about using a simpler contractual approach for many educational functions. Many of the tasks involved in running a school—transportation, food service, maintenance—are well suited to simple contracting.[37] But for many aspects of public education, including many of its most troublesome dimensions, contracting is an awkward and error-prone approach. It is difficult to specify in advance the details of the work to be done. It is also more difficult to evaluate performance with sufficient promptness and precision to enforce accountability through contracts. As we discuss elsewhere, the fundamental barrier to improving education through contractual outsourcing is the chronic difficulty of measuring the pedagogical value added by the intervention. And meaningful competition is hard to engineer. None of the key criteria for accountable contracting really apply. Those who are inclined to place large bets on charter schools, thus, are implicitly or explicitly embracing two precepts: first, that private organizations promise superior productivity in the education sector; and second, that conventional contracts are inadequate instruments for harnessing private advantages within the contexts of dysfunctional schools.

Production Discretion as the Hallmark of Charters

The charter movement highlights the defining features of collaborative governance. A public entity (the chartering authority) delegates a public task to a private entity through an explicitly codified relationship (the charter) marked by shared discretion. The central issue, as always, is the public value gained through the granting of production discretion to a private collaborator minus the public value lost due to payoff and preference discretion.

The public partner establishes the process for requesting a charter. It can accept, reject, or call for changes in the initial charter for each school. It can impose rules that circumscribe the school's options: that establish lottery protocols for admitting students, set a minimum

---

[37] In principle, such tasks can be outsourced quite readily, though this occurs rather rarely in practice. See Donahue, *The Warping of Government Work*, 101–136, for some evidence and observations on this issue.

number of school days, delineate some curricular requirements. It can decide at what level to reimburse schools for the students they enroll, and can regulate to what extent they can supplement public funds, whether through student charges or donations. And it can punish the school by declining to renew its charter, and in extreme cases revoking the charter before it expires.

The school managers have broad freedom to develop their own pedagogical approach in the charter application. This application typically lays out the school's proposed governance and management structure, educational philosophy, goals, and the means by which performance will be demonstrated. Once the charter is accepted and signed, this dimension of discretion narrows sharply; the managers are obliged to deliver on the terms of the charter, but they retain a significant range of discretion over the ways they pursue this mission.[38]

By exercising their production discretion, charter schools can create public value in several ways. To start, they reap simple improvements in operational efficiency. Free from the intricate network of personnel regulations that bind conventional public schools, a charter can select and reward teachers on the basis of performance rather than seniority. It can choose curricular material, and revise its choices, on the basis of teachers' judgments rather than requirements handed down by the school board or some central administration. It can experiment with unconventional schedules, team teaching, class sessions that integrate math and science or history and languages, classes that are combined or subdivided relative to the K-12 norms, heavy reliance on technology-based methods, and so on. Compared to their conventional counterparts, many charter schools have longer school days or longer school years. Many pay their teachers less, and quite a few pay them more. Positive results for charters could be either the same performance at lower costs or—more germane to most charter advocates' priorities—higher performance for the same level of resources.

Charter schools can also create public value, not just by doing the same thing better, but by doing different things, namely, providing

[38] In the language of Chester Finn and his colleagues, "Although answerable to outside authorities for their results ... they are free to produce those results as they think best." Chester Finn, Jr., et al., *Charter Schools in Action* (Princeton University Press, 2000), p. 15.

learning in areas important to their students' development, but slighted in public schools. This ability to tilt the objectives is what motivates many enthusiasts of the charter movement. Charter schools can accelerate improvements in the standard version of public education, accommodating new goals and seizing new opportunities more rapidly. And, perhaps more importantly, they can offer a diverse menu of educational approaches. Charter-school advocates shun pedagogical homogeneity and prize diversity, as Chester Finn explains: "The charter idea assumes that schools should differ from each other so that the diverse needs of a pluralistic society can be met. It allows for 'back to basics' schools, 'progressive' schools, virtual schools, Montessori schools, Waldorf schools, Comer schools, Core Knowledge schools, Advantage schools, Hope Academies, schools for at-risk kids, alternative schools, and all manner of public-private hybrids."[39]

Anyone well acquainted with more than one child is likely to agree that children have different learning styles. An educational system catering to many ways of learning ought to be able to serve a heterogeneous student population better than could a system offering a single approach, or one differentiating only by sweeping categories like "special needs" or "gifted and talented." While charter advocates care about simple efficiency and expect charters to outperform conventional schools, they tend to care more about educational diversity. The notion that charters create educational value by expanding the options available to students and parents is at once central to the appeal of this collaborative approach and, as we now relate, the source of one of its gravest risks.

Payoff and Preference Discretion

Payoff discretion refers to the flexibility that a private collaborator can use, either to augment the total pool of value or to claim for itself a larger share of that pool. This variant of the dark side of discretion tends to be a more serious hazard when the private partner is for-

---

[39] Ibid., pp. 70–71.

profit, and thus tends to be a smaller problem for the nonprofit-dominated charter-school movement. Nevertheless, a few states permit for-profits to apply for charters themselves, and all states allow charter holders to delegate the day-to-day operations of their school to a profit-seeking management firm.[40] To the extent that discretion falls to the management firm, the classic tensions of payoff discretion can arise as operations are subtly nudged into alignments that swell private rather than public surpluses.

Nonprofit collaborators can also exercise payoff discretion. Even without pressure from profit-hungry owners, nonprofits still need to cover their costs and generally prefer larger to smaller financial reserves. They may exercise payoff discretion to benefit not the institution but the *individuals* within it—managers or other employees who are in a position to capture greater benefits for themselves, rather than produce the greatest possible public value.

But preference discretion—the ability to do things the way the private collaborator wants to do them—is likely to be the greater source of the tension in the charter-school domain. It arises from the characteristics of both the private collaborators and the task. A nonprofit seeking a charter may be uninterested in financial gain, but it is likely to be organized around fervently held and distinctive educational beliefs. Those on the private side of the collaboration are likely to be passionate about their preferences, laying the foundation for conflicts between public and private priorities.

At the same time, the characteristics of the task make it difficult to distinguish between legitimate and illegitimate pedagogical diversity in practice, and frequently even in principle. This difficulty arises from the ambiguous nature of the public stakes in an individual child's education. At its narrowest, education may be seen as just one among many services that people can choose to consume for their

40 SRI International, "Evaluation of the Public Charter Schools Program: Final Report," Report prepared for the Office of the Deputy Secretary (U.S. Department of Education, November 2004), p. 32. As of 2002, nearly one-fifth of charters relied on management firms for at least some services See also Alex Molnar et al., *Profiles of For-Profit Education Management Organizations 2004–05*, Seventh Annual Report (Education Policy Studies Laboratory, Arizona State University, Tempe, Arizona, April 2005), p. 13, table 2.

own benefit, with the community requiring only that each consumer receive a minimum share of the service.[41]

A slightly broader construction would still view schooling as an investment geared to produce overwhelmingly private benefits, but one in which individual preferences may be flawed. Families might be myopic not just about the right amount of education to obtain for their children, but also about the right kind. Some may underrate the future payoff from studying languages and social sciences relative to math and technology (or vice versa); others may erroneously predict that a deep grounding in a child's culture will matter more for her future well-being than high earning power (or, again, vice versa). Even if they can correctly rank the value of alternative educational products, families may have difficulties distinguishing between competent and incompetent providers of each option.

Such a reading of the market's limitations for K-12 education implies that one important government role could be to help families be smart shoppers. It could provide information about the test performance of different schools, the strengths and weaknesses of their curricular offerings, how alumni fare in future schooling and careers, and so on. It can also take more intrusive steps to circumscribe educational choices. The state might bar charter schools that teach contempt for democracy or for capitalism, or that run classes exclusively in Spanish or Ebonics, on the grounds that such curricula are bad for children even if they appeal to parents, just as the state bars the sale of LSD even though some people want to consume it.

A still more ambitious version of the rationale for public financing interprets education as a hybrid good offering both individual and collective payoffs. By this view, the community has stakes in an individual's schooling because other people's future welfare will be affected by the amount and nature of education that person receives,

[41] In this view the community has no quarrel with whatever definition of "education" a family happens to embrace, but simply wants to make sure they consume at least a certain amount of it per child. If *this* is the only rationale behind public spending on K-12 education, the exercise of preference discretion by charter schools is not really a problem, since any educational vision that attracts students is as valuable as any other. Note, though, that if this is the only rationale behind public spending for education, a shift to pure school vouchers would be a simpler and equally valid reform strategy.

an interest that can be separate from, or in conflict with, the priorities of students and their families. A couple might want their child to be educated in ways that maximize his own future income, while the rest of us might put priority on preparing him as well to be a reliable subordinate or a trustworthy coworker or an honorable boss. Or parents might want their child to grow up sharing their preference for contemplative cultural pursuits over grubby practicality while the rest of us—mindful of the national debt to be serviced and the tumbling ratio of workers to retirees—would like her to absorb a strong work ethic and a pragmatic cast of mind.

More broadly, and no less importantly for this interpretation, public spending for education may be motivated by a common interest in shaping not just competent producers and consumers but responsible, informed, and respectful citizens as well. Aspiring charter holders who propose to celebrate one ethnic heritage at the expense of others, or to slight history and civics in the curriculum to make room for more courses in technology and marketing, could have preferences that match those of a sizable group of parents but that conflict with essential criteria that justify taxing one citizen to finance the education of other citizens' children. As we move along the spectrum of alternative conceptions of educational value—from strictly private to significantly public—the complexities, both conceptual and practical, of implementing a charter-school initiative proliferate.

The Governance Challenge Presented
by the Charter Movement

The difficulties of conventional education management are chiefly tactical (juggling staff, space, and schedules; ensuring that curricula mesh across grade levels; making the buses run on time) and political (coping with school boards, soothing unhappy parents, navigating the rapids of bureaucratic politics). Charter schools introduce governance requirements of a significantly different nature. Their management—on behalf of the citizenry at large—must be strategic, since it involves overseeing and at times guiding independent institutions with both their own motives and substantial spans of discretion. The manager's task is to weave a fabric of information flows, constraints, and incentives that maximizes the gains from production discretion while minimizing the losses from payoff and preference discretion.

Public officials overseeing a charter system must meet several challenges at once. The first is to get the right individuals and organizations to create and run the charter schools. This means inducing organizations with the appropriate goals and capacity to apply for charters, and then issuing charters to high-potential applicants while denying those less promising. Government officials orchestrating charter systems must also negotiate charter terms, monitor performance, and renew or revoke charters in ways that intensify the incentives to foster public value.

Most charter advocates hope and expect that charter schools can provide not just a superior organizational technology for producing homogeneous educational value, but also a diversified portfolio of educational approaches tailored to a range of needs and priorities. But if we want charters to approach education differently from conventional public schools—as well as doing the same thing in different and presumably better ways—then governing a network of charter schools becomes far more challenging. It is not enough to attract and grant charters to well-suited applicants, set test-score targets, and reward or punish charter schools in accord with their students' performance. Public managers must also calibrate the value of the educational vision embodied in each charter application, judge whether the applicant's motives and capacity accord with that vision, comparatively rank applications that propose to deliver value in very different currencies, and then monitor matters to determine how well each charter school is actually delivering on its distinctive promises.[42]

Students and their families can also exercise discretion, and their preferences interact with those of charter operators in ways that can

---

[42] If test results captured all that matters about charter performance, and if a sturdy accountability structure motivated charter schools to maximize test scores, then dealing with preference discretion would be a minor chore. It would not matter whether a charter school's teachers and administrators inwardly cherished ethnic pride, the Socratic method, phonics, self-esteem, traditional values, artistic creativity, or Esperanto. They would either align their preferences with the production of high test scores, or suppress them. However, management becomes much more complex as the spectrum of legitimate educational missions widens, implying that tests can capture only a fraction of what matters.

either ease or complicate governmental efforts to minimize the abuse of preference discretion. Two key issues apply here: first, the balance between parents' preferences and other considerations in defining education's public value, and, second, parents' capacity to distinguish effective from ineffective charter-school operations. The simplest case applies when we merely stipulate that a good public education is whatever parents want for their children, and when we are confident that parents can identify schools that will deliver a high-quality version of their brand of education. In this simple world, charter operators can offer whatever model of education they prefer, and the schools finding favor with parents are, by construction, legitimate producers of public value. If we believe that parents are *exclusive* and *knowledgeable* arbiters of educational value, in other words, there is little need for worry about preference discretion on the part of charter schools. Parental choice will be all we need.

Let's agree that parents are important but not exclusive arbiters of value, and also that a school must contain some nucleus of public purpose if it is to receive public funds. The content of this nucleus, the political and institutional procedures by which it is defined, and the share of the curricular space it occupies will differ across communities, between levels of education, and over time. But in any case, under this scenario, some sets of educational agendas will qualify for public funding, and some will not, even *if* they find favor with parents. To the extent that this more demanding standard for tax-funded education prevails, the public officials responsible for school chartering must not only be able to understand, evaluate, and manage the preferences of charter operators. They must also have a thorough and concrete grasp of what makes education "public" in the eyes of the community that pays for it, and be able to distinguish between legitimate and illegitimate curricular diversity.

Realizing the Potential of Charter Schools

There have been dozens of studies of charter schools, including a score or so summarized in an extensive empirical addendum that we make available online: http://press.princeton.edu/titles/9401.html. The studies target different pieces of the puzzle, use different measures of success, employ different analytical strategies, and are done by people with differing degrees of skill, objectivity, and perhaps candor. So it is not surprising that you can find a published study to support just about any assertion you might care to make about the merits of charter schools. A number of studies, however, are quite rigorous and objective, and their most important finding is clear: a significant number of charter schools do deliver substantially superior outcomes, as measured by test scores—including outcomes for low-income and minority students. If we can find ways to follow the path of the top-tier schools, the charter movement has great potential to improve American education.

One key issue in assessing performance concerns how to surmount a fundamental barrier to fair comparisons: the difference between students at charter schools and those attending regular schools. Students at charters—who affirmatively choose their schools, or whose parents do so for them—are certainly not the same as students who continue with the local public school. The question is *how* they differ, or rather the relative weight of the various ways they differ, beyond measures such as race or income or locale. Some families opt for charters out of desperation, when a child was faltering badly at her prior school. Some families opt for charters out of ambition, since many charters (and not so many regular schools, especially in poor neighborhoods) both require and reward active parental involvement. If the former effect predominates, charters will have more than their share of weak students, and simple comparisons will underrate their ability to create educational value. If the latter, charter students will be abler than average, and test scores will overstate their success.

A rich enough data pool could overcome this barrier. If we had a national system for tracking every student's test scores over time—like the national system for tracking every worker's income—then jumps or slumps in performance as a student moves from one school to another would provide a lot of leverage for isolating the "school effect" from the student effect. Or if an experiment could randomly assign large groups of students to either charters or regular schools, we could get a fix on charter performance unpolluted by hidden differences in student populations. But neither remedy is on the horizon, forcing researchers to improvise ways to "control for" student characteristics using coarse and partial measures. Fortunately, there is sometimes a near equivalent to a randomized controlled trial. In many jurisdictions, students must be admitted to charters by lottery among all applicants. Then, by comparing the performance of those who won the lottery and those who lost, as a number of conscientious studies have done, we get something very close to such an experiment.[43]

One thing *can* be said at this stage, with a fair degree of confidence: there is no large and systematic difference, on average, between charters and regular schools in the educational results they deliver. If charter schools as a group enjoyed a large performance edge over other schools, or suffered a large performance deficit, we would know by now. There is already too much experience with charters, and too many avid partisans anxious to prove the case either way, for a dramatic average difference to remain hidden.

The key word in the prior sentence, though, is "average." In principle, a small average difference could mean that all or most charters are trivially better, or trivially worse, than conventional schools. Alternatively, a small average difference could mean that some charters are a great deal better, and others are a great deal worse, than conventional public schools with the big wins and big losses pretty much canceling out in the aggregate.

Both common sense and the overwhelming weight of the empirical work to date suggest that the second interpretation is far more plausible than the first. Some charter schools use their freedom to create curricular offerings that deliver tremendous performance by the metric of test scores, and even more public value that eludes the coarse empirical nets of standardized testing. Some charters deploy their discretion opportunistically or cynically, collecting private benefits at the expense of public value. And some—no doubt many—sincerely intend to deliver high educational performance but simply bungle the job.

---

[43] Nitpickers could observe that inferior performance by lottery losers might be due to some discouragement effect, not an inferior education. Alternatively, inferior performance by winners might be due to laziness, because they "knew" they would be lucky in life.

Winnow, Expand, and Replicate

There is actually good news—at least conditionally good news—in the evidence that some charter schools are terrific, some are terrible, and the average is close to a wash. The fact that great charter schools exist—Parker and Westminster and the Academy of the Pacific Rim and many, many more—suggests a powerful strategy for making the most of the charter movement: winnow, expand, and replicate. The logic is simple. Experiment with dozens or scores or hundreds of different kinds of charter schools. Assess the results with an honest eye. Shut down what doesn't work. Scale up and reproduce what does. Repeat as needed.

That's the ideal. But today's reality is that the charter movement presents a blend of stellar and subpar schools with little net benefit, on balance, to American education. This is *not* a refutation of the notion that collaboration with discretion-wielding private partners can create public value in the educational realm. Still less is it an indictment of the private sector; of *course* education entrepreneurs cover a wide range of motives and competence. Rather, it reflects regrettable shortfalls in *governance*.

If the officials responsible for the public side of this collaboration did a better job on their key governance tasks—selecting the right charter applicants and motivating them appropriately—the range of charter performance would be narrower and higher. Suppose the officials authorizing charter schools were more consistently successful at weeding out the weak and shady applicants, and at granting charters to the good bets—even diamonds in the rough with solid fundamentals but shaky marketing skills. Suppose the officials overseeing charter schools were able to loosen or tighten the reins of discretion in light of performance, requiring laggards to mend their ways and letting the stars innovate unfettered. In such a scenario—without assuming any changes whatsoever in the private-sector population of potential charter operators—we could realistically expect far clearer, and far more positive, evidence that the charter movement was delivering on its promise.

Subpar governance, on the public side of this experiment in collaboration, is not in the least surprising. Most states have failed to recognize the public-sector challenges that charter schools entail, and have grievously underinvested in governance capacity. The Government Accountability Office (GAO) found in 2005 that only eleven states provided any funding whatsoever for oversight by local districts or other charter-school authorizers.[44] When states were surveyed in 2004 about the personnel dedicated to charter-school oversight, the most common response was that the state had a single full-time-equivalent staffer on the job. Arizona's two staffers were overseeing nearly 150 charters each.[45] Among all the public entities entrusted with authorizing charters—including state boards, universities, and the most common, local governments—just one-third had any identifiable staff unit devoted to charter oversight.[46]

The charter movement has been widely misconstrued as lifting from government's shoulders, and shifting to private actors, the responsibility for creating public value. But it actually represents a transformation, more than a diminution, of government's role. A shift from conventional public schools to charter schools entails different tasks for government, but those tasks are vital ones. To maximize the odds that private discretion works in the service of public value, government must choose, enable, motivate, and oversee its collaborators. If charter schools, as a group, are failing to deliver the clear-cut performance gains that advocates anticipated, it may be less because we have overestimated the power of private-sector innovation than because we have misconstrued the governance work to be done.

[44] U.S. Government Accountability Office, Report to the Secretary of Education, "Charter Schools: To Enhance Education's Monitoring and Research, More Charter-School Level Data Are Needed," GAO-05-5 (January 2005), p. 21, table 4.

[45] SRI International, "Evaluation of the Public Charter Schools Program: Final Report," p. 18.

[46] Ibid., p. 38 and p. 50, exhibit 4-8. It is also worth noting that an American Federation of Teachers study found that in California and Connecticut, states with generally more rigorous oversight, average charter performance was better than in jurisdictions with less oversight (Texas, Arizona, Michigan, DC, and Colorado). F. Howard Nelson et al., "Charter School Achievement on the 2003 National Assessment of Educational Progress" (American Federation of Teachers, August 2004), 13–15, tables 8 and 9.

Skills for Successful Governance

If the charter movement is to deliver its full potential, the public party to the collaboration must have several skills and the authority to use them.

- Chartering officials must set requirements and establish procedures that encourage applications from qualified candidates while discouraging both incompetents and those whose educational agendas are beyond the pale.

- When processing charter proposals, government must strive to avoid both errors of commission (granting charters to applicants unable or disinclined to deliver public value), and those of omission (declining charters to promising applicants).

- It must ensure that each charter describes goals and expectations clearly enough to distinguish between success and failure, and lay out the terms by which performance will be judged.

- Where charter requirements are fully specified, it must monitor operations to ensure that they are being met.

- Where requirements are imperfectly defined, it must monitor operations to calibrate the balance between production discretion and payoff and preference discretion.

- It must base decisions to renew or revoke a charter on clear criteria, objective evidence, and transparent procedures. Absent clarity, politics will swamp reason.

- Government should disseminate scorecards for schools. This will facilitate choices by parents, and will help other schools to follow the best.

- Finally, government must revise and refine policies and procedures in all of these areas as experience accumulates.

It is unrealistic and unfair, of course, to expect every jurisdiction experimenting with charters to possess all of these governance capacities. After all, the parallel requirements for public-school governance are rarely met nearly in full, and governance imperatives—and, in particular, *management* imperatives—tend to be afterthoughts in charter initiatives. Still, if these tasks are performed reasonably well, adding charter schools to the educational menu of a state or district will result in a broadly positive collaboration. If these tasks are performed badly, or simply ignored, payoff and particularly preference discretion will flourish. Production discretion will yield lower benefits than it would had the managers selected the right charter applicants and presented them with the right monitoring-and-incentive scheme. The charter movement will fall short of its potential.

A well-governed charter movement, by contrast—blending private productivity and diversity with wise public stewardship—has the potential to dramatically improve the quality of American education, particularly in the poor urban areas where current performance tends to be lamentably low. If Westminster and Parker and the Academy of the Pacific Rim prove to be harbingers of the future—if we are wise and honest enough to make the most of what the charter option offers—then the charter movement will be the poster child for boosting productivity in the creation of public value through collaboration.

Chapter 5

◇◇

Collaboration for Information

$\mathbf{B}$ring the knowledgeable party into the tent. That is the generic argument for collaborations motivated by information. When government lacks information essential to the accomplishment of a public mission—and private actors possess it—collaboration is an imperative, not an option. To go it alone is to travel blind. This is not so, of course, if government can easily acquire the necessary information. But vital data sometimes cannot be obtained with reasonable speed, at reasonable cost, and with reasonable reliability. The private sector may, for reasons good or bad, refuse to divulge everything it knows. Or information may be so deeply embedded in a private organization, so hard to provide or interpret correctly outside its context, that even the most willing private player cannot fully or effectively share it with government. Or government may suspect (again, for reasons good or bad) that information transfers would be biased, incomplete, or distorted so that public officials cannot be confident that they have the truth at all, much less the whole truth and nothing but. In such circumstances, turning to better-informed partners can be a powerful motive for collaboration. But it also means that government starts off with a built-in information deficit relative to its private-sector counterparts, suggesting special challenges in the pursuit of efficiency, accountability, and fairness.[1]

---

[1] The challenges presented by incomplete information flow have motivated an extensive literature in economics. The classic article is George J. Stigler, "The Economics of Information," *Journal of Political Economy* 69, no. 3 (1961): 213–225. See also Joseph E. Stiglitz, "The Contributions of the Economics of Information to Twentieth Century Economics," *Quarterly Journal of Economics* 115, no. 4 (2000): 1441–1478. Major contributions to this field have been made by George Akerlof, Kenneth J. Arrow, and A. Michael Spence. All authors cited here have won the Nobel Prize for their work.

Federal job-training policy provides an example, already cited, in which collaboration grew out of private industry's almost inevitably superior understanding of how to pursue a public mission. America's long-standing reliance on private actors in workforce development has roots in all four rationales for collaboration: productivity, information, legitimacy, and resources. But the strongest and most consistent argument in this area is the private sector's characteristically weighty information advantage. Equipping willing workers with the skills that can take them from minimum-wage to middle-class employment is a public mission endorsed across a wide expanse of the political spectrum. But advancing that goal efficiently requires detailed information about the future labor market, particular knowledge about individual workers, and practical links to employment opportunities.

Suppose a low-skilled worker—let's call her Betty—walks into the office of a government agency responsible for worker training. Betty is stuck in a dead-end job. She meets the eligibility requirements for subsidized training to improve her earning power. How can the government best get Betty the training she needs? To illustrate the interplay of interests and information in the human-capital arena, and the elusiveness of any perfect solution, consider three options.

First, the governmental agency could deliver the training itself. Worker training is somewhat akin to primary and secondary education, after all, which is an entirely conventional public-sector mission. And direct governmental training has been a factor in workforce development in most times and places, and in some settings it remains the dominant model. If the agency opted to train Betty itself, it could start by consulting its voluminous collection of official statistics. The data banks show that manufacturing work tends to be well paid, and that some jobs within manufacturing resist the general trend of job losses to automation and outsourcing. Standardized tests show that Betty has the intellectual ability to succeed as a process-control technician. Her current company employs many such technicians, at wages three times what Betty earns in her present unskilled job. If she can get the requisite skills, a bright future awaits. So the training agency checks the schedules of its upcoming process-control programs and assigns Betty to the next available slot.

A second option would give Betty a voucher and let her buy her own training. Her motivation to make the right choices is clear, and she has more detailed information about her own ambitions and abilities than does anyone else. This is the model we tend to apply to college students—grants and subsidized loans can be spent on whatever curriculum students prefer, within very wide limits. Medicare, similarly, also allows beneficiaries to pick their vendor. It will pay for their care at any accredited hospital. But the voucher approach is less common for adult-worker training, largely because of government's concerns that workers cannot find and process the information necessary to advance their own interests. If the public officials responsible for workforce development were confident that Betty would use her voucher to gain marketable skills from competent training providers, vouchers would be the magic bullet.

The third pure form would give private-sector actors already at hand—for example, Betty's employer—the responsibility (and the public funding) for upgrading her skills. This approach has powerful information advantages. Her employer would surely know much more than does the government about the premium the labor market would pay for particular skills, about Betty's strengths and weaknesses, and about the match between them. The employer might know, for example, that Betty is bad at math but great with people. More importantly, the employer will be aware (as government will not) that much of the assembly line is slated to move to Malaysia, leaving the local office to concentrate on domestic distribution. Information unavailable to the government would point to marketing communication, not process control, as Betty's best option.

Far less drastic situations could still give Betty's employer a major information advantage. Perhaps the assembly line, while staying in place, will soon be incorporating new technologies that will change the nature of the process-control job and the skills needed to perform it. The employer may be loath to reveal this fact to the government—lest it leak to competitors—yet it could easily train Betty for the jobs that will be available in a year's time.

For all of these reasons American job-training policy relies heavily on private-sector employers for workforce development—not just to deliver training, but to exercise discretion in determining what skills are best suited to particular workers. At the same time, this information-driven assignment of discretion creates predictable tensions. Betty and society at large might benefit were she to undergo more extensive training that would equip her for a much higher-paying job. But the employer might find cause to question this approach, particularly since the new skills might equip Betty to decamp for a rival employer. The firm might exercise its discretion to tilt payoffs toward itself, minimizing its share of the cost of training Betty and maximizing its benefit—for example, by categorizing actual work as "training" to be subsidized by taxpayers, and by focusing on skills that are useful only within the firm itself so that Betty won't be tempted to leave (or to demand a raise as the price of staying).

A training system that relies on private collaborators requires painstaking management in order to maximize the gains of production discretion net of the losses from payoff discretion. Frequently, this requires a careful balancing approach. One common tactic is to vest discretion in business-dominated boards that direct the allocation of public training funds, rather than in individual firms. Such boards fragment the flow of information and complicate decision making, but they weaken the potential for payoff discretion to drain value from the public. Another tactic is to require reporting on the results of training once completed—the employment and earnings of program graduates—to impose accountability without interfering with the application of private-sector information advantages.[2]

Workplace Safety

"Management-based regulation" is the apt term our colleagues Cary Coglianese and David Lazer apply to a broad domain of information-

---

[2] There is a large literature, both theoretical and empirical, on the advantages and risks of the characteristically American collaborative approach to workforce development. For an excellent empirical overview, see Howard Bloom et al., "The Benefits and Costs of JTPA Title II-A Programs: Key Findings from the National Job Training Partnership Act Study," *Journal of Human Resources* 32, no. 3 (Summer 1997): 549–576.

motivated collaboration in the regulatory arena.[3] In some regulatory settings, the public sector's information deficit is so great that government, acting alone, risks creating regulations that do too little to protect public interests, or that overly burden private enterprise, or both. Giving regulated businesses an opportunity to employ their privileged perspective can reduce both risks and costs. But giving managers an active role in regulation because of their information advantages almost inherently means granting them a large range of discretion. The classic challenge of collaboration thus applies: balancing the upside and the downside of private discretion.

The federal Occupational Safety and Health Administration (OSHA) has conducted a range of experiments with collaborative approaches. Standard practice for OSHA in the early decades after its establishment in the 1970s had been to inspect workplaces—either randomly, or in response to an accident or complaint—and to punish employers when violations of federal health and safety rules were identified. But OSHA's corps of inspectors has always been tiny relative to the number of regulated firms. Workplaces could go decades without an inspection, so incentives for compliance were weak. Another problem, and one that would have persisted even in the unlikely event of a massive increase in budgets and workforce at OSHA to allow frequent inspections, was the imperfect fit between workplace hazards and OSHA's specifically enumerated rules. Some OSHA requirements and prohibitions—drafted, of necessity, for general applicability—were needlessly costly in some settings. (Stephen Breyer, now a Supreme Court justice and never any sort of free-market fundamentalist, has spoken derisively about cowboys being forced to bring along toilet facilities owing to OSHA rules.)[4] Conversely, many workplaces faced significant but idiosyncratic risks that had never been recog-

---

[3] Cary Coglianese and David Lazer, "Management-Based Regulatory Strategies," in *Market-Based Governance: Supply Side, Demand Side, Upside and Downside*, ed. John D. Donahue and Joseph S. Nye, Jr. (Brookings Institution Press, 2002).

[4] Justice Breyer's Harvard Law School class, taught with Richard Zeckhauser from the 1970s till the 1990s. Background and basic information on the Cooperative Compliance Program can be found in "Motivating Job Safety," chap. 10 of *Making Washington Work: Tales of Innovation in the Federal Government*, ed. John D. Donahue (Brookings Institution Press, 1999).

nized by the statute books, or had risk patterns so distinctive that applying economywide standards would overregulate in some areas and underregulate in others.

In the mid-1990s, OSHA attempted to address these informational shortcomings by testing a collaborative approach to workplace safety regulation. Starting with regional pilots, and then moving to a full-scale operational shift, OSHA experimented with regulatory models that depended on managers' judgment and de-emphasized federally mandated rules in setting priorities for workplace safety.

This strategic shift began with an experiment in Maine. OSHA sought to induce and empower managers to use their knowledge—knowledge the government did not have—to tailor safety regimes that would be best suited for their individual workplaces. This Cooperative Compliance Program encouraged firms to develop health and safety programs that addressed the profile of risks prevailing in each office, factory, or construction site. Firm-specific plans were developed with extensive worker input and often went well beyond government requirements. OSHA personnel operated as consultants as firms developed their plans, and then as episodic auditors once plans were in place, to ensure that the terms were met. Where the law permitted, OSHA staffers were empowered to ignore technical violations of rules that had been sensibly downplayed in a company's plan. Where the law required strict compliance with such rules, OSHA applied the mildest possible sanctions. But a firm that violated its own safety plan faced the likelihood of severe consequences.

Early indications hinted that this strategy of relying on firm-specific expertise about firm-specific risks and mitigation options brought major advantages in both safety and cost. "We fixed a lot of things OSHA inspectors would have walked right by," claimed the safety manager of a major paper company.[5] But some industry groups objected that OSHA was imposing unspecified obligations by the implicit threat of traditional inspections for firms that refused to cooperate. A coalition led by the U.S. Chamber of Commerce filed suit against

[5] Quoted in ibid., p. 123.

OSHA on procedural grounds, and a federal appeals court shut down the Cooperative Compliance Program in 1999.[6] It is hardly obvious that the Chamber's short-term victory, which eliminated some regulations but precluded further cooperative rule making, produced an outcome in the long-term interest of most of its members, much less of the broader business community. OSHA's experiment with shared discretion over workplace safety plans was far sounder than its abrupt and disappointing ending might suggest. In contrast with OSHA's traditional approach, it recognized the diversity of regulated firms and the substantial realm of common interest in achieving any given degree of workplace risk reduction in the most efficient way possible. We hope and expect that comparable approaches to regulation—models that capitalize on the information advantages of private firms—will become more common, within and beyond occupational health and safety.

This foray into collaborative governance was tripped up by regulatory politics that featured the traditional fight over *how much* protection should be required, a fight that can rage even when business and government make peace over *how*. The Chamber of Commerce seized an opportunity to win a round over "how much" at the expense of a superior resolution over "how." The Chamber—displaying a myopia all too common among ideological combatants on both the left and the right—was so focused on the fight over the level of regulation that it foolishly strangled a promising innovation in the means of regulation.

Infrastructure Security

One of America's most pressing problems, now and into the foreseeable future, is protecting itself against terrorist attacks. In this area, the private sector will frequently have a sharp information advantage that can motivate a collaborative approach. Consider the challenges of protecting mostly private infrastructure assets, such as chemical

---

[6] Susannah Zak Figura, "Safer Days Ahead," *Government Executive*, March 1, 2000.

plants, power utilities, and major office buildings. These vital physical assets must be protected, not least in order to prevent wider public devastation that would accompany an attack on them. But against what risks? And by what means? And by whom? And at whose expense? These questions do not lead to easy answers.

Security can be provided by the public sector, the private sector, or some blend of the two.[7] The ability to separate finance from delivery further multiplies the options. For example, protection can be provided publicly but funded privately (through special tax levies on affected industries), or it can be provided privately but funded publicly (through tax subsidies or direct grants for security guards or equipment), or with a dizzying array of alternative arrangements along both the financing and delivery dimensions.

This profusion of delivery models is far from hypothetical. Property owners defend against fire risks in part through private efforts—alarms, extinguishers, sprinkler systems, fireproof materials—and in part through reliance on government firefighters. Public police forces and private security services coexist, though—a little-known fact—the private force, in the aggregate, is far larger in the United States. Dividing lines can blur, as when public cops perform off-hours paid "details" for private clients. Airline security arrangements have skittered across the delivery-model spectrum in recent years, from for-profit contractors employed by airports and paid for by airlines, to a federal agency partly funded by special taxes, with some recent moves toward a mixed system involving both public and private players. (More on this shortly.)

Alas, there is small hope that the path of least resistance provides a glide path to the right arrangements.[8] Collaboration for infrastructure

---

[7] Each sector faces its own sequence of decisions over how to handle its share of the work. Within the public sector, how should responsibilities be parceled out across federal, state, and local government, and between military and civilian units? Within the private sector, should each company handle its own security, or should industry-spanning associations defend against shared threats?

[8] The woefully inadequate and terribly coordinated policies in the few days surrounding Hurricane Katrina in August 2005 show the impossibility of developing effective collaborative arrangements predominantly on the fly. Hurricanes are different, to be sure, from terrorism threats, but in many ways simpler. For example, they give considerable advance warning.

protection is all but inevitable, since neither sector on its own is likely to possess the requisite mix of information, resources, and incentives. But rarely is the best approach to risk reduction, or the fair allocation of the burden, obvious at the outset. Private owners of vulnerable assets, reasoning that war (including "war on terror") is government's responsibility, expect the public sector to do the heavy lifting. Government, in turn, sees firms' concentrated stakes in valuable assets as providing ample private incentive for them to invest in protection against low-probability but high-loss events. Efficient collaboration will be not the default outcome, but the result of analysis, careful transactional architecture, and painstaking management.

Debates over physical security have long featured both a bias toward the government in principle, and a blend of public and private responsibilities in practice. Max Weber explicitly defined government as "the human community that successfully claims the monopoly of the legitimate use of physical force,"[9] and Hobbes reluctantly prescribed submission to Leviathan as the only remedy to the "warre of every man against every man."[10] Providing protection against a common enemy is often presented as the quintessential public good. Yet the U.S. Constitution—often considered the blueprint for the modern state—was written in the wake of a war fought in part by extragovernmental forces. The Hessian mercenaries on the British side are featured prominently in the history books. Much less well-known are the "Pennsylvania Associators," a private force organized by Benjamin Franklin to substitute for the state militia that Quaker Pennsylvania balked at mustering under public authority.[11] And few realize to what extent the feisty American naval forces in the Revolution were made up of privateers, motivated by a mélange of patriotism and hunger for the "prize money" that followed successful raids on British shipping.[12] Private armies are still common in failed or fragile

---

[9] From "Politics as a Vocation," in *From Max Weber*, ed. H. H. Gerth and C. Wright Mills (Oxford University Press, 1946), p. 78.

[10] Thomas Hobbes, *Leviathan* (Oxford University Press, 1881), p. 95.

[11] The Pennsylvania Associators figure in David Hackett Fisher, *Washington's Crossing* (Oxford University Press, 2004). Their origins and organization are described on pp. 26–28.

[12] Robert H. Patton, *Patriot Pirates: The Privateer War for Freedom and Fortune in the American Revolution* (Pantheon Books, 2008).

states, and dismantling or assimilating extragovernmental forces has been a major theme in the transitions, or attempted transitions, to legitimate democracy of Afghanistan, Northern Ireland, and Nicaragua. That theme will be repeated in Lebanon, Iraq, Palestine, and many African and some South American states if and when they become stable democracies. Even the United States, with the mightiest army in the world, has relied on private forces in Iraq and elsewhere for functions that are at best marginally distinguishable from classic combat operations.[13]

Given the blend of approaches in a mission so close to the heart of government's responsibility, it is unsurprising that private forces also play a role in more mundane domains of public protection. Most large universities, for example, have their own police forces to maintain order on campus and protect prominent (and, in particular, controversial) guests. When public figures who are potential targets of disrupters or assassins visit our own university, they are protected by a mix of public and private forces. A senior federal official might be guarded by the Secret Service and Harvard police while he gives his speech, with a phalanx of off-duty local police paid by the university monitoring entrances and exits, and a state-police escort to and from the airport.

In many policy arenas, collaboration between the public and private sectors is one option among many, an option that may or may not turn out to be superior to direct provision, regulation, simple contracting, or autonomous voluntarism. Infrastructure protection, in contrast, by its very nature usually involves some degree of interorganizational, and often cross-sectoral, collaboration. In the United States, all chemical factories and airlines, most power utilities and electricity transmission assets, and many port operations and nuclear facilities are privately owned. Collaboration thus becomes a necessity, rather than an option—though the nature and terms of that collaboration can vary over a wide range.[14]

[13] Peter Singer, *Corporate Warriors* (Brookings Institution Press, 2002).

[14] Sometimes the choice of public or private security arrangements is less consequential than it seems. Paul DiMaggio and Walter Powell have argued that institutions performing similar tasks tend to conform to similar models of operation, whatever their formal structure. Paul J.

A substantial private role in infrastructure protection is all but in-evitable. The extent and contours of collaboration, however, are open issues, in part because our experience with large-scale domestic ter-rorism threats is recent and limited, and in part because collabora-tion in the protection arena is quite distinctive, so that lessons from other domains may not apply without modification. The debate over airport security screening in late 2001, for example, illustrates a ten-dency to give government the benefit of the doubt in the security arena, which departs from Americans' general presumption that the private sector holds an efficiency edge.

The events of September 11, 2001, touched off a heated debate about the relative efficacy of public and private protection services. The ex-isting system of private passenger screening was suddenly, and with near unanimity, denounced as inadequate. A public mission that was newly perceived to be of paramount importance—ensuring that no-body bent on destruction could board an airliner armed—was at the mercy of a cheap, rickety delivery system. Public scrutiny clarified that the airlines, many of them chronically on the verge of insolvency yet required to provide passenger screening, bid out the work to a highly competitive industry of private security firms. In order to eke out any profit from their lean contracts with the airlines, these secu-rity firms scraped their workers from the bottom of the labor pool. Screeners' wages were paltry; their benefits were generally negligible; standards, naturally, were low and turnover high. No recipe for iron-clad security, and on September 12, 2001, no longer acceptable. What was to replace this rejected status quo? One option was to declare that it had been an error to split off passenger screening from the govern-ment in the first place, and to move it back to where it belonged—alongside other crucial security functions carried out directly by the public sector. The other option was to continue to delegate screening to specialized private providers, but with more funding, far higher standards, and direct oversight by government. Politics and psychol-ogy, and not necessarily a dispassionate evaluation of the best system,

---

DiMaggio and Walter W. Powell, "The Iron Cage Revisited: Institutional Isomorphism and Collective Rationality in Organizational Fields," *American Sociological Review* 48, no. 2 (1983): 147–160.

played a major role in the creation of a new federal Transportation Security Authority responsible for virtually all airport safety screening duties. It is difficult to judge whether this allocation of responsibility was the best choice.[15] On the one hand, there have been no airplane hijackings or acknowledged near misses on TSA's watch. On the other hand, trial tests suggest that many weapons still get overlooked. A successful future hijacking could push the inspection task back toward the private sector.

On the broader issue of infrastructure security, all four generic justifications for private roles come into play, though several give mixed signals. The productivity argument is less one-sidedly in favor of delegation here than in many other functions. A case can be made for government itself to handle quite efficiently the many functions associated with infrastructure protection.[16] Similarly, it is not clear whether private-sector involvement would notably augment the resources available for infrastructure security. As our discussion in chapter 7, "Collaboration for Resources," will make clear, the net increment of security resources (relative to the baseline of exclusive

[15] Security is very likely better than it was prior to September 11, 2001—though the rarity of hijacking both before and since makes quality in general and risk levels in particular hard to measure—but it is less clear that the increment of safety is worth the sharp increase in costs, or that the TSA performs better than would have an upgraded private system. The gross flaws in the previous contractual model did not preclude structuring a sturdier arrangement. The work, however vital, is readily specified: inspect every passenger and every piece of luggage to ensure that no weapon can be smuggled onto an airplane. Contractual provisions could mandate (at a commensurate price) that screeners be citizens, college graduates, psychiatrists, or martial-arts experts, or meet whatever other qualifications are judged essential. Evaluation is much more straightforward for airport screening than for many other functions that are delegated contractually. The performance of individual screeners can be gauged through devices, now routinely in use, that periodically project the phantom image of a gun, knife, or bomb onto an innocent X-ray screen. The performance of screening contractors could have been evaluated, to almost any desired degree of stringency, by a corps of plainclothes inspectors constantly testing security with dummy weapons or bombs and levying painful financial penalties for any lapse. Several large firms already operate in the industry, and entry is relatively easy, making airport screening far more competitive than many other outsourced functions. Such arrangements are not merely hypothetical; they were and are the norm in many European countries that are sadly familiar with terrorism.

[16] The public's attitudes toward the appropriate provision of security may be strongly shaped by the most recent dramatic failure. Government efforts to deal with Hurricane Katrina, which bring to mind many comparisons with protection against terrorism, may have dampened enthusiasm for government as the guarantor of security. High-profile failure may promote a "throw the rascals out" attitude that drowns out analysis.

governmental responsibility) will depend on the details of the relationship between public and private collaborators, and can range from very large to approximately zero. Considerations of legitimacy make both extremes untenable. It is almost unimaginable that the public sector would be entirely absent from infrastructure security arrangements. Even independent of the prudential arguments—that is, could a security regime with *no* links to government actually work?—such an arrangement might not comport well with citizens' views of the private sector's proper role. On the other hand, a purely governmental arrangement could raise questions about needless expansion of state authority and, on quite different grounds, about the propriety of sparing private organizations from—and burdening taxpayers with—the costs of providing security benefits that are concentrated on valuable but vulnerable private assets.

The most consistently valid argument for a collaborative approach to infrastructure security, however, turns on information. Government itself is almost certain to lack the fine-grained understanding of particular assets, and the role they play in complex chains of production and distribution within the economy, that is necessary to determine the appropriate level of protection or to mount the most robust and least costly defenses. The private organizations that own, operate, or depend on physical assets will generally possess far more information about how to protect those assets, and how vital such protection is, than government can command in advance or readily obtain. For example, if the government merely asks about the economic value of resources so as to allocate its protection resources efficiently, private parties will surely exaggerate the values of those they own. The government's information deficit causes problems for protection and, even more so, for recovery. Priorities for restoring production after an attack, for example, are likely to depend on highly proprietary considerations—which products are least profitable and which most, which inputs have ready substitutes and which are indispensable, which plants should be left in ruins since they are nearing obsolescence and which are cutting-edge—that firms will quite understandably be loath to reveal in the service of contingency planning.

Risks of Collaborative Infrastructure Security

The risks of a collaborative approach involve both payoff and preference discretion. The most obvious vulnerability associated with payoff
discretion concerns the allocation of costs. The managers of private
firms engaged in collaborative security efforts—if they are faithful
stewards for their shareholders—would prefer to have government
bear more of the protection bill, including costs incurred for security
that benefits the firm itself rather than the public at large. This logic
extends to firms' natural desire to reduce any cost-increasing or profit-
decreasing constraints on their operations. For example, suppose that
building a triple-fence security perimeter patrolled by National Guardsmen would reduce by 90 percent the public risks of an attack on a
chemical plant, at a total cost of $100 million. Suppose, further, that
a reformulation of the plant's product line, or strict security vetting of
all employees, could achieve the same reduction for a mere $70 mil-
lion. If government would pay most of the cost for the first option
and the firm would pay all for the second, we could expect the private collaborator to use its discretion to tilt the decision toward the
perimeter patrol.[17]

Similarly, firms will generally wield their discretion to favor antiterrorism measures that offer ancillary private benefits. Installing
floodlights throughout a port can deter petty theft and vandalism,

---

[17] A systematic hazard involving payoff discretion is embodied (though experts differ as to
the degree) in the Terrorism Reinsurance Act of 2002 (TRIA). This law was enacted in response
to complaints that private terrorism coverage had become expensive, and sometimes unavailable, in the wake of the 9/11 attacks. There were respectable arguments to be made for and
against major government participation in the insurance market. TRIA ended up socializing
the upper range of losses from terrorism damage to property, that is, making the government
reimburse such losses. Therefore, insurance companies will get little payoff for reducing their
exposure to the catastrophic risks for which government bears most of the cost. This will
dampen those companies' incentives to price their services high enough to motivate the in-
sureds to invest in risk reduction. Kent Smetters of Pennsylvania's Wharton School has suggested that under TRIA, private owners of vulnerable assets will underinvest in security when
much of the cost of a catastrophic incident falls to government. TRIA's origins, provisions, and
incentive effects are discussed in Smetters, "Insuring against Terrorism: The Policy Challenge"
(paper prepared for January 2004, Conference of the Brookings-Wharton Papers on Financial
Services, draft of February 4, 2004).

not merely terrorism. A report from the Office of Inspector General at the Department of Homeland Security suggests that such payoff discretion has been at work in the allocation of public port-security money. A port proposed and received a grant for surveillance equipment that auditors found to "support the normal course of business" rather than respond to realistic terror threats.[18] Each firm in an industry would like shared security regimes to be structured in ways that favor its own business strategies, rather than those of its competitors. A nuclear plant that has been operating for a long time, with a twenty-year accumulation of spent fuel rods stored on the premises, will push for protection policies that focus on nuclear waste; a newer plant will see more payoff in policies that concentrate on threats to the reactor itself. Requirements for a half-mile buffer zone around ports handling hazardous cargoes—accompanied by limited grants to buy adjacent land—would be devastating to a port in the middle of a dense, pricey city, but quite acceptable (and possibly even conferring a competitive edge) to a port in an isolated community.[19]

Infrastructure security poses fewer obvious conflicts in preferences among collaborating parties than do some other arenas of public-private collaboration. In social services, for example, some people consider it a very good thing if religious messages accompany substance-abuse counseling, and some people consider it a very bad thing. In matters of infrastructure protection, interests surrounding salient choices are reasonably aligned. Yet even here there is room for preferences to diverge at the margin, and private discretion can entail public costs. Private firms may also value the *perception* of security as well as its reality. Customers and possibly investors may find it hard to gauge levels of or changes in risk, and may respond to visible risk-reduction measures more than to effective but obscure reductions in the probability of a damaging attack. Private collaborators, moreover, will also prefer arrangements that give them privileged access to pub-

[18] Eric Lipton, "Audit Faults U.S. for its Spending on Port Defense," *New York Times*, February 20, 2005, sec. 1, p. 1.
[19] This would be the case whether the urban port is owned by a private firm or by a public agency such as New York's Port Authority.

lic security resources. To the extent that a major employer can shape the contingency plan for a regional alert, it will send more police and Guardsmen to its chemical plant and fewer to the local hospital, school, or armory.

Given that the public and private producers are sure to be tussling over costs, responsibilities, and credit, and that their interests diverge, each will have an incentive to provide its own estimates of the perils it confronts and of the benefits that its own efforts provide. Difficulties in estimating the probability or severity of an attack—in the face of massive uncertainties—magnify any natural tendencies to distort estimates to serve one's own purposes. These inherent uncertainties complicate the challenge of structuring a fair and feasible accommodation in the context of what are sometimes called "security externalities." This term refers to the tendency for measures meant to protect one asset to alter the risks confronting other assets. The effect can be positive or negative. A snarling guard dog in one property owner's yard might scare burglars away from houses nearby, offering positive externalities to his neighbors. But once the burglars have targeted the neighborhood and are determined to pull off a heist, the presence of the guard dog in front of one house raises the risk to those lacking canine protection.

The balancing of burdens and benefits and the management of payoff discretion will always be technically challenging, and vulnerable to both political and psychological disruptions. Suppose government is able to structure an arrangement with a major port operator that features just the right blend of public and private expenditure and just the right pattern of risk-reduction investment at the start of the deal. The port operator is compensated just enough, and on just the right terms, to induce it to recognize the security externalities associated with its operations. Suppose, then, that many years pass without a major domestic terrorist attack. The port operator will be tempted—to the extent that the terms of the deal and government's vigilance permit—to use its discretion to tilt security expenditures away from risk reduction and toward activities that boost profitability —for example, installing attractive lighting in its tourist areas and illuminating less in the shadows beyond. To the extent that this occurs, collaborative infrastructure protection is likely to be viewed as "corporate welfare" and to lose its political legitimacy.

Efforts to protect vital infrastructure in the coming decades will almost certainly involve extensive interaction between business and government, frequently featuring the shared discretion that is the hallmark of collaborative governance. These arrangements could turn out to be flexible and effective, or rigid and lame. They may make a limited claim on resources and allocate costs in ways that are both fair and efficient, or they may bloat costs in ways that tilt burdens toward the government, undercut private prudence, and sap the public's willingness to pay for security. Which of these possibilities becomes reality will depend on many factors, including information yet to come on the nature and extent of terrorism risks.

Payoffs and Pitfalls

Without ever using the particular vocabulary we employ, economists have long studied the allocation of discretion. The usual challenge they address tends to be the risk that agents will slack off when continuous monitoring of their work is not practical.[20] Our challenges are different: deterring the illegitimate seizure of resources or the redirection of output—respectively, payoff and preference discretion. Moreover, our agents tend to be organizations rather than individual workers, the economists' standard. But the sources of the classic principal-agent problem, and our discretion-related problems, are the same. The private agent is better equipped to undertake a responsibility than is the governmental principal, frequently because he has superior information. And the agent's knowledge and actions cannot be fully monitored.

The diverse examples touched on in this chapter—from safer jobs to smarter training and terror-resistant factories—hint at the variety,

[20] John W. Pratt and Richard J. Zeckhauser, eds., *Principals and Agents: The Structure of Business* (Harvard Business School Press, 1985; paperback, 1991).

and the scale, of the potential payoffs from shared discretion when private parties have a major information advantage over government. But that information advantage is a doubled-edged sword. Private players can exploit it to tailor measures to their interest, and thereby to siphon resources—often invisibly—from the public at large.

Collaboration is essential when private players know and government does not what should be done and how. Being alert to the possible pitfalls of granting responsibility to self-interested entities is the best way to minimize losses.

Chapter 6

◇◇

Collaboration for Legitimacy

Colin Powell has a deep appreciation of the concept of a "force multiplier." In military usage this term (which we invoked fleetingly in chapter 1) is any capability—whether technological, organizational, or managerial—that augments the effectiveness of a military unit. As chairman of the U.S. Joint Chiefs of Staff, Powell was an enthusiastic and effective advocate of force multipliers—battlefield computers, precision-guided munitions, and night-vision technology, among others—and employed them to drive Iraq out of Kuwait in the 1991 Persian Gulf War.

But Powell extended the concept beyond the battlefield. In his subsequent civilian role as secretary of state, Powell implemented a thoroughly collaborative approach to foreign aid that he likened to a force multiplier. In May 2001, Powell unveiled what became known as the Global Development Alliance in testimony before Congress. The goal he set forth was to allow the U.S. Agency for International Development to partner with private institutions in alliances marked by what we call shared discretion. The government would play a role analogous to that of a venture capitalist, seeking out and funding private organizations presenting plausible propositions for creating public value. He described the GDA as a portfolio of procedures that would leverage U.S. dollars with the money and energy that private collaborators could bring to bear to create "a force multiplier for our development goals and objectives."[1]

Why did Powell choose to use this collaborative approach to USAID?

---

[1] House Appropriations testimony of May 10, 2001, quoted in Kirsten Lundberg, "Smarter Foreign Aid?" KSG Case Program, C-15-04-1778 (Harvard University, 2004), p. 8.

Part of the answer is that he had an intuitive grasp of the resource, information, and productivity rationales for collaboration. As we have noted, multiple rationales usually apply in any particular collaboration, and the foreign-aid arena offers many opportunities to boost effectiveness through private involvement. But the origins of the Global Development Alliance also lay in an urgent search for legitimacy. Foreign assistance is chronically short on domestic political support and, under Powell's tenure, was taking increasing fire from its critics in Congress. Powell anticipated that crucial constituencies involved with aid would look with more favor if the delivery model were collaborative.

This chapter examines how utilizing the private sector to produce public value can foster legitimacy in a variety of contexts. The legitimacy of a given collaborative effort—the extent to which a society approves of the collaboration and its goals—is in the eyes of the beholders. Some societies seem to have few reservations about direct state action and prefer that their government do its work itself. Other cultures hold the public and private sectors in equally high (or low) regard, and display no systematic preference for direct or indirect delivery. And some—particularly, but not exclusively, the United States—tend to be chary about government's overall size as well as its weight in particular domains.

Perceptions of legitimacy can also vary over time within a single society as events shape citizens' sense of what arrangements are right and proper. In the early part of the last century, a series of events—Wall Street's collapse, the Great Depression, the New Deal, and World War II—severely eroded confidence in the private sector and raised government's standing in the eyes of most citizens. FDR's massive Works Progress Administration, which would have been widely denounced in less troubled times, enjoyed considerable public support. In subsequent decades, conversely, government's relative standing was undercut by solid private-sector performance and high-profile examples of governmental shortfalls—from much-derided public employment programs under Carter to the catastrophically inept response to Hurricane Katrina under George W. Bush—to the point that a huge state-run program such as the WPA would have been a hard sell.

Recent rounds of financial trauma have once more dented the private sector's legitimacy advantage, but America's cultural inclination toward private solutions still runs deep.

Politics inevitably plays a huge role in shaping perceptions of legitimacy. The public is rarely unanimous about a given mission's value, nor is the public consistent in its judgment from one mission to another. Ideologues, politicians, and interested providers use loaded language, dueling anecdotes, and selective statistics to burnish their favored approach to public service and batter rival approaches. In short, legitimacy is a contentious and perennially contested issue.

Yet despite the sometimes fierce ideological battles that legitimacy entails, the shifting balance of power between different approaches to government buffets and reshapes, but does not destroy, efforts at public-private collaboration. Cultural shibboleths about what is and isn't legitimate broadly represent the distillation of practical judgments about what does and doesn't tend to work. The preference to provide low-income Americans with vouchers that let them obtain food aid through private retail outlets reflects not merely cultural distaste for government-run soup kitchens, but also evidence that the private distribution network is reasonably effective. Similarly, considerations of legitimacy can usually be trumped by sound arguments that private delivery, however culturally congenial, is too costly or too risky or unlikely to work in some particular case. When a hurricane shatters a region's retail network, few people object to having a governmental entity such as the National Guard distribute food to survivors. Legitimacy, in other words, generally follows efficiency—though it typically follows a few paces behind and has a tendency to wander. Wrangles over legitimacy can often be tamed if the parties abandon debates about the absolute propriety of a large public or private role, and shift to a *comparative* analysis of which functions are more suitable, and which less, for each implementation model. (We will explore this "comparative advantage" theme in detail in chapter 9.)

Many collaborations are motivated in part by the private sector's legitimacy edge in a particular arena. In some cases legitimacy is the central motive, though pragmatic and philosophical considerations are virtually always interwoven in any concrete case. The most extensive example examined in this chapter, the Joint Commission on the Accreditation of Healthcare Organizations and its pivotal, legislatively hardwired role in Medicare, reflects productivity, resource, and (especially) information motives for collaboration, alongside that of legitimacy. Yet without gainsaying the influence of other factors, we now consider a few cases in which legitimacy looms large in the choice of the means for achieving some public mission. We begin with the foreign aid example that opened this chapter, and move to an examination of how considerations of legitimacy established a costly bias toward private, rather than governmental, delivery of student loans. Contrasting approaches to the development and use of land that suddenly became available in two large urban areas constitute our third illustration. Then we close with a detailed review of how the creation of the Medicare and Medicaid programs hinged on a collaborative effort to assess the quality of hospitals, an arrangement easier to explain by reference to legitimacy than by the analytics of optimal performance.

Foreign Aid: From Procurement to Alliance

Jesse Helms saw his chance.

With George W. Bush set to assume the presidency in a matter of days, Senator Helms seized the moment to resurrect a favorite proposal that had died in committee five years earlier. In a speech to the American Enterprise Institute on January 11, 2001, Helms, a longtime conservative scourge of the U.S. Agency for International Development (USAID), proposed that the agency be eviscerated. Rather than a governmental agency applying its own judgment—inherently and irredeemably flawed, in his view—to foreign aid projects, Helms called for transforming USAID into a simple financial conduit, a grantmaking arm of the State Department that would distribute resources to private aid groups.

"The time has come to reject what President Bush correctly labels the 'failed compassion of towering, distant bureaucracies' and, instead, empower private and faith-based groups who care most about those in need," Senator Helms thundered. Citing USAID's refusal to make a grant to Nyumbani, a Kenyan orphanage for children suffering from AIDS, he accused the agency of "cold, heartless bureaucratic thinking." And he repeated his frequent charge that government-organized assistance under USAID had only "lined the pockets of corrupt dictators, while funding the salaries of a growing, bloated bureaucracy."[2]

Helms's renewed attack on USAID was disheartening to the agency's embattled staff. Since 1993 USAID had seen its budget shrink from $14.1 billion to a paltry $7.6 billion. Its staff, mostly foreign nationals working in USAID missions abroad, had fallen from 10,000 to 7,000 in that same period and the agency had closed 30 of its 110 missions.

USAID's longtime agenda of accelerating progress and ameliorating misery in less-favored countries reflected a real humanitarian impulse on the part of the American people. The mission had also always been partly strategic, of course, and had its roots in the Cold War. It represented a bid for the good opinion of populations overseas. During the height of the ideological struggle between capitalism and communism, a favorable image abroad was seen as vital. But as the emblem and the instrument of one side in that struggle, USAID was meant to embody the principles of democratic capitalism. Though the level of orthodoxy and intensity varied from one administration to the next, USAID was always expected to favor market-based over state-centered solutions when providing advice and resources to developing countries. And it was expected to operate, to the greatest feasible extent, through private agents, both for-profit and nonprofit, when carrying out its work. Private partners also provide a much-needed U.S. constituency for an agency whose intended beneficiaries—poor foreigners—carried no political weight with Congress.

But while USAID had long relied on delegation to get its work done—operating with few employees relative to the size of its budget, and many contractors and grantees—that philosophy was rarely

---

[2] Quoted in Stephen Mufson, "Holmes Calls for Abolishing AID, Increasing Support for Taiwan," *Washington Post*, January 12, 2001, p. A6.

well articulated. Even before Helms launched his renewed attack, the agency was facing pressures both to intensify and to alter the nature of its reliance on private partners. USAID managers were becoming increasingly aware of the practical downsides to their customary forms of dealing with private agents. When the agency procured goods and services, contract officers sought to pin down every detail in legally binding requirements. And when it issued grants to non-profits, its standard practice was to articulate goals and expectations with as much precision as possible. In short, USAID was accustomed to maintaining a near monopoly of discretion. Any example of seri-ous discretion in the hands of a private agent was regarded as a man-agement failure to be remedied.

That in-control attitude was felt strongly among the contractors and grantees that worked with USAID. After canvassing many of the nongovernmental organizations that had relationships with USAID, Holly Wise, a senior USAID official, paraphrased what the NGOs had been telling her: "You [USAID] decide what the problem is, you de-cide what the solution is. You put out a call for vendors, you control us, you resource us to do your bidding.... This is a master-slave rela-tionship, this is not a partnership."[3]

So while reliance on the private sector was well established within USAID, the disadvantages of the characteristic *form* of interaction were already apparent. There was a poor fit between the standard model of tight, fully specified agency relationships and the highly un-certain challenges that characterize the typical development setting. Private contractors and grantees often had much better information about opportunities an aid project presented and the constraints it would face. In addition, they sometimes had expertise far beyond what USAID possessed. Even apart from the mounting political pressures, some thoughtful USAID officials came to see considerable merit in experimenting with expanded private discretion.

The result was that the agency's own concerns about its legitimacy, as much as the political pressures, drove USAID managers not merely to continue the agency's reliance on the private sector, but to elevate

[3] Holly Wise, quoted in Lundberg, "Smarter Foreign Aid?" p. 5

the external profile of its indirect-delivery model as well. Operational considerations also called for changing the model away from simple procurement and toward more strategic approaches that capitalized more fully on the benefits of private initiative. Simply put, the agency sought to move decisively along the spectrum of discretion, shifting in a very conscious way from contracting to collaboration. Previous programmatic innovations had rendered the term "partnership" at once tainted and hopelessly vague within USAID. The officials, struggling to frame a new sort of approach and aware of the importance of terminology, anchored the new approach on the term "alliances."

Andrew Natsios, a veteran public administrator, was charged with executing the effort to bolster USAID's effectiveness through more extensive collaboration. Natsios had been appointed as administrator of USAID early in 2001 and was ideally cast to lead the transformation from procurement to alliance. He had years of experience, from an earlier stage of his career, as a senior USAID manager. He was an authentic intellectual quite capable of crafting principles to ensure that "alliances" became something more than a catch phrase. And his conservative bona fides earned him a certain degree of latitude from Bush administration overseers.

Natsios's philosophical convictions had been tempered by his work within and beyond the foreign aid field, especially a stint managing the massive reshaping and submerging of the Boston area's major highways that was known as the Big Dig. By the time he took the helm at USAID, Natsios had lost any romantic illusions about the private sector. He knew that private partners could cannibalize as well as catalyze a governmental undertaking. He also knew that the success or failure of a cross-sectoral undertaking depended to a great extent on the quality of the public officials managing the project. And there was no one better at that than Andrew Natsios. His hard-nosed and analytical approach to relationships between government and its corporate and nonprofit partners would serve him well as the new initiative took shape.

Changing the procedures and culture of USAID to make the organization amenable to a new way of implementing its mission wasn't easy. The agency had to overcome suspicions and doubts not only among its own staff, but also among the contractors and grantees that had become accustomed to doing business with USAID the old-fashioned way. Congressional overseers were also skeptical that USAID would really change. The alignment of private energies with public goals involved a subtle new architecture that evolved away from the old partnerships in which two like-minded organizations—USAID and CARE, for example—shared their resources and goals under USAID's direction, and toward alliances in which distinctly different organizations with notably different goals came together to accomplish a mission. Holly Wise, the career foreign service officer who turned GDA from a slogan into a live operation, described a hypothetical alliance with IBM: "You don't start off being the same, and your goal isn't to be the same at the end.... We come together to do this one specific thing. We have a pre-nuptial [i.e., a formal alliance agreement] to keep us safe. We define what our common cause is, we work on that common cause, and then we go back to being IBM and AID."[4]

The GDA's founders, Andrew Natsios and Holly Wise, have moved on to new challenges, as has Colin Powell, the cabinet secretary who provided counsel (and cover). But as of mid-2010—well into the Obama administration—the GDA continued to thrive. A joint effort hinging on hardware giant Cisco had trained thousands of information-technology workers in forty-seven poor countries. An alliance involving multiple banks and credit unions in the United States and overseas was easing the flow of vital remittances from workers based abroad to their families back home. The creative talents behind the children's television show *Sesame Street*, backed by big donations from corporate sponsors and guided by USAID into cooperative agreements with education ministries, were strewing adaptations of their successful preschool educational broadcasting model across the airwaves of poor countries around the world.[5] The GDA model was becoming entwined with USAID's organizational DNA, and the

---

[4] Quoted in ibid., p. 11.
[5] Global Development Alliance, 2008 report, USAID, December 2007.

logic of alliances—whether or not the label endured—promised to become a long-term refinement in USAID's repertoire for getting its work accomplished.

Byzantine and Broken

It's a banker's dream: return with no risk. It is a loan program that guarantees not only that a bank will receive higher-than-market-rate returns on the loans it makes, but also that if the borrower can't or won't repay the loan, the government will do so. Welcome to the world of federally guaranteed student loans, a program that has proven helpful to students, costly to taxpayers, and a gravy train for banks.

In contrast to other countries where higher education is an entitlement (at least for the qualifying elite) and tuitions are low, American colleges and universities charge their students substantial sums. Over the course of more than half a century the federal government has provided or promoted a wide array of grant or loan programs to help students pay those large tuition bills. Since the passage of the revered Serviceman's Readjustment Act, or "G.I. Bill" in 1944, government-backed student aid programs have varied widely in their financial terms and their criteria for the eligibility of both students and institutions. More pertinent to our purposes, there have also been heated debates about the legitimacy of various organizational mechanics for delivering student aid, and wild swings from one delivery model to another.

Student aid offers a useful window for examining questions of legitimacy because the task itself is straightforward: get money to students to cover college costs; get it back, with interest, once they're in the workforce. There are few obstacles, at least in principle, to operating at almost any point along the public-to-private spectrum. Indeed, much of that spectrum has been occupied in practice at some stage of the sixty-year history of student lending. By far the most common approach, however, has been delegated delivery, with banks doing the actual lending while benefiting from various governmental inducements and supports. In the absence of a compelling pragmatic case for direct governmental action, legitimacy favored a prominent private role. Yet, as we will see, there can be downsides, sometimes serious, in delegated delivery, especially when private discretion outpaces public monitoring capacity.

The G.I. Bill, the government's first widespread effort to encourage and aid people to get a college education, was a resounding success. Universities that fully embraced the program saw their enrollments triple from prewar levels. An additional program, the National Defense Student Loan Program, was passed in 1958 to provide subsidized loans to students in participating schools. Then in 1965 Congress took a major step toward expanding aid for postsecondary education. The Guaranteed Student Loan Program was enacted as part of the comprehensive Higher Education Act. Loans were to be made by banks and repayment would be guaranteed by the federal government, usually acting through guaranty agencies. Those intermediary agencies would be either private entities or organizations established by individual states. The program failed to attract as many banks as had been anticipated. So in the 1970s, seeking to spur banks' interest in participating, Congress offered a further incentive—a promise of supplemental payments from the federal government—to top off the interest rates that students paid in the event that the rate ever fell below market levels any time before the loan was fully repaid. Guaranteeing both the yield and the repayment of student loans had the desired effect. By the early 1990s, several thousand private financial institutions were participating in the program, issuing billions in loans every year.

Like any large financial program, the student loan system drew reports of waste and abuse. Critics accused banks of making excessive profits for carrying out simple administrative chores free of any real risk. Concerns were voiced that all participants—students, banks, and other players—were tempted into carelessness since all the risk fell to an essentially passive government. And a congressional investigation of the Education Department's controls over guaranty agencies found an array of deficiencies, starting with extensive overbilling and inept record keeping. As a result, the Clinton administration proposed shifting to direct student loans, bypassing the banks. The administration, the General Accounting Office, and the Congressional Budget Office all predicted that a simpler administrative structure that better aligned risks and responsibilities would save significant sums.[6] In 1993 Congress passed legislation authorizing the Department of Education to issue loans directly. The legislation envisaged a gradual but definitive shift from delegated to direct government lending, with subsidized bank lending phased out by the end of the 1990s.

But in 1994, well before the direct loan program could be fully implemented, the political context shifted. Republicans captured control of Congress and became the new arbiters of legitimacy. Bitter challenges to direct student lending were inevitable, and legislation was quickly introduced in both houses to eliminate it. The lead Senate sponsor, Dan Coats of Indiana, warned that unless the Clinton initiative was reversed, "Americans will have nowhere else to turn but the largesse of the Department of Education when it comes time to finance their college education." Coats urged "colleagues who support limited Government and prudent fiscal restraint" to cosponsor his bill, which would abolish the deviation from private-sector delivery of tuition aid.[7]

Representative Ernest Istook, when introducing parallel legislation on the House side, anchored his motives even more explicitly in legitimacy, stressing that "the Federal government should only carry out those responsibilities that cannot be performed by the private sector."[8] The eventual compromise was new legislation that kept banks in the student loan business and curtailed, but did not eliminate, the experiment with direct lending. Both channels remained open, and a decade later there was a total of about $250 billion outstanding in guaranteed tuition lending by banks. Lending by the federal government itself, which had been expected to dominate the system when it

[6] General Accounting Office, "Student Loans: Direct Loans Could Save Money and Simplify Program Administration," HRD-01-144BR (September 1991).

[7] Statements on Introduced Bills and Joint Resolutions, Senate, August 11, 1995, *The Congressional Record* via THOMAS, accessed November 24, 2005, http://thomas.loc.gov.

[8] Extension of Remarks, June 9, 1995, *The Congressional Record* via THOMAS, accessed November 24, 2005, http://thomas.loc.gov.

was introduced, had been driven down to less than one-quarter of total loans by 2007.[9]

It is revealing to note that what is universally referred to as a "direct" federal lending program is in fact administered by a private information-processing firm—currently a unit of Xerox—though under a conventional contract with minimal discretion.[10] This suggests that practitioners implicitly recognize the affinities between "direct" delivery—that is, action undertaken by people working in government agencies who exercise little independent discretion—and delegation through well-specified contracts, that is, work done by people employed by government contractors who exercise little independent discretion. And it highlights the contrast between *both* of these approaches and collaborative models featuring shared discretion.

The respected GAO estimated that the guaranteed-loan program cost the government an average of $9.20 per $100 loaned, while the "direct" program cost $1.70 per $100 loaned, less than one-fifth as much. Banks and their associations lobbied to block legislative provisions that would have made direct loans more convenient or less expensive, and deployed lawyers to file lawsuits against Education Department practices they saw as threats to subsidized, government-insured bank lending.[11] The banks' political efforts were amplified by a diffuse but potent sentiment that government should steer clear of the lending business, so long as there is any plausible private alternative.

The sentiment would prove to be costly to taxpayers, in part because of a seemingly sensible move to keep inflation from scaring banks away from the lending program. In 1980, during a period of high inflation that prompted complaints from banks about their returns on student loans, Congress guaranteed that certain types of student loans would return no less than 9.5 percent. When interest rates later fell, Congress moved to end what had become a windfall for

[9] Jonathan D. Glater and Karen W. Arenson, "Lenders Sought Edge against U.S. in Student Loans," *New York Times*, April 15, 2007.

[10] General Accounting Office, "Student Loans: Direct Loan Default Rates," GAO-01-068 (October 2000), p. 8.

[11] Glater and Arenson, "Lenders Sought Edge against U.S. in Student Loans."

lenders. The 9.5 percent guarantee was eliminated, save for loans initiated before October 1, 1993. Surprisingly, the federal payments to banks for those older loans *rose* substantially in the next several years instead of falling as would have been expected as the loans were repaid. An investigation discovered that banks were using a variety of techniques to repackage loans in ways that enabled them to meet the technical terms of "pre-1993" transactions eligible for the 9.5 percent guarantee. The result: far from fading away as lawmakers intended, the volume of 9.5 percent loans grew to more than $17 billion late in fiscal year 2004 from $11 billion in fiscal year 1995. Estimates put the cost to taxpayers of these economically sterile subsidies at more than $1 billion. When subsidies are available, crafty actors will capitalize. Subsidy chasing, the flip side of the more familiar tax avoidance, should be anticipated when collaboration relies on financial inducements to attract partners.

Worse was to come. A wave of investigations revealed that banks were routinely lobbying and pressuring universities—and in many cases offering financial inducements of borderline legality—to encourage students to opt for private instead of direct loans. Some cases crossed the line into clear-cut corruption, as banks offered trips, gifts, and other incentives to university employees in a position to influence students' choice of lenders. Financial-aid officials at Columbia, Johns Hopkins, the University of Southern California, and the University of Texas were found to have ownership stakes or lucrative consulting arrangements with the banks to which they steered student borrowers.[12] So, it later emerged, did at least one senior staffer at the federal Department of Education tasked with overseeing private lenders.[13] But education secretary Margaret Spellings claimed that bad laws and regulations, not bad apples, were the main barriers to reining in abuses by private lenders. Her department, she argued, was enforcing as much accountability as the law allowed. "The system is redundant," in Spellings's words; "It's Byzantine, and it's broken."[14]

[12] Karen W. Arenson, "Columbia to Pay $1.1 Million to State Fund in Loan Scandal," *New York Times,* June 1, 2007.

[13] "The Widening Student Loan Scandal" (editorial), *New York Times,* April 8 2007.

[14] Sam Dillon, "Spellings Rejects Criticism on Student Loan Scandal," *New York Times,* May 11, 2007.

By mid-2007 lawsuits, regulatory revisions, and legislative reforms at the state and federal levels had narrowed the discretion of private lenders, and tilted the mixed student-loan system back somewhat toward direct lending. The Obama administration, in its first budget, called for scrapping guaranteed private loans entirely in favor of the cheaper and simpler direct-lending channel. In 2009—rather narrowly, and almost entirely along party lines—Congress passed legislation phasing out the private lending channel, with the $80 billion in estimated ten-year savings earmarked for low-income student scholarships.[15]

A River Ran Through It:
Approaches to Governing New Land

"Buy land. They've stopped making it."

Mark Twain's famous assertion seems reasonable enough, but on rare occasions it overstates the case. In the spring of 1957 relentless rains drove the river Turia up to and beyond the bridges linking the two sides of Valencia's historic city center. Water ran sixteen feet deep in some of the streets, and much of Spain's third-largest city was devastated. Determined to avoid a repetition of the deadly flood, Valencia undertook a massive project to divert the Turia from its ancient course, paying for the required excavations with a sharp increase in local taxes. The diversion project made Valencians safer, but it also posed an unconventional challenge: what to do with the strip of vacant land, formerly the riverbed, running through the middle of the city?

With little fuss or hesitation the Generalitat (regional government) took responsibility for the undertaking. After briefly considering a proposal to build a large roadway, the government instead developed a master plan for a ten-kilometer stretch of parkland. Over the decades the Generalitat struck shifting alliances with both lower and higher levels of government—the local authorities of Valencia, Spain's national government, and the European Union—to assemble financial

---

[15] Tamar Lewin, "House Passes Bill to Expand Student Aid," *New York Times*, September 17, 2009.

and logistical support for an increasingly ambitious urban-renewal project featuring gardens, paths, art installations, and playgrounds. The capstone was the City of the Arts and Sciences, an architecturally daring and quickly world-famous museum complex, built and run by a public corporation wholly owned by the Generalitat.[16]

Sluggish traffic, not rising waters, posed a similar challenge to Boston in the 1980s. The Central Artery, an elevated six-lane highway built in the 1950s through the center of downtown, was overwhelmed by traffic. Planning for the Big Dig, an ambitious plan to widen the Central Artery and bury it in a skein of tunnels, began in the 1980s, and construction started in 1991. Once the last stretch of elevated highway was demolished, there would be nearly thirty acres of open space in a city center that had been congested since colonial days. What should be done with Boston's first big swath of vacant terrain in two centuries?

Formally the Commonwealth of Massachusetts owned the land, but it had the authority to delegate its management as it saw fit. That left a wide-open question about the governance of what would be called the Greenway. It could be managed by some existing unit of state or city government. Either or both levels of government could establish a special authority tailor-made to govern the Greenway. Or management could be delegated to one of the many private nonprofits already operating in the area. Certainly government—a vast tangle of official agencies at multiple levels were involved—would have some influence in the decision-making process. At the federal level, the Department of Transportation, the Environmental Protection Administration, and the Army Corps of Engineers would each have their own opinions. The Commonwealth of Massachusetts would receive input from the legislature, the governor's office, the Secretariat for Environmental Affairs, and the Massachusetts Turnpike Authority. Finally, Boston would advance ideas through the mayor's office, the city council, the zoning commission, and the Boston Redevelopment Authority. And those were just the most prominent agencies involved at each level.

[16] Leslie Crawford, "Valencia's Formula for Getting Ahead Is by Thinking Big," *Financial Times*, October 26, 2005, p. 6, and "Historia de las ciudad de las artes y las ciencias," at http://www.cac.es/historia/index.htm, accessed November 2005.

But it was inconceivable in the United States that decisions with such far-flung economic and cultural stakes would be left to government alone. A vast network of private organizations, some long established and others created for the purpose, were involved in determining what to do with the new land. Some groups were organized geographically, associated with a particular stretch of land or block of buildings abutting what used to be the elevated highway. Others cohered to embody some set of priorities. The Boston Greenspace Alliance, for example, was an umbrella group for a cluster of organizations determined to maximize open space and minimize construction on the new land. Arguably the most powerful private group was the Artery Business Committee, or ABC. Years before ground was broken for the project, the ABC was formed by a group of business people alarmed about the prospect that the construction work would make downtown impassable for a decade or more. As the project neared completion, the ABC morphed into an organization with a broader interest in how the new Greenway would be used.[17]

Governor Mitt Romney proposed a New England version of Valencia's governance solution for the old riverbed—direct control of the Greenway by the state's Department of Conservation and Recreation.[18] That model found little support beyond the governor's office. After endless rounds of political wrangling, marked by the quiet backroom scheming and noisy public recriminations de rigueur for any enterprise in Boston, a solution emerged: the Greenway would be governed by a "conservancy," an independent private organization with a ten-member board dominated by business leaders.[19] One factor supporting the consensus for such a private model was that no self-respecting Boston political leader could let anybody else's public agency win control. But an additional and probably more important reason was that a private organization had the potential to inspire confidence among potential funders of the Greenway. A core task, for

---

[17] Kirsten Lundbert, "Too Many Parents: The Governance of the Rose Kennedy Greenway," Kennedy School Case Program, 2006.

[18] Anthony Flint, "City, Pike Seen Near Parks Plan; Dismantling of Artery Spurs Race for Role," *Boston Globe*, February 21, 2004, p. A1.

[19] Thomas Palmer, "10 Named to Govern and Raise Money for Greenway," *Boston Globe*, December 1, 2004, p. C5.

whoever had charge of the Greenway, would be raising resources to ensure its maintenance over the long run in an uncertain environment for public funding. Analysts estimated that an endowment of around $50 million would be needed. In Valencia, the state-owned corporation that built a museum complex where the Turia once flowed had no great difficulty attracting private donations to supplement its government funding. Not so in Boston. As an editorial in the *Boston Business Journal* warned, private donations would be forthcoming only if the organization running the Greenway were seen as sufficiently independent of government.[20]

Fragmented arrangements for managing contributed to the long-awaited Greenway's disappointing debut. Fund-raising and investment have been erratic and behind schedule. The Greenway works, after a fashion, as a pedestrian corridor where traffic once roared. But as a cultural asset it has turned out to be ... well, pedestrian. The art and landscaping are mostly lackluster, programming is meager, and many of the intended cultural amenities have failed to materialize.[21] Legitimacy can come at a cost.

Lost Opportunity:
Medicare, Rating Hospitals, and Legitimacy

It was one of the strangest fights Madison Square Garden had ever hosted. The legitimacy title was on the line.

The Kennedy administration landed the first blow. It was eager to build popular support for a proposed new program called Medicare that would insure the health of America's elderly. It was the spring of 1962, and the administration filled the Garden with supporters aged sixty-five and older to watch the president deliver a speech promot-

---

[20] "A Problem with the Greenway Solution," *Boston Business Journal*, July 16, 2004.

[21] An Armenian Heritage Park, with a fountain and sculpture in remembrance of the Armenian genocide and all subsequent genocides, and a labyrinth in grass and stone that represents life's journey and that will take thirty minutes to traverse, was expected to add some interest when it opens in late 2010.

ing Medicare. The speech was carried live by all three networks and was coordinated with simultaneous Medicare rallies in forty-five other cities.

Two days later the American Medical Association delivered its dramatic counterpunch. The AMA also booked Madison Square Garden —but left it empty, to symbolize what the physicians viewed as their underdog status. AMA president Dr. Edward Annis stood alone at the podium in the darkened hall while network cameras broadcast his speech. Kennedy's Medicare plan, Annis warned, "would put the government smack into your hospitals! Defining services, setting standards, establishing committees, calling for reports, deciding who gets in and who gets out, what they get and what they don't ... and imposing a federally administered financial budget on our houses of mercy and healing.... It will stand between patients and their doctors. And it will serve as the forerunner of a different system of medicine for all Americans."[22]

The empty Garden won. A few weeks later a key vote failed in the Senate 52–48, and thus evaporated any hope of passing Medicare in that Congress. Three years later—in the wake of Lyndon Johnson's landslide victory, and after the murdered president's mythic status gave posthumous impetus to Kennedy's social agenda—the political environment permitted another attempt at Medicare's passage. Enactment was no sure thing.

Fully aware that anything even mildly redolent of socialized medicine faced an uphill battle in American politics, officials in the Kennedy and Johnson administrations repeatedly adjusted the Medicare proposal to maximize—and advertise—the private role. As one scholar observed, Medicare's architects viewed their central challenge as designing "administrative arrangements ... for expanding the state's role in financing hospital care without arousing uneasiness over state interference. The central thrust of this bid for legitimacy was to ensure that the actual delivery of care would remain in private hands. But

---

[22] The 1962 speech is excerpted, and its context described, in Edward R. Annis, *Code Blue: Health Care in Crisis* (Regnery Gateway, 1993), pp. 67–70.

another element was deliberately to avoid hierarchical control over the cost and quality of care under the new program."[23]

The contest over Medicare represented an epic struggle for legitimacy in the delivery of health care. A major skirmish concerned who would make sure that the quality of Medicare-financed hospital services to the elderly met minimum standards. After all, the government would be spending huge sums of money, and the quality of hospitals was very difficult for lay people to assess. The history of Medicare provides some perspective on how that question was resolved when responsibility for quality oversight was imposed on a private organization called the Joint Commission on the Accreditation of Healthcare Organizations (JCAHO). The complicated role the JCAHO has played in this massive federal program shows how the quest for legitimacy can complicate the pursuit of top performance.

Lots of Money, Little Information

The United States paid $697 billion in hospital bills in 2007, representing one out of every three dollars the nation spent on health care.[24] (Doctors' bills, nursing homes, and prescription drugs were the other big items.) Hospitals claimed a slightly greater share of America's public and private resources than did elementary and secondary schools (which spent $624 billion) and considerably more than did colleges and universities ($383 billion). Government paid over 55 percent of the total hospital bill—compared to the nearly 40 percent paid by private insurance, and the 3.5 percent patients paid out of their own pockets. Medicare alone accounted for more than $196 billion in federal hospital spending. Yet for all that there is no federal institution to oversee hospital quality.

Of course spending, even of vast sums, doesn't automatically provide sufficient reason to undertake close scrutiny of the institutions receiving the money. The government buys lots of paper but doesn't

[23] Lawrence R. Jacobs, "Institutions and Culture: Health Policy and Public Opinion in the U.S. and Britain," *World Politics* 44, no. 2 (1992): 203.

[24] All figures in this paragraph are drawn from or calculated from data in *Statistical Abstract of the United States 2010*, tables 127, 134, and 215.

find it necessary to inspect paper mills. Paper, however, is not like hospital care. There are three major differences, each suggesting the government may have a role in providing information to the market. First, paper is easy to evaluate; hospital care is not. Second, the consequences of poor quality differ greatly: for paper trivial, for hospitals and their patients dire. Third, the government uses paper directly, and large agencies can judge quality for themselves. Hospital care under Medicare is selected by millions of individuals, acting in isolation.

And in contrast to the case of many other markets—where individuals can become smart shoppers, savvy about quality—it is hard for people to assess hospital performance. Guidance offered by physicians and insurance companies is sometimes shaped by self-interest. A physician is not likely to recommend a hospital where she does not have admitting privileges. Insurance companies have favored relationships with selected providers. Word of mouth is not a reliable guide to hospital quality. Most people, and their friends and relatives, have only very few encounters with a hospital. Good or bad outcomes in any hospital may turn on any number of factors—the severity of the illness or injury, or the patient's other conditions—that are beyond the hospital's control. And quality differentials do not alter outcomes for sure. They only affect probabilities, which makes it hard to judge quality from a few encounters. If rigorous sterility controls mean a 3 percent chance of postoperative infection, while sloppy practices mean a 5 percent chance, even the most attentive layman will be unable to infer much about quality from his own and friends-and-family experiences.

Today, state health authorities monitor and regulate some aspects of hospital operations, but the federal government has steadfastly eschewed that role. The federal agency most closely linked to hospitals is the Centers for Medicare and Medicaid Services (CMMS), but it does little more than write checks, and has virtually no capacity to assess the quality of the care behind the bills that it pays. This shortage of institutional incapacity is no accident. CMMS is required by law to delegate the quality-oversight responsibilities for hospitals that receive Medicare payments to JCAHO, a private concern. Once accredited by JCAHO, a hospital is deemed to be in compliance with

Medicare's conditions of participation. While Joint Commission accreditation is not the sole route to Medicare participation—a hospital can instead seek certification from state health authorities, and in 2008 a private rival was authorized to nibble away at the franchise—but it is the route chosen by the vast majority of hospitals. And Medicare looms so large in hospital revenues that the ability to admit Medicare patients is a de facto operating license.

Legitimacy and Medicare

In Medicare's formative days, the Kennedy and Johnson administrations struggled to overcome deeply embedded worries over government's role in health care. Private polling conducted at Kennedy's request found that while "people want something done" about health costs for the elderly, "they have doubts about the method."[25] More than four decades later, the Obama administration and his congressional allies encountered much the same public views when they grappled with extending coverage to the uninsured.

Opponents of an expanded governmental role in the medical system were skilled then, as they are today, at both stoking and invoking such doubts. These opponents were drawn from two overlapping groups: first, politicians and others with sincere substantive objections to governmental intrusions on terrain they viewed as best reserved for the market, and, second, those with economic stakes—mostly physicians—who believed their autonomy and incomes would be imperiled by greater government involvement in health care. Looking back from today, one might assume that it was doubt about the government's capacity, not concerns about legitimacy, that drove the decision toward the private sector. But the first half of the 1960s was the high-water mark of Americans' belief in the *competence* of government. Direct federal administration of Medicare was not rejected on grounds of effectiveness. Indeed, officials at the Bureau of the Budget —the predecessor of the Office of Management and Budget—made a strong substantive case that a sophisticated federal administrative in-

---

[25] Quoted in Jacobs, "Institutions and Culture," p. 197.

frastructure for Medicare was essential for accountability. Analysts and political officials at the time were acutely aware of the risks of delegating to a private organization the major managerial functions for a program with such large financial consequences for the government.[26]

But there were other calculations to be considered. Robert Ball, head of the Social Security Administration, explicitly made the case that maximum reliance on private organizations to administer Medicare offered "public relations advantages which might outweigh some of the basic advantages of greater speed, flexibility, and control that come from a direct-line operation."[27] Political calculations, heavily shaped by perceptions of legitimacy, rather than technical assessments of the most effective administrative arrangements, dominated the institutional draftsmanship of Medicare in general and its accountability mechanisms in particular.

Thus when the Social Security Amendments of 1965 formally established the new program, they featured extensive reliance on private organizations. The law's dry language noted that while Medicare was the responsibility of the secretary of Health, Education and Welfare (the predecessor agency to Health and Human Services), the "Secretary may perform any of his functions under this subchapter directly, or by contract ... as the Secretary may deem necessary."[28] While the means for performing most functions were left open in the law, technically speaking, it was as well understood as it was inevitable that private insurance companies—notably the Blue Cross/Blue Shield network—would be responsible for most aspects of the money flow from Washington to health-care providers.

The legislation went even further, however, in specifying the delivery model for one crucial function—determining a hospital's eligibility to participate. One part of the law laid out a lengthy set of criteria to be met before a hospital could bill the federal government for a

[26] See ibid., pp. 203–204 and 207, for specific illustrations of Kennedy and Johnson officials opting for indirect management of Medicare on legitimacy grounds, not because they doubted the feasibility of direct administration.

[27] Robert Ball memo of 1961, quoted in Jacobs, "Institutions and Culture," p. 204.

[28] USC 42, chap. 7, subchap. XVIII, sec. 1395kk.

senior citizen's health care.[29] A separate part simply stated that any institution accredited by the Joint Commission on Accreditation of Hospitals (as the organization was then known) "shall be deemed to meet the requirements"[30] with no questions asked. As one scholar later put it, in order to placate those most opposed to or skeptical about this expansion of the state, the design of Medicare's administrative arrangements "spared professionals and providers the indignity of dealing with the federal government."[31]

What the Joint Commission Does

Were the Kennedy and Johnson administrations correct in their assessment that political expediency required an indirect approach to Medicare management? Our discussion about this governance model and its perceived legitimacy begins with the observation that the Joint Commission, essentially a private group that plays the pivotal role in overseeing the quality of hospitals, fulfills a central function of government—providing information to improve market efficiency. Moreover, it fulfills that function in a market in which the government is a massive participant.

Direct governmental performance certainly does not guarantee effective quality control. After all, the Federal Savings and Loan Insurance Corporation spectacularly failed to prevent the thrift industry meltdown of the 1980s. At the same time, private certification is by no means rare, even for matters of considerable public consequence. Accounting firms validate a corporation's financial statements. Bond rating agencies assess the quality of corporate, municipal, and sovereign debt securities, although the major rating services signally failed in the run-up to the 2008–9 financial meltdown. The International Organization for Standardization—better known by its scrambled acronym, ISO—verifies that manufacturing operations hew to estab-

---

[29] USC 42, chap. 7, subchap. XVIII, sec. 1395x(e).

[30] USC 42, chap. 7, subchap. XVIII, sec. 1395bb.

[31] Timothy Stoltzfus Jost, "Medicare and the Joint Commission on Accreditation of Healthcare Organizations: A Healthy Relationship?" *Law and Contemporary Problems* 57, no. 4 (1994): 25.

lished specifications. Some of these private rating and regulatory arrangements break down, to be sure, as we saw with the failure of debt-rating agencies in the subprime mortgage crisis, but we should not let recent breakdowns, however vivid, obscure how well such private arrangements often work. There also are many instances in which public and private quality-control models operate side by side in the same domain at the same time, sometimes in parallel isolation and sometimes in complicated symbiosis. Both the (public) National Highway Traffic Safety Administration and the (private) Insurance Institute for Highway Safety test-crash cars and publicize the results. The oldest and most familiar quality certification in the United States is the UL logo attesting that any of a broad array of products meets the standards of the Underwriters' Laboratories, a private organization established in the late 1800s by the insurance industry. Nearly all product categories tested by UL are also subject to regulation by the federal Consumer Product Safety Commission, and from time to time the standards of the public and private organizations collide.[32]

Two factors distinguish the Joint Commission from other private organizations in the ratings business. First, it provides the green light for the expenditure of vast public resources. Second, its personnel—particularly doctors and nurses—are the lifeblood professionals of the very institutions it is certifying, and those institutions employ a major fraction of such professionals. The question is whether the relationship between JCAHO and the public authorities ultimately responsible for Medicare—whatever the origins of that relationship—offers a reasonably accountable and efficient implementation model for this particular public mission. Engaging this question requires addressing the characteristics of the private organization, the nature of the task, the nexus between public and private players, and how the organization actually functions. It especially requires some close attention to the form and the degree of discretion JCAHO commands.

To obtain accreditation a hospital must undergo a JCAHO survey evaluation. JCAHO's fees are modest—in the tens of thousands of

---

[32] Barry Meier, "Sparks Fly over Industry Safety Test," *New York Times*, December 22, 1995, p. 3-1.

dollars, depending on an institution's size and complexity, not the hundreds of thousands—but not trivial. Hospitals occasionally cite cost as a reason for switching from JCAHO accreditation to state-agency certification.[33] Softening the pain, the federal government considers JCAHO fees to be legitimate costs of operating a hospital, and permits them to be included in the formulas used to calculate spending eligible for reimbursement.

A survey team generally spends three days, and sometimes more, inspecting a facility, interviewing its personnel, and reviewing its records. A few months later JCAHO issues its report. In all but a few cases the hospital receives accreditation. The Joint Commission is thus more a doorkeeper than a scorekeeper. It determines who's in and who's out, but has little to say about who's up and who's down.

A Mandate to Collaborate

The determination of which hospitals can participate in Medicare involves what is, objectively speaking, a joint venture between CMMS[34] —the agency that administers Medicare and Medicaid—and JCAHO. But it is an odd collaboration, mandated by legislators rather than designed by managers. Neither the private nor the public collaborator was consulted as the relationship took shape. Neither CMMS nor its predecessor existed when the legislation was written, and the Joint Commission learned it had been tapped to handle quality control only after Medicare legislation was enacted.[35]

JCAHO is a private party performing an essential public function— authorizing hospitals to bill the federal government for a staggering quantity of services. Medicare hospital bills are roughly equivalent to the combined total outlays of the departments of Commerce, Energy,

---

[33] Susanna Duff, "Two Vermont Hospitals Abandon JCAHO Accreditation," *Modern Healthcare*, August 19, 2002, p. 20.

[34] The Center for Medicare and Medicaid Services was long known as the Health Care Finance Administration.

[35] See "Remarks by Dennis O'Leary, M.D." from July 20, 2004, reproduced at http://www .jcaho.org/news+room/press+kits/gao/talkingpoints.htm.

Homeland Security, Interior, Justice, Labor, and State.[36] But JCAHO is not in any meaningful sense accountable to the public collaborator. CMMS, which pays the bills, has no authority over the standards the Joint Commission applies. Beyond refusing to pay bills for unaccredited facilities, CMMS is not authorized to make any direct use of the data from these validation studies. The inspector general's office of the Department of Health and Human Services has characterized CMMS's actual stance toward the Joint Commission as "more deferential than directive."[37] In terms of the framework we have employed throughout this book, JCAHO commands an extreme degree of discretion, while its governmental counterpart has very little.

The lopsided allocation of discretion also reflects some particular characteristics of the public partner, the CMMS. A former general counsel of the Department of Health and Human Services has stressed the significance of CMMS's origins as a unit of the Social Security Administration. Its organizational culture orients it to perform as a check-writing agency whose missions are to determine when people can receive money for doing something, and then to pay that money when they do it. Historically, it has not viewed itself as a regulatory agency and has resisted legislative efforts to transform it into one.[38]

Given that culture, CMMS can be expected to strongly prefer to delegate quality certification, even independently of legislative strictures. In contrast to the conventional wisdom that bureaucracies are inherently imperialistic and turf conscious, CMMS has never displayed much desire to control quality certification, possibly fearful of claiming terrain that it could not easily master. Indeed, it appears that CMMS is more comfortable than is the Joint Commission with the imbalance in the allocation of discretion between the two. In 2004,

---

[36] FY 2005 outlays for these seven agencies combined were about $154 billion, as calculated from Office of Management and Budget, *Budget of the United States, Fiscal Year 2006*, historical table 4-1, "Outlays by Agency 1960–2010."

[37] Office of the Inspector General, "The External Review of Hospital Quality: The Role of Accreditation" (Department of Health and Human Services, July 1999), p. 13.

[38] Michael J. Astrue, "Health Care Reform and the Constitutional Limits on Private Accreditation as an Alternative to Direct Government Regulation," *Law and Contemporary Problems* 57, no. 4 (1994): 75.

JCAHO president Dennis O'Leary bluntly expressed his concern with the lack of any mechanism for receiving guidance from the government: "When we introduced our new accreditation process, we briefed CMMS staff on several occasions.... What we would have liked to have had was their blessing, their approval. But there is no statutory authority for them to do that."[39]

A Governmental Disadvantage

CMMS would be poorly equipped to judge the quality of hospitals. Inspecting hospitals is a technically demanding task. It is not clear that CMMS would be up to even exercising detailed control over the Joint Commission. To oversee such work—to inspect the inspectors and to guide them when necessary—would call for personnel with technical and managerial abilities at least equivalent to those of the surveyors being assessed. Those surveyors, in turn, would have to meet the capabilities of the staff of the institution being overseen. It is simply unrealistic to expect CMMS to be able to hire and retain top-flight technical and managerial personnel given the salaries it is able to pay. The head of the Joint Commission earned more than six times as much as the head of CMMS, as of 2003.[40] While disparities are narrower below the top level, there is a substantial compensation shortfall between public and private pay scales for virtually all professions relevant to hospital accreditation.

More important to our discussion, governmental organizations are often highly reluctant to produce finely differentiated quality judgments. They tend, instead, to prefer basic pass-fail assessments. Partly that is due to formal rules, such as the Administrative Procedures Act, that require exhaustive justification if an agency attempts to treat one individual or organization any differently from all the rest. But

---

[39] July 20, 2004, O'Leary remarks from press release cited above, n. 35.

[40] Dennis O'Leary's compensation of $860,000 from *Modern Healthcare*, May 2, 2005, p. 26; Mark McClellan's of just under $137,000 from Committee on Government Reform, U.S. House of Representatives, 108th Congress, 2nd session, "United States Government Policy and Supporting Positions, 2004 Edition" (U.S. Government Printing Office, 2004).

fundamental patterns of bureaucratic behavior also play a role. There is a natural aversion to risk and confrontation when no prospect of reward balances the downside. This tendency is evident across a broad range of government agencies. The Federal Deposit Insurance Corporation treats banks as either sound or unsound. The Pension Benefit Guarantee Corporation perennially faces congressional opposition when it attempts to differentiate among employers even on quite clear-cut measures of funding risk. State unemployment insurance organizations are seldom able or willing to charge firms known to churn their workforces at rates much higher than those paid by historically stable employers whose workers rarely claim insurance. The Consumer Product Safety Commission treats products as either safe (requiring no action) or unsafe (and subject to immediate recall) in contrast to the fine gradations in assessment applied by private groups such as Consumers Union.

Performance Incentives

Under Medicare, the Joint Commission was given wide latitude in its approach. At first blush that latitude would seem to raise questions about diligence. Perhaps the JCAHO would cravenly rubber-stamp the applications of the hospitals that pay its bills. But experience clearly shows the Joint Commission is no pushover. In recent years it has shifted from long-scheduled inspections to a short interval between the scheduling of a visit and the arrival of inspectors to conduct completely unannounced reviews, in the spirit of pop quizzes keeping students on their toes. This trajectory is in the right direction, from the public's perspective, but cannot be popular with hospitals. And while it is relatively rare for a hospital to be denied accreditation, it is far from unknown.

Even were we to ascribe only the crassest motives to JCAHO, servility is not in its interest. Most hospitals, after all, aspire to and attain reasonably high quality standards. They want JCAHO accreditation to send a signal to prospective patients, who would be expected to complain if accreditation became automatic and thus empty. Even if JCAHO were cheerfully ready to sacrifice patients' interests in pursuit of hospital fees, there is no reason to believe its own personnel would tolerate such a trade-off. Surely such laxity would boomerang once academia and the media—and ultimately the public—discovered it. Rubber-stamping the accreditation bid of a bad hospital brings in survey fees of a few tens of thousands of dollars—almost surely too little to compensate a rational economic actor, even one utterly unconstrained by scruples, for imperiling its reputation.

Assume for the moment that the Joint Commission's officials had only the selfish goals of preserving their good incomes, status, and a quiet, predictable professional life. It still remains obvious that the biggest threat to those goals would be losing the franchise as the main gatekeeper for Medicare money. It would be a calamity for the Joint Commission to be stripped of its accrediting authority, and an only slightly lesser calamity to lose its dominant role in the accreditation business. This is far from a hypothetical danger. Legislation passed in 2007 opens the door to alternative private accreditation, and while rivals so far have made only minor inroads, a few well-documented instances of slipshod accreditation—especially instances linked to patient harm—could lead to a successful assault on the franchise. Slips of this sort could quickly wither JCAHO's legitimacy in its role of impartial judge; unsavory accusations of pandering to the payers could quickly emerge. Potential litigation from suffering patients over sloppy monitoring is surely an additional concern. The Joint Commission thus has powerful incentives to be rigorous enough to maintain its reputation and legitimacy, even if the application of adequate rigor at times annoys some of the institutions that provide its revenues.

The private Joint Commission, moreover, has shown itself able to accomplish some tasks that neither government, nor hospitals acting independently, would be able to do as well, or at all. For example, its standards for mental health facilities recommend "spiritual assessments" to determine whether and how a mental patient's faith can serve as a source of strength and aid to recovery. Governmental organizations, appropriately cautious about transgressing boundaries between church and state, might be leery of making such recommendations.[41] JCAHO's accomplishments include undertakings that are clearly valuable in retrospect, but that would have been difficult or impossible to anticipate in a fully specified contract. Aggregating experience from low-probability, high-cost events across a great many hospitals, it discovered that the abbreviation IU for "international units" could be mistaken for the number 10 when scribbled by a careless physician. This abbreviation joined other error-prone terms on an "official do-not-use list" that JCAHO disseminated. Only the largest and most attentive hospitals would have been capable of assembling such a list from internal evidence alone.

Sins of Omission

But not every aspect of the complex collaborative arrangement between JCAHO and the government produces the results it could and should. Consider first some of the simpler and more predictable costs of this legitimacy-driven implementation model. There have been episodic press exposés of conditions to be found in JCAHO-accredited hospitals, with all the wince-inducing details one might expect.[42] Various critics periodically raise concern about the potential for conflicts of interest, especially when JCAHO is conducting high-stakes inspections of a hospital while simultaneously offering that same hospital the chance to buy the services of its consulting subsidiary. Yet these concerns seem, on balance, less weighty than they at first appear. The fact that problems can be found at accredited hospitals does not prove the charge of laxness on JCAHO's part. Conditions may change after the survey team leaves; there is often room for honest disagreement about the degree or even existence of a quality shortcoming; and *any* inspection system run by human beings is going to have the occasional failure. And while one could imagine a somewhat extortionate marketing strategy for JCAHO's consulting

[41] David R. Hodge, "Spirituality and People with Mental Illness: Developing Spiritual Competency in Assessment and Intervention," *Families in Society* 85, no. 1 (January–March 2004): 36–44.

[42] Walt Bogdanich, "Small Comfort: Prized by Hospitals, Accreditation Hides Perils Patients Face," *Wall Street Journal*, October 12, 1988, p. 1; Gilbert M. Gaul, "Accreditors Blamed for Overlooking Problems," *Washington Post*, July 25, 2005, p. A-1.

subsidiary, it is noteworthy that the Joint Commission sets its own fees for surveys. If it wanted to extract the maximum from every hospital it inspects, it could simply raise these fees, rather than "laundering" the protection money through a consulting subsidiary.

The most profound weakness to be found in this collaboration has nothing to do with such risks. Rather, the major cause for dissatisfaction with this collaborative arrangement is that it delivers results no better than those that would be eminently achievable with a conventional governmental quality-control system. JCAHO follows the path of public guarantors of quality in applying only a coarse filter. The problem is not that a horrible hospital on occasion can win or retain accreditation—that is a likely defect of any plausible model—but that there is so little meaningful differentiation among accredited hospitals. A pass-fail approach necessarily strips out most of the important distinctions among America's wildly diverse health-care institutions. Patients, insurers, physicians, and other pertinent audiences get essentially the same signals from JCAHO about run-of-the-mill and truly exceptional health-care institutions. There is no easy way for patients to distinguish among acceptable, excellent, and exceptional hospitals, and thus less potent motives than there might be for institutions to strive for excellence. It requires more sophistication, more incentive, and more doggedness than virtually any patient could possess to extract the nuanced information that would permit one to draw any distinctions among the institutions, and much more courage than JCAHO demonstrates to make easy-to-interpret differential grades.

The Joint Commission's ratings approach provides little incentive for hospitals to improve, apart from the few at the borderline of acceptability. (In colleges, the downside to grade inflation is not merely that the slothful get by, but that grades are squashed at the top, and the incentives they would otherwise provide for excellence are eroded.) Thus a chronic problem of conventional governmental certification and licensing systems shows up, lamentably, where it need not. More precise distinctions among hospitals could generate very large benefits. Health-care institutions vary widely in the quality of care and the health gains achieved from the marginal dollar spent. Even a relatively rudimentary performance-incentives system could save large sums or improve average quality levels, or both. Such a system might divide the "accredited" category into five quality quintiles, thus imposing a requirement that 20 percent fall into each category, and varying reimbursement rates somewhat between quintiles.[43]

The lack of quality gradation suggests that Medicare's architects paid a high price for legitimacy. If the political climate at the time had allowed them to build an in-house accreditation capacity, they might have been able to obtain better results in terms of the amount and quality of the information provided about hospitals. It would require a great deal of analytical and, particularly, empirical work before we could conjecture responsibly about whether a government-run or a delegated model for hospital quality assessment would be, on balance, more appropriate. The evidence at hand *does* suggest, however, that in JCAHO we may be getting the downside of delegation—extra costs, ambiguous accountability, and some inevitable measure of abused discretion—without harvesting the potential benefits of more meaningful ratings. JCAHO, unlike CMMS, should be sufficiently insulated from political pressures to establish a more finely differentiated rating regime. As a private organization, demonstrably able to pay its personnel as it sees fit, it could motivate assessors (in ways a government agency cannot) to undertake the extra effort required to issue and justify differential scores.

Why does the private JCAHO, entrusted largely on legitimacy grounds with an important public task, pursue its work in ways that seem rather close to those a public agency would choose? It seems likely that maintaining an essentially pass-fail regime, with almost everyone passing, is the most comfortable operating model for JCAHO, promising a minimum of controversy and stress.[44] The benefits of a finer-grained accreditation system, after all, would fall to the public

---

[43] In 2004, the Massachusetts Group Insurance Commission initiated a system under which health plans had to rate their doctors in different categories based on both quality and economy. Patients going to doctors in lower-ranked categories incur higher deductibles. See http://www.pioneerinstitute.org/pdf/ROE13.pdf. The main Web page for the initiative is http://www.mass.gov/gic/annualreportb.htm.

[44] In parallel fashion, teachers quickly learn that their interests are not served if they give failing or even marginal grades.

(who would get better care) and to top-performing hospitals (who would get more patients), rather than to the Joint Commission. At best, JCAHO would have to work harder. At worst, it would see its market shrink as institutions opted for accreditation by state agencies or even lobbied for the authorization of other, less demanding private accreditation organizations. It is not surprising that JCAHO would not undertake anything beyond pass-fail on its own initiative. And the weak public party in the collaboration, CMMS, lacks both the authority to require a more precise assessment system and the capacity to establish such a requirement or to determine whether JCAHO is meeting it. Thus the Joint Commission remains a doorkeeper, not a scorekeeper, to the public's quiet loss.

A Concluding Word on Legitimacy

When a new program comes into being, legitimacy derives from expectations rather than experience. Expectations may flow, however, from a sector's past performance with related or even not-so-related tasks. Thus the successes of collaboration we chronicle with charter schools and public parks make the public more amenable to private-sector production in other arenas. Similarly, failures, such as the Panglossian scoring by financial ratings agencies before the 2008 meltdown, make citizens more skeptical, in this case of private raters generally. We refer to the flow of reputations from one party to another as *reputational externalities*. The phenomenon is general—we extrapolate behavior across African presidents or corporate chieftains —but applies with special strength to the relative legitimacy of the private and public sectors.

Historical accidents and half-conscious stereotypes, rather than cold reason, may at times motivate legitimacy-based decisions to adopt a collaborative model. But this merely rearranges, rather than diminishes, reason's role. The altered analytic job is to develop the best possible version of whatever delivery model concerns of legitimacy allow. When practicality and politics both precluded a simple governmental approach to governing Boston's new Greenway, public and private collaborators—after considering plenty of other options—eventually improvised a politically salable if operationally subpar arrangement. The Joint Commission works better than it might—though not as well as it could if a little more creativity and a lot more discipline were invested in making the most of a model that considerations of legitimacy made imperative. Americans wanted their foreign aid to be delivered in a way that celebrated private enterprise rather than bureaucracy. It's easy to imagine clumsy and unaccountable and corruption-prone ways to accommodate that preference, making it all the more remarkable that Andrew Natsios and his team found so elegant a solution. Whatever the origins of a collaborative approach, clear thinking can always make it better. Astute analysis and scrupulous attention to the evidence can soften the trade-off between ideological preference and practical performance. Legitimacy and effectiveness can advance in tandem.

Chapter 7

◇◇

Collaboration for Resources

Once a trash-strewn, crime-ridden wasteland, Central Park underwent a remarkable renaissance as a welcoming oasis. Its famed Literary Walk exemplifies the park's elegant and harmonious blend of nature and art. Today, in any but the least clement weather, at almost any hour, New Yorkers and tourists alike can be found strolling among the carved-stone literary greats beneath the arching elms. But not so long ago Robert Burns and Sir Walter Scott and their granite comrades mostly sat lonely and graffiti-scarred, wind-whipped litter piling up against their pedestals. Things have changed in Central Park over recent decades, very much for the better, and collaborative governance is at the heart of the story.

If we had to flag a single turning point in that transformation, the best date would be 1980. That was the year that New York City's parks department hired Elizabeth Barlow (Betsy) Rogers to run Central Park. Her marching orders from the mayor and the parks commissioner were clear: reverse the decay of New York's long-term icon. Business as usual had plainly failed, and Rogers had the go-ahead to try new approaches. What she was not given, and could not even remotely hope for, was any significant increase in public resources. New York City's budgetary situation, while a notch less desperate than it had been five years earlier, remained forbiddingly tight. Parks and playgrounds were treated as dispensable frills; cops, firefighters, and ambulances took priority. The parks department's budget had fallen by nearly a third, on top of the erosion inflicted by inflation, since 1974. More than half of the workforce had been laid off or had retired in the previous six years, and no replacements had been hired.

Rogers could do things the old way and almost certainly fail. Instead, she sought to build a culture and an institutional structure for enlisting private resources in the rescue of a beleaguered public park.

The challenge Rogers faced is found in many quarters. Scarce resources are a fact of modern government. The total cost of all the things that citizens would like government to do far outstrips the tally of taxes that citizens are prepared to pay. A particularly common motive for collaboration, thus, is to augment government's own resources with those of private partners who have an interest in a particular governmental endeavor.

The level of resources that government can muster to advance some task, of course, depends on popular perceptions about the goals to be served, the efficiency with which the task is addressed, and the fairness with which the costs and benefits are shared. Each of these factors, in turn, can be affected—for better or for worse—by whether government pursues the goal directly or taps private capacity. This chapter will look at three revealing situations in which a major motive for collaboration with private parties was the hope of securing private resources to support public endeavors. They involve New York City's parks; the Partnership for a New Generation of Vehicles, a Clinton-era campaign to increase the efficiency of American cars; and the Food and Drug Administration's efforts to speed the approval of new pharmaceuticals without sacrificing safety.

New York City's Parks

Before we delve into examples of how some specific New York City parks were transformed by collaborative approaches, we must set the stage. And no one bestrides that stage like Robert Moses, the man for whom the term "edifice complex" was coined.[1] The famed builder and power broker was a fixture in New York government from 1924

[1] Some parts of this section are adapted from John D. Donahue, "Parks and Partnership in New York City," Kennedy School of Government Case Program CR16-04-1743 and CR16-04-1744 (Harvard University, 2004).

to 1968, for most of this time serving as New York City's parks commissioner. From this improbable bureaucratic perch Moses assembled a formidable political base and transformed the face of the city. The parks department under his leadership evolved from a backwater of city government into a municipal powerhouse. At its peak in the Great Depression, it boasted a workforce of seventy-five thousand (mostly paid with federal funds), including eighteen hundred designers and engineers.[2] Moses reconfigured vast swaths of Queens to accommodate a World's Fair in 1939, and did the same thing again in 1964. He carved out new parks and reshaped old ones, and dotted the city with playgrounds, beaches, pools, fountains, and recreation buildings. He doubled the total acreage of New York's parks and significantly improved the quality of equipment, amenities, and maintenance. Parks, beaches, and zoos were not enough to quench Mr. Moses's ambitions. He expanded his domain to include roads, bridges, Lincoln Center, the United Nations building, and housing projects throughout the city.

Moses was creative, relentless, and at times ruthless in assembling the resources required to build and feed his empire. He played the municipal budget game hard and well, often claiming improbably large shares of city revenues. He also learned how to tap every legitimate state and federal source of support (as well as some whose legitimacy was decidedly borderline). His most audacious move was to render his empire largely self-supporting by extracting tolls and rents from any plausible payer.

Some observers and historians praised Moses for his drive and vision; others denounced his naked use of power. Both assessments have merit, and all agree that Moses was a tough act to follow. Other New York City park commissioners—less ambitious, less brazen— saw Moses's unconventional revenue streams slip from their grasp. Without those vast resources it was not possible to come close to success on Moses's terms. So for a long time, those who followed Moses mostly failed.

---

[2] Moses's workforce shrank considerably from this federally funded high-water mark during the Great Depression and by 1963 was only around ten thousand.

Robert Moses left a high-maintenance legacy. As New York (like other American cities) entered an era of malaise and turmoil in the 1970s, maintaining the prodigious investment built up over the Moses years became ever harder. The flight of middle-class families to the suburbs chipped away at the city's financial base. Crime soared. New York, fiscally out of kilter as a result of ill-advised borrowing, stumbled into a full-blown financial crisis in 1975. The vivid urban mayhem unleashed by a 1977 power failure sealed New York's image as a city in decline: dim, disorderly, and dangerous.

In that environment it was inevitable that park management would slip another notch. The parks were seen as a second-order public function, and the parks department suffered from the view that its mission was discretionary. Its budget and staff were cut repeatedly from the mid-1960s onward. Those charged with maintaining the parks, both officials and staff, felt crushed between today's meager means and yesterday's vaunting mission.

The sheer scope of the parks department's mandate overmatched the fiscal capacity of modern New York. In 1980, the department was responsible for 900 playgrounds, 709 athletic fields, 535 tennis courts, 104 swimming pools, 15 miles of beach, 14 golf courses, and 3 zoos. It had 572 separate parks in its portfolio, with a total acreage exceeding that of all Manhattan by 50 percent. The parks department's budget plunged from $139 million in 1974 to $96 million (in inflation-withered dollars) in 1980. The workforce dwindled by more than 50 percent between 1965 and 1980.

The "Partnership" Strategy Takes Shape

In 1978, when Gordon Davis was appointed by Mayor Ed Koch as New York's first African American parks commissioner, he inherited a bedraggled empire. New York's halting fiscal recovery allowed the Koch administration to slightly increase the parks department's budget, but Davis knew that no plausible increase in money and manpower would allow his department to maintain, on its own, the legacy left by Moses. Instead, Davis initiated a campaign of tactical retreat to a manageable core mission. In a policy that came to be called "load-shedding," Davis and his team shifted functions away from the parks department and toward corporations, nonprofits, and other units of government. Golf courses and refreshment stands were turned over to private firms that would run them as concessions. Although such efforts may have offered modest efficiencies, they did not attack the core problem: many parks, little money.

Cutting costs could not do enough. Davis recognized that he had to figure out some way to ramp up resources. He suspected that the citizens of New York were collectively willing to pay much more to provide for its parks than the parks currently received. But that didn't matter: citizens cannot direct their tax money to their favored activities. To achieve his goal of more money for parks, Davis shifted tactics from load-shedding to strategic load-*sharing*. The load-sharing strategy reframed the parks department's mission and means. It came to bear the label of "partnerships." What would become a guiding theme of collaboration with corporations, private organizations, and citizens at large took shape under Davis. Responsibility for the zoos in Central Park, Flushing Meadows in Queens, and Prospect Park in Brooklyn was shifted to the New York Zoological Society, a venerable private nonprofit organization that was already running the Bronx Zoo.

But such ad hoc efforts, however innovative and promising, did not yet cohere into an overall strategy, Davis realized. He commissioned a team of external consultants to develop bold ideas for a ten-year recovery plan. They urged Davis to develop and exploit opportunities for sharing responsibility with individuals and organizations beyond the parks department. The idea resonated with Davis's instincts. "It's a direction we're actively pursuing," he told reporters, "but we don't know whether we can do it as quickly as the city's fiscal condition requires."[3]

The partnership approach became the linchpin of the parks department's operating strategy under Davis and then his successor, Henry Stern. Stern's early moves were the self-explanatory Adopt-A-Monument and Historic House Trust. He then established a separate and far more ambitious nonprofit, the City Parks Foundation, to raise

[3] Anna Quindlen and Michael Goodwin, "New York City Park System Stands as a Tattered Remnant of Its Past," *New York Times*, October 13, 1980, p. 1.

private money for sports, arts, and other cultural programs, environmental education, and physical improvements systemwide. A spin-off, the Partnership for Parks, was later launched to supplement financial resources with organizational assistance, facilitating the formation of local volunteer and support organizations that in turn attracted additional resources in an ever-widening virtuous circle.

By the early 1990s, partnerships with the private sector—for capital investments, for volunteer labor, for contracted services, for political support—had matured from an improbable experiment into the strategic mainstay of the parks department. Evening and weekend meetings with volunteer groups became part of the job for department officials. Identifying grant opportunities, nurturing volunteer organizations, and cultivating the wealthy and well connected had become core competencies for senior managers. But the creative cultivation of deep-pocketed private partners had to keep pace against the rapid dwindling of public resources in the early 1990s. New York City was entering another fiscal swoon, less dire than the mid-1970s crisis, but nevertheless severe. In 1990 the department's share of city funding had been $195 million. It would not approach that level again for a dozen years. The operating budget slipped to $185 million in 1991, then plunged to $133 million in 1992. On a single dark day in 1992, more than eight hundred parks workers received pink slips. The parks department's full-time workforce, which had recovered to around five thousand people in the mid-1980s, commenced a sustained slide that would take it well below two thousand.

This was the setting for the systemwide foray into experiments with collaboration to shore up New York's parks. We now turn to three specific examples of these arrangements, illustrating different aspects and different outcomes. These experiments were part of one of the largest and most explicit efforts to produce public value by leveraging private capacity.

Park Story One: Central Park and the Conservancy

What would become the parks department's proudest example of the partnership approach grew from modest beginnings. When Betsy Rogers took the new post of Central Park administrator in 1980, she

chose a strategy that defied the reigning belief that New York's elite—
with other options for access to greenery and fresh air—were inherently indifferent to the city's public parks. As a blue blood herself, she
was thoroughly familiar with upper-crust cultural institutions, such
as the Metropolitan Museum of Art, the New York Public Library, and
the Metropolitan Opera, that had long enjoyed the support of groups
of prominent citizens who donated their own money and time, and
used their connections and stature to energize fund-raising. These
New Yorkers not only cared intrinsically about art or books or music,
but also valued the opportunity to deepen established social connections and form new ones in a civic-minded setting, both parading
their status and raising it.

Why shouldn't something similar work for Central Park? Rogers
found the question compelling. She was a landscape designer, and
had written extensively about both Central Park and its creator,
Frederick Law Olmsted. With the blessings of Commissioner Davis
and Mayor Koch, Rogers approached William Beinecke, a distin-
guished philanthropist who had done much for Yale, and asked him
to serve as the founding chairman for a group to be called the Central
Park Conservancy.[4] Beinecke agreed. He then helped to recruit other
founding trustees and raise seed money, and the Conservancy was
incorporated as a private nonprofit oriented toward, but separate
from, the public asset of Central Park.

Rogers established a visitors' center in a newly refurbished building in Central Park, to be staffed by Conservancy volunteers. It started
by providing maps and answering questions, but the center's services
grew to staging art exhibits, small-scale musical performances, and
educational programs for children. Meanwhile the parks department—
using a conventional mix of city and state funding—was completing
several urgent rehabilitation projects in Central Park, including the
restoration of the dilapidated Sheep Meadow. This set the stage for a

---

[4] Details on the formation of the Central Park Conservancy are drawn from interviews; from
a lengthy presentation by Elizabeth Barlow Rogers, now on the faculty of Bard College, available electronically at http://www.elizabethbarlowrogers.com/lecture/index.html; and from historical material on the Conservancy's Web site at http://www.centralparknyc.org/thenandnow/
cpc-history/.

three-year campaign of comprehensive planning for Central Park's renewal, culminating in public forums and a full-length book laying out both the goal and the organizational means to reach it.[5] Betsy Rogers was the indisputable point person for this effort. Even so, it was hard to say whether the department or the Conservancy had the lead, because since 1980 Rogers had worn two hats, serving simultaneously as the department's administrator for Central Park and as the president of the private Central Park Conservancy. To add to the tangle, her salary as administrator was paid from private funds. Potential conflicts of interest abounded; yet all the evidence suggests she assiduously served the public's priorities.

In New York, the best gauge of a civic organization's standing is its fund-raising prowess. Here, the success of a 1983 Conservancy awards luncheon—where park supporters made hefty contributions for the privilege of seeing colleagues honored—announced that a major new institution was on the scene. The Conservancy showed itself to be a fund-raising powerhouse, not just a passel of enthusiasts. Five years later, the Conservancy raised a $25 million endowment for the Greensward Trust—fancy charity terminology for a park maintenance fund. The Conservancy thus solidified its bid to be a permanent fixture in the constellation of prominent New York City civic organizations. It became an increasingly vibrant nonprofit, with an ever more ambitious agenda, during the 1990s. Fund-raising efforts exploded, providing resources both for major investments and renovations and for ongoing maintenance. And the prestige of being a supporter of the Conservancy grew as approving mentions in the society pages cemented the cause's cachet.

The Conservancy was now able to refurbish some Central Park facilities that had been quietly crumbling since the Robert Moses era. New committees and initiatives were established to link unmet park needs with citizens' latent readiness to donate time, money, or both. Volunteers put in tens of thousands of hours each year, and their efforts increasingly were supplemented by paid Conservancy employees. Yet the Conservancy essentially remained a private voluntary

---

[5] *Rebuilding Central Park: A Management and Restoration Plan* (MIT Press, 1986).

organization providing discretionary support for a city-run park—a large-scale version of the "friends of the park" associations that were increasingly common around the nation and especially in New York.

Given the major resources that were flowing from the Conservancy, the structure of the collaborative relationship with the parks department was unbalanced. Resources and responsibility were out of alignment. In the context of the enormous contributions it was making, the Conservancy simply had too little discretion. All parties recognized that something would have to change. In 1998, following extensive yet amicable negotiations, New York City's government agreed to a sharp shift in discretion: it transferred stewardship of Central Park to the Conservancy. Mayor Rudolph Giuliani, Commissioner Henry Stern, and Conservancy Chairman Ira Millstein signed a legal agreement formalizing the Conservancy's new role.[6]

Superficially the agreement resembled a conventional service-procurement contract, of the sort New York or any other city routinely signs with providers of construction or consulting or social services. It required the Conservancy to "provide, or cause to be provided, services specified for maintaining and repairing Central Park to the reasonable satisfaction of the Commissioner." The Conservancy was required to submit a detailed operating budget to the commissioner, subject to his written approval before the plan could be considered final.[7] The agreement also delineated which facilities (such as the parks department's headquarters building, the Arsenal), which prerogatives (licensing and collecting money from private concessionaires), and which park functions (including law enforcement, and control over public streets passing through the park) remained with the city. Nearly a tenth of the agreement dealt with procedures for procurement contracts, including the requirement for competitive bidding and bars to financial dealings with any relatives of Conservancy employees.[8]

But the critical collaborative element of the document gave the Conservancy great latitude to determine how to carry out its tasks, a

---

[6] "Agreement between the Central Park Conservancy and City of New York, Parks and Recreation," dated and signed February 11, 1998.

[7] Ibid., pp. 5–6.

[8] Ibid., pp. 29–33.

stark contrast to the tight language on financial conflicts of interest. New York officials felt safe granting the Conservancy so loose a leash because they were confident that their collaborators substantially shared the city's goals. The authorizing document departed radically from past city practice, and from cut-and-dried contracting in general. The specification of the tasks to be accomplished, for example, was left remarkably vague. Litter was to be removed and grass to be mowed "as needed." Snow and ice would be cleared "within a reasonable period of time." Plants were to be fertilized "as appropriate." When the technical characteristics of the task permit specificity—as here they did—conventional contracts tend to be far more precise. This is both to permit fair competitive bidding and to provide an unambiguous basis for judging (if necessary, in a courtroom) whether a contractor's obligations have been met. The language of the park-management contract would give a New York City attorney little to work with if it ever came to a legal fight over the Conservancy's performance, much less how it chose to manage the park, say, in its choice to fill an expanse with graceful landscaping instead of a ball field. And the legal language, however loose, was still more imposing than either party's expectation of how much the parks department would actually meddle in the Conservancy's efforts. While the relationship was technically contractual, this was far from the usual competitive contract. The Conservancy faced no rivals in its particular domain, since no other group had the history, the reputation, or anywhere near the financial clout.

The financial provisions of the Conservancy–parks department deal were even more peculiar. Contracts usually specify sums to be paid by the city. But this agreement dealt at more length with the money the Conservancy would *bring* to the party than with any monies it would *get* from the city. It required the Conservancy "to raise and expend annually a minimum of $5 million" for "maintenance, repairs, programming, landscaping, and the renovation and rehabilitation of existing facilities."[9] The parks department, for its part, would pay the Conservancy an annual stipend of $1 million, plus an incentive payment, an extra fifty cents for every private dollar raised

[9] Ibid., pp. 9–10.

and spent beyond $5 million.[10] Despite its contractual status as a minority funder, the parks department had the right to inspect the Conservancy's financial reports, program records, board meeting minutes, and other documents.[11] And in a curious reversal of the usual public relations arrangement—whereby the public entity acknowledges support from the private—the Conservancy was required to "conspicuously acknowledge the involvement" of the parks department in all its press releases, reports, and other communications involving Central Park.[12]

Midway through the eight-year agreement, Central Park had passed from gloom to bloom. It had not merely regained but, in most respects, surpassed the standard set by Robert Moses in the days of flush public budgets, an accomplishment none would have expected and few would have believed possible a decade earlier. Around twenty-five million people visited the park in 2002. The number of people using the Conservancy's visitors' center was approaching a million a year; more than half a million participated in its sports, cultural, or nature programs. At least one multimillion-dollar restoration project was brought to completion nearly every year. Many of them won design awards for excellence in architecture or landscaping. Fashion photographers and film crews once again were drawn to Central Park, with more than two thousand photo or film sessions annually, using the park's well-tended landscapes and iconic statues and buildings as backdrops.[13] Most remarkably, sweeping expanses of the park were reclaimed by pedestrians for nighttime use.

The Conservancy managed the park more aggressively than had the parks department in earlier days, but also quite differently. Employee morale was taken seriously; every one of the 150-some staff (from Belinda Adefioye to Jonathan Zelkind) was listed by name in

---

[10] In the third year and beyond, the Conservancy would also receive half of any increase, over a baseline, in net revenues the city earned from concessions in the park, but total city funding was capped at $4 million.

[11] "Agreement," pp. 15–16.

[12] Ibid., pp. 37–38.

[13] Nearly forty major movies have filmed scenes in Central Park under the Conservancy's stewardship.

the Conservancy's glossy annual report.[14] The Conservancy's employees were strictly nonunion—a detail that rankled the parks department's workforce—hired after interviews and reviews by both the human resources and the operations departments, and retention was contingent on performance. Graffiti were scrupulously removed the same day they appeared; trash barrels were emptied daily; the night's accumulation of litter disappeared by 9 a.m., and uniformed staff riding nearly silent electric carts patrolled manicured paths, ever alert for the stray coffee cup or candy wrapper. Few fences marred the view, though a system of discrete "red flags" was used to warn visitors away from vulnerable areas such as ball fields temporarily closed to let the turf recover.[15]

Maintaining Central Park to these exacting standards was an expensive proposition. Fund-raising, fortunately, remained a Conservancy strong suit. "Associate membership" cost a mere $35 a year—the 2002 annual report pointed out that "passion for Central Park ... is not dependent on income"[16]—but the categories of membership ranged upward to the "Chairman's Circle" at $25,000 a year. Higher-level membership brought various amenities (from tote bags and commemorative paperweights to private tours and VIP treatment at Central Park festivities), but the more potent motives seemed to be affection for the park itself and the shoulder-rubbing benefits resulting from the Conservancy's lofty status in Manhattan society. Its board of trustees was studded with prominent people from New York's financial industry and other circles in which big-ticket philanthropy was a routine part of life.[17] (Billionaire Michael Bloomberg had been a Conservancy trustee before he was elected mayor.) Most trustees wrote large checks themselves and, just as important, leveraged further contributions by boosting the Conservancy's social cachet. The Conservancy capitalized on the intricate philanthropic reciprocity

---

[14] *The Many Faces of Central Park*, Central Park Conservancy Annual Report, Fiscal Year 2002 (2003).

[15] This section draws on the 2003 brochure cited above, as well as on one author's observations in the fall of 2003.

[16] *The Many Faces of Central Park*, p. 13.

[17] Ibid., p. 28.

in which New York's elite cements relationships by supporting each other's favorite charities. Contributions in fiscal 2002 exceeded $18.6 million, dwarfing the $2.8 million in government money the Conservancy collected under its agreement with the parks department.[18]

This gusher of cash let the Conservancy spend $15.8 million in 2002 to restore and maintain Central Park's 843 acres, or nearly $19,000 per acre, roughly three times the per-acre budget for the parks department in general. While the Conservancy provided the bulk of the resources for Central Park, the city government still retained a role. The parks department had twenty-three employees dedicated to various Central Park functions that had not been delegated to the Conservancy. Parks also contributed to the support of the Central Park Zoo, while the New York City Police Department, as would be expected, continued to do the heavy lifting on park security.

Skepticism, and from some quarters blunt hostility, had greeted the 1998 agreement delegating Central Park's maintenance to the Conservancy, including a *Village Voice* feature denouncing the "sellout" of the park to "a private philanthropic elite."[19] But the delegation arrangement won wider acceptance as the park blossomed. Occasional grumbling was heard about private events appropriating a building or meadow. More serious were complaints that opportunities to throw a ball or Frisbee in Central Park were being progressively restricted in favor of the bucolic atmosphere favored by private donors—a textbook example of preference discretion at work. But the topflight programming, award-winning renovations, and meticulous maintenance delivered by the Conservancy were evident to anyone who visited Central Park, and more than counterbalanced feelings that the elite was tilting too many benefits toward itself. No informed citizen with anything like mainstream tastes about the purpose of urban parkland could think he would be better off if the Conservancy were removed from its role.

[18] Ibid., p. 14.
[19] Guy Trebay and Eddie Borges, "Central Park Sell Out: With Little Public Input, a Private Elite Is Set to Take Over the Crown Jewel of Urban Parks," *Village Voice*, October 14, 1997, p. 44.

Putting the Central Park Conservancy in charge of New York City's premier green space represents a remarkably successful example of collaboration for resources. Shrewd public officials figured out how to unleash vast latent constituencies to produce a better Central Park. As private leaders proved able and willing to galvanize efforts to improve the park, government learned to step into the shadows. An eclectic menu of motives—economic stakes on the part of nearby homeowners and landlords whose property values rose and fell with Central Park's quality; the opportunity to shape priorities for the use of the park; the social luster to be gained as the Conservancy found a niche among New York's high-status charities; and an undeniable quotient of pure civic-mindedness—was tapped to attract and cement commitment to the cause. Private resources poured in, and in many cases were deployed much more productively than government could have managed on its own. As a result, a highly visible, hugely valuable public asset experienced an improbable resurrection.

The complicating factor we term "payoff discretion"—the tendency of the private collaborator to line its own pockets—has been somewhere between a trivial problem and wholly absent. The contract was structured to avoid conflicts of interest, and it helped that the Conservancy is a nonprofit organization that shares city government's stakes in an excellent Central Park. Financial scandal has never tainted its efforts. But preference discretion—the tendency of private collaborators to impose their own views about what's most valuable—has made more of a mark on the collaboration. Donors' priorities definitely have affected the facilities of the park. There are more flower beds and fewer playing fields, more Shakespeare and less soccer, and an upscale tilt to the park's image, amenities, and regulations. But only the most passionate of populists would claim that this is an unreasonable price to pay for the radical rehabilitation of an asset open to all.

In short, the gains in public value engineered by the Central Park Conservancy outweigh, by many multiples, any losses from preference discretion. And while the private collaborators are the more visible stars of the success story, dedicated and painstaking government officials, weaving subtle skeins of incentives, continue to labor behind the scenes to make the collaboration work. Kudos to all.

Park Story Two: Harlem's Swindler Cove Park
and Peter Jay Sharp Boathouse

Bette Midler is one of America's most enduringly popular entertainers. This talented, versatile, and resolutely outrageous singer and actress parlayed a cult following among New York City's demimonde into mainstream success in movies, recordings, and concert tours. After gracing Los Angeles for more than a decade, Midler returned to New York in the mid-1990s. In an interview with *Good Housekeeping* magazine—complete with a demure cover photo that must have raised eyebrows among her early fans from New York's gay bathhouses—she reflected on her homecoming: "I was very disappointed in how parts of the city looked. I was so upset, I didn't sleep for weeks. I love New Yorkers, and I'm like them—I'm noisy, I have my opinions—but I'm not used to the kind of carelessness and waste that I was seeing. People were throwing their garbage out the window, leaving their lunches on the ground. Finally, I realized I needed to actually do something, even if I had to pick up the stuff with my own two hands."[20]

Midler ended up doing just that. In 1995 she organized a squad of volunteers to clear accumulated trash from Harlem's Fort Washington Park. Shortly thereafter she formed a nonprofit called the New York Restoration Project to raise funds and muster volunteers for neglected public parks. She concentrated on parks in rough neighborhoods far from the prosperous core of Manhattan. As she explained to the *New York Times,* "There were already enough rich stupid white women like me who could save their own parks."[21] A five-acre plot on the Harlem River soon caught her attention. The site was in the far north of Manhattan, directly opposite the Bronx, owned by the city but tended by nobody. It had become an informal garbage dump for a nearby public housing project. Household trash, discarded plumbing fixtures, and other odd detritus (including a two-thousand-pound safe) lay scattered among the flotsam washed ashore by the river. In

---

[20] Bette Midler interview in *Good Housekeeping,* October, 2000, reprinted on New York Restoration Project Web site, http://www.nyrp.org/, accessed January 2004.

[21] Peter Hellman, "On Harlem River, Hope Floats," *New York Times,* October 30, 2003, p. D-9.

1996 Midler organized a few dozen friends, and friends of friends, to clamber over the rocky shore bagging decades' worth of refuse. "Picking up the garbage with Bette is a very insider club," noted New York State parks commissioner Bernadette Castro.[22]

The neighborhood surrounding the city-owned riverfront lot was very far from prosperous. Median household income was about $23,000, and more than a quarter of the households earned less than $10,000. Single mothers heavily outnumbered two-parent families, and nearly half of the female-headed families lived below the poverty line. Only around half of the neighborhood's adults had even completed high school, and only 40 percent had a job. Among the four thousand people living in the census tract, the grand total of homeowners was seventeen.[23]

Once the worst of the debris had been removed, Midler and her associates decided that the lot should be a proper park. They persuaded the city and state park authorities to invest $10 million to transform the site into Swindler Cove Park, named for Billy Swindler, a community activist who, until his death from AIDS in 1997, had run gardening projects in the vacant lot for children from the nearby public school. With public money supplemented by private donations and volunteer labor, Swindler Cove Park soon boasted a landscaped pond, a small beach, ornamental gates and fences, a boardwalk traversing well-tended wetlands, and a community garden in the care of Public School 5 students. In 1998 then parks commissioner Henry Stern presented Midler with the first "Lifetime Friends of Parks" award for her work on Swindler Cove and four other north-Manhattan parks.[24]

Midler was proud of her accomplishments in Harlem, but far from satisfied. Something more was needed. Suddenly she realized what it was: rowing. Joseph Pupello, the president of Midler's New York Restoration Project, recalls the day he and Midler saw a rowing shell

[22] Ibid.

[23] Figures are from census data accessed in December 2003 from http://www.census.gov/main/www/cen2000.html: Data Set: Census 2000 Summary File 4 (SF 4)—Sample Data Geographic Area: Census Tract 289, New York County, New York.

[24] http://www.nycgovparks.org/sub_about/parks_history/historic_tour/history_reinventing_parks_recreation.html, accessed December 2003.

from Columbia University coursing down the Harlem River. "A group of kids from the projects were glued to the balustrade fence watching the rowers with total intensity."[25] Competitive rowing—whether in fragile single shells or powerful eight-oared crew boats—was a decidedly obscure, indeed rather snooty sport. Most Americans thought of rowing (if they thought of it at all) in connection with Oxford, Cambridge, and the Ivy League elite. Early in the twentieth century, though, rowing had been more popular among the general public, the focus of weekend regattas on urban rivers through much of the East, including the Harlem River.

"I saw pictures of the number of people engaged in sport on the Harlem River in its former incarnation," Midler recalled, "and then I saw the ghost town it had become. If it existed once, why not again?"[26]

The New York Restoration Project got to work planning a rowing program for Harlem high school students, to be supplemented by a boat-building program for middle school children. Midler and Pupello reasoned that rowing would not merely connect Harlem youth to their river, but could also provide an entry ticket to college. Title IX, requiring progress toward gender equality in the number of athletes playing college sports, was driving growth in women's college rowing programs. A large women's crew team could provide Title IX cover for football and other cherished men's sports at a relatively low cost per athlete.[27] Within five years after women's rowing became an official National College Athletic Association (NCAA) sport, around one hundred colleges fielded women's crews, and the Ivy League could no longer count on dominance by default.[28] In principle—and the principle was inspiring to Midler—rowing scholarships could deliver convoys of Harlem kids into college, and from there into middle-class

[25] Hellman, "On Harlem River, Hope Floats.".

[26] Ibid.

[27] Dianne Pucin, "For Women, It's a Whole New Ballgame," *Los Angeles Times*, November 30, 1998.

[28] 1997–2005 championship information at http://www.ncaasports.com/rowing/womens/history, accessed November, 2005. In 1997, when women's rowing first gained official NCAA status for Title IX purposes, Ivy League schools had won sixteen of the twenty-two past national championships. Dan Brown, "Scholarships Threaten Ivy's Success in Women's Crew," *Yale Daily News*, April 8, 1997.

prosperity. In practice, though, few schools offered any substantial scholarships to rowers, much less reached the NCAA ceiling of twenty rowing scholarships. And men were not eligible for rowing scholarships at all.[29] Midler was undeterred by—or, more likely, unaware of—these details.

To do the rowing program right, Midler decided, Harlem needed a real boathouse. Spotting the architect Robert M. Stern at a party, Midler persuaded him to donate the services of his world-famous firm to design a boathouse for Swindler Cove Park. She then set out on a round of fund-raising, eventually gaining major commitments from the Peter Jay Sharp Foundation and the Warnaco Corporation, generously supplemented with contributions from her and her network of friends (including superstars such as Paul Newman and Yoko Ono).[30] The New York City Department of Transportation agreed to pay for the $300,000 barge on which the boathouse would float. By the end of 2003 the final touches were being put on a magnificent $3 million structure to be called the Peter Jay Sharp Boathouse, owned and run by Midler's organization as the centerpiece of Swindler Cove Park. The program's Web site proudly announced the impending opening of the new sports facility:

> The boathouse will provide access to the Olympian sport of rowing through programs for underserved high school students. A secondary school rowing program may provide a means of attaining athletic scholarships to college for inner-city teens. Further, it is hoped that the boathouse will become a destination for New Yorkers who wish to watch practices and races from the upper deck and the promenade of nearby Highbridge Park.

"[The Harlem neighborhood of] Washington Heights should have a championship rowing team," Midler told a reporter. "We've got spirit. We've got pluck. Why not us?"[31]

The Peter Jay Sharp Boathouse was opened with star-studded festivities and a fireworks display by the famed Grucci Brothers. Inch for

---

[29] http://www.ncaasports.com/rowing, accessed December 2003.
[30] NYRP Web site, http://www.nyrp.org/boathouse.htm, accessed December 2003.
[31] Hellman, "On Harlem River, Hope Floats."

inch, it was as elegant a new building as New York had seen in a long time. It also proved to be a bustling operation almost from the day it opened. New York's first new boathouse in a century became a powerful magnet for rowers from around the city. The venerable New York Rowing Association, dating from 1866, set up headquarters in the new boathouse to run the Urban Rowing Initiative, as well as recreational and competitive rowing programs for youths and adults. Since rowing enthusiasts tend to be graduates of elite colleges, and since membership started at $1,000, most members came from more favored precincts than Harlem.[32] The boathouse hosted races by New York–area alumni of Oxford and Cambridge to accompany the traditional black-tie Oxford-Cambridge race dinner. It also launched the Head of the Harlem Regatta, which attracted scores of boats from rowing clubs around the region, as well as an invitational scholastic regatta for teams from a dozen rowing clubs and schools, most of them private.

But there was one disappointment: the clientele for the new boathouse departed considerably from the original vision of a focus on Harlem youth. As planned, it offered an Urban Rowing Initiative for middle and high school students. Participants were enthusiastic, though relatively few, with only around one hundred showing up in the first year of operation. Some did come from the Washington Heights area, but most participants were from public schools elsewhere in the city.[33]

There is not the slightest doubt about the sincerity of Bette Midler's motives or the hugely positive impact, overall, of her engagement with New York's parks. But there is reason to question her and her allies' assessment that a first-class boathouse was a top priority for the kids of Washington Heights. A major motive was to improve access to college through rowing scholarships. But the scale of this benefit depends on three factors: first, the number of kids—or rather girls,

---

[32] Information on Peter Jay Sharp Boathouse programs, including the regattas, from the New York Rowing Association Web site at http://www.nyrowing.org/peterjaysharprc/rowing _programs.html, accessed in November 2005. Information on the Oxford-Cambridge alumni races from http://www.oxalumny.org/pastevents/archives/2005/04/, accessed November 2005.

[33] "Rowing Gains a Following," *New York Newsday*, November 5, 2005.

since boys are not eligible for rowing scholarships—who get involved with rowing through the program; second, the share of these Harlem girls who turn out to be good enough to get a rowing scholarship; and third, the average difference between a rowing scholarship and alternative sources of tuition assistance (such as Pell Grants and other need-based aid) for college students from Washington Heights. It is not particularly cynical to suggest that the boathouse crowd—their hearts assuredly in the right place, but their heads perhaps focused elsewhere—substantially overestimated all three factors.

Swindler Cove Park—a transformed trash dump—provides a terrific amenity for the local community. The boathouse within it surely offers some benefit for the young people of Washington Heights. But it is probably not the most valuable thing, from their perspective, that could have been done with $3 million or so in private money. From the intended beneficiaries' point of view, private resources are not free. Three million dollars for a boathouse represents a drain on the finite willingness of generous people to write checks to help poor kids. For the major benefits to go instead to Amherst, Yale, and Cambridge alums represents a hard-to-measure but very real loss to disadvantaged youth. And the project soaked up $300,000 of discretionary public resources—the city's spending on the barge—or about $3,000 in very scarce governmental money for each youth involved in the rowing program.[34] In this case a strong argument can be made that, despite good faith all around, granting private collaborators wide discretion in exchange for more resources turned out to be a bad bargain.

This skeptical assessment of one boathouse by no means undercuts the overall soundness of the partnership strategy for New York's parks, or indeed the assessment that Swindler Cove Park overall represented a dramatic improvement for the local community. The right amount of private discretion on average will be too much in some fraction of the cases. And the mix of public and private control that

---

[34] The federal and state governments also lost tax revenues when donors to the boathouse subtracted their gifts from taxable income. But whether these deductions should be added to the public cost of the boathouse depends on whether donors increased, or simply redirected, their charitable giving at Midler's urging.

should, by all odds, work out best will sometimes turn out badly not because of payoff and preference discretion but owing to bad luck or bad judgment. It probably would have been better for all concerned—including poor kids in Washington Heights—if parks department officials had raised a few uncomfortable questions about the appropriateness of a top-of-the-line boathouse. Perhaps their reluctance to speak up was due to Midler's celebrity. Perhaps it reflected their respect for her doggedly persistent work on behalf of parks in poor neighborhoods. Or maybe they made the same miscalculations as did Midler and her friends. In any case, they deferred to her judgment in an area where there was no reason to expect her judgment to be particularly sound. Good hearts and good intentions, alas, are no guarantee of good outcomes in every case.

Park Story Three: The Bryant Park Restoration Corporation

The New York Public Library, guarded at the entrance by Patience and Fortitude, its famed marble lions, has an elegant park as its backyard. Bryant Park embraces the library, and provides a compact urban oasis bounded by Fifth and Sixth avenues to the east and west and by Fortieth and Forty-second streets to the south and north. The nine acres of grass, trees, paths, and terraces break up an overwhelmingly commercial stretch of Manhattan, with a dense concentration of some of the city's more expensive office space. It is the only green gap in a vast expanse of concrete, and one of the most elaborately maintained swaths of greenery in all New York.

Until the early 1800s, this tract made up part of the city's semirural northern fringe and served as a pauper's graveyard. As New York expanded to the north, a reservoir replaced the cemetery. The Public Library was completed in 1911 at the corner of Fifth Avenue and Forty-second Street, and around the same time the green space behind it was named in honor of the poet William Cullen Bryant. Bryant Park remained a rather bedraggled affair until Robert Moses reshaped it into a classical terrain of lawns, terraces, and hedges as part of his park-building boom during the 1930s.

As money and ambition ebbed following the Moses era, Bryant Park deteriorated even more than did the overall park system. The neighborhood—heavy with offices, scant on housing—had few residents to press Bryant Park's claim on tight city budgets for either park maintenance or police patrols. When the office workers departed for the night, the more downtrodden and lawless elements of an increasingly troubled New York emerged. Bryant Park came to be deserted by day and dangerous by night. Flourishing commerce in illicit drugs brought it the unwelcome moniker "Needle Park." Muggings and even murders were frequent enough to lead all but the reckless, lawless, or clueless to shun Bryant Park, especially once the sun set.

In 1980, the Rockefeller Brothers Fund (headquartered a few blocks away) created the Bryant Park Restoration Corporation, naming Andrew Heiskell as its chair. Heiskell, the Brahmin titan heading media giant Time Inc., led the board of the New York Public Library.[35] Daniel A. Biederman, an ambitious Harvard MBA who was beginning to build his reputation as an urban-development consultant, was hired to be the executive director of this new organization. With the support of the parks department and money from foundations, the Bryant Park Restoration Corporation experimented with various tactics to break the vicious cycle of desertion and danger—removing litter; installing booths where people could buy books, flowers, and discount theater tickets; and offering free lunchtime concerts. The tactics worked, to a degree. By the early 1980s, workers from surrounding offices flocked to Bryant Park at lunchtime on pleasant days. But the *New York Times* still attributed "a Jekyll and Hyde character" to the park. Though sometimes vibrant by day, especially in good weather, when night fell or the weather turned sour, "the crowds disappeared and the park resumed its sinister appearance."[36] Kiosks and cleanup simply weren't enough. Something bigger would be required to reclaim Bryant Park. By the mid-1980s, this something bigger began to take shape.

[35] Historical section of Bryant Park Web site, http://www.bryantpark.org/history/bryant-park -today.php, accessed January 2004.

[36] Deirdre Carmody, "Vast Rebuilding of Bryant Park Planned," *New York Times*, December 3, 1983, p. 1.

Since his first days at the Restoration Corporation, Daniel Bieder-man had been developing a "master plan" for Bryant Park, and late in 1983 the basic structure of that plan was made public. It started with a transformation of the landscape. The bold blueprint, prepared by a premier landscape designer, started with a call to rip out the ancient, tall ornamental hedges that provided such inviting cover for illicit doings. The plan envisaged gravel paths threaded through the park to welcome strollers; lampposts to dispel shadows; and an array of amenities to lure visitors. Those amenities included a foun-tain with reflecting pools, upgrades and additions to terraces and plazas, outdoor tables and thousands of chairs, and world-class pub-lic bathrooms.

But the environs were just the start. Biederman's grand vision also featured a glittering glass-and-steel restaurant with twenty-two-foot ceilings, huge dining rooms to seat one thousand people, and an out-door terrace. Celebrity restaurateur Warner LeRoy, who was initially enlisted by Biederman to create the ritzy eatery, explained his con-ception: "What we are building is a grand cafe that can be imagi-natively lit in the evening and that will help make the park a great, wonderful, public gathering place. It could be a great scene, like the Via Veneto or the Piazza San Marco."[37] (The famously flamboyant LeRoy was seen as merely eccentric when he sketched this image— Bryant Park rivaling Venice's magnificent central piazza—which in other voices would have sounded delusional.)

The price tag for this vision of Bryant Park—at least $18 million for the capital investment alone—was spectacularly beyond what New York City's Department of Parks & Recreation could sink into a single small park. But government funding wasn't what Biederman had in mind. Most of the money he envisioned would be private. Warner LeRoy would build the grand glass restaurant at his own expense, an investment he would recoup through future profits, and he would also contribute $2 million toward the landscaping plan. Millions more would come from foundations and other private contributors solic-ited by the Bryant Park Restoration Corporation. Public funds from

[37] Ibid.

New York City were expected to cover barely 5 percent of the total capital-investment package.

Biederman anticipated that the new Bryant Park would require over a million dollars each year for horticultural work, maintenance and cleaning, restroom attendants, and a substantial private security force. The parks department was prepared to contribute no more than $250,000. Thus private money would have to cover most of the operating costs as well. The restaurant would pay a half million every year as rent, and the Restoration Corporation committed to provide another $250,000 on its own. But a further stream of reliable annual cash was needed if Bryant Park were to be maintained at the standard to which it would be constructed. Biederman had a solution to this final piece of the financial puzzle. It was the most novel part of his plan.

Business organizations in a few of New York's commercial areas had been experimenting with a new institution called the "business improvement district" (BID). The basic idea was to carve out special jurisdictions within New York City that would charge taxes beyond the rates assessed on property in the rest of the city in order to provide correspondingly higher levels of public services.[38] Biederman proposed stretching the BID concept to apply to Bryant Park. An excellent park, he observed, offered real economic benefits to surrounding property owners and business operators, and it was entirely reasonable for them to pay for these special benefits with special taxes.

Biederman unveiled his master plan to broad acclaim, mixed with some skepticism. There were still many millions of dollars to be raised, and at least eight stages of official review to be navigated, before ground could be broken on the project.[39] Parks commissioner

[38] A business improvement district—or "BID," as it came to be called—would seek the consent of a majority of businesses within a geographically bounded area to levy an incremental tax, or "assessment." (Legally only 49.5 percent of property owners had to consent to a BID before assessments would be mandatory for all businesses in the district, but in practice officials required more like 70 percent agreement before endorsing a BID.) Each BID had to be approved by the state legislature. But once the legislature blessed the arrangement, the supplemental taxes became legal obligations, collected by the government and passed on to the private BID to fund extra street sweeping, security patrols, or other "public services" within the boundaries of the district.

[39] These included an environmental impact statement; the Uniform Land Use Review Procedure; hearings before Community Board 5; the blessing of the City Planning Commission, the

Henry Stern said his department was "watching this carefully," though he pronounced himself reassured by the involvement of the New York Public Library (which shared both terrain and a chairman with the Bryant Park Restoration Corporation).[40]

Enthusiasm for the plan was hardly universal. For the doubters, according to the *New York Times*, the "sticking point" was "the idea that a public park would be managed by a private group." Park advocates, including the nonprofit Parks Council, generally found the notion "repugnant," and were particularly concerned that dependence on BID financing would make Bryant Park beholden not merely to a private group, but to a group made up of business interests.[41] This is a pattern we frequently see: before a collaboration is put in place, the principled concerns—or, to put it less diplomatically, ideological shibboleths—of both supporters and critics outweigh pragmatic assessments. Only the evidence generated by actual operations can trump preconceptions about what will or won't work, what is or isn't fitting.

The vehemence of critics' objections was softened, though only to a degree, by the blunt fact that the status quo was so very far from satisfactory. Despite a general upturn in New York City, Bryant Park was still mostly empty except on sunny weekday afternoons. Its well-received concerts were wildly outnumbered by the scores of drug arrests each month. The charge that private control threatened to corrupt a fine public park seemed rather hollow in the circumstances.

The logic of letting Biederman try it his way eventually prevailed, and his way ultimately transformed the park. While the details of timing and dollars differed considerably from the original plan, the reality of a remade Bryant Park turned out to conform fairly closely to Biederman's vision. In mid-1985, the Restoration Corporation signed a deal with New York City granting the corporation "the exclusive license and privilege to operate and manage the Park." The city balked at giving the corporation legal control of the terrain itself. Thus

---

Board of Estimate, the Landmarks Preservation Commission, and the Art Commission; and approval by the State Legislature. Carmody, "Vast Rebuilding of Bryant Park Planned.".
[40] Ibid.
[41] Ibid.

no lease was granted, and the dry wording of the agreement specified that the corporation "shall manage and operate the Park at all times on behalf of the City."[42] The next year the legislature approved a business improvement district surrounding Bryant Park and authorized assessments to pay for park maintenance. Not until well into 1988, though, did the rebuilding plan receive the last of the required sign-offs. The park closed for three years to permit construction.

The new Bryant Park had its debut in a grand ceremony in the spring of 1992. Cast-bronze lampposts flanked each entrance. The monuments had been refurbished and the paths relaid. The grass of the great central lawn was fastidiously manicured. Flood lamps beaming down from atop adjacent office buildings, along with powerful streetlights on Forty-second and Fortieth streets, illuminated the park. The hedges had been ripped out, as planned, and openings were artfully cut into the interior balustrades. More than $150,000 had been spent renovating the bathrooms alone; these, ten years later, according to the Bryant Park Restoration Corporation, were voted "best in America" by subscribers to an online travel service. Eight security officers—half of them New York cops, the other half private guards hired by the corporation—patrolled the nine-acre park during the day; four more guarded it after the gates were closed at night. Discounted tickets for concerts and Broadway shows could be purchased at what Daniel Biederman declared "the best-looking ticket booth in the United States."[43]

When the centerpiece restaurant opened a little later, it was under the control of Ark Restaurants—which ran Lutèce, Sequoia, and other high-end eateries—not that of Warner LeRoy, but its high-ceilinged, glass-walled splendor was at least the equal of the original plans. With Mediterranean-themed dining rooms opening onto an umbrella-dotted terrace, the new Bryant Park Grill could seat 1,100 people and offer them fare that was refined even by Manhattan's lofty standards. Kiosks selling ice cream, cappuccino, and pastries supplemented the

[42] "Management Agreement for Bryant Park between the City of New York and Bryant Park Restoration Corporation," July 29, 1985, signed by Mayor Ed Koch, Parks Commissioner Henry Stern, and BPRC Chairman Andrew Heiskell, sec. 4, pp. 7–8.
[43] Ibid.

Grill, and three more restaurants opened their doors over the next few years.

Bryant Park's outdoor bar quickly became a fixture of Midtown's after-work singles scene; lunchtime crowds on the benches and lawn routinely numbered as many as four thousand. On summer evenings, Home Box Office sponsored free movies that drew ten thousand people a time; and the former drug bazaar had become "Manhattan's town square."[44] Alexander Garvin, a Yale professor of urban planning, called Bryant Park "a success that surprised a lot of us. If you had asked me two years before they opened whether you could eliminate the population that used the park by redesigning it, I'd have laughed in your face. And I'd have been wrong. Totally wrong."[45] (Crime was beginning to decline citywide, but in Bryant Park the decline was precipitous.) The reshaped park won a cluster of design prizes, including recognition from the Municipal Arts Society, and an award for excellence from the prestigious Urban Land Institute. Herbert Muschamp, the longtime architecture critic for the *New York Times*, pronounced the resurrected Bryant Park "one of the nicest things New York City has done for itself in a long time." There was a touch of ambivalence in his assessment, however. Much as he admired the design, Muschamp was rueful about what he termed the emerging "Business Class" version of New York exemplified by the new Bryant Park.[46]

The grand reconstruction plan turned out to require more public money than originally envisaged. Excluding the restaurants, which as planned were privately funded, the restoration cost about $9 million, of which two-thirds came from New York City and only one-third from private sources.[47] But private funds would indeed cover the bulk of the annual operating costs, with the parks department's contribution limited to the agreed-upon $250,000. Through the business improvement district, surrounding businesses were initially charged eleven cents for each square foot of commercial space, for a total of

[44] Bruce Weber, "Town Square of Midtown," *New York Times*, August 25, 1995, p. B-1.
[45] Ibid.
[46] "Remodeling New York for the Bourgeoisie," *New York Times*, September 24, 1995, p. B-1.
[47] Weber, "Town Square of Midtown."

about $850,000 in the new park's first year. Rent charged for the restaurants and other fees were expected to add the final slice of the estimated $1.2 million operating budget.

The Restoration Corporation's mission statement declared its commitment to "run our operations using the best techniques of private business."[48] With an eventual budget approaching a half million dollars per acre it could afford far more intensive nurturing than any publicly run park, but Bryant Park's managers also displayed creativity to complement financial brute force. Hoping to attract more families, Biederman installed an elaborate carousel on the park's southern edge.[49] Bryant Park became one of the country's first outdoor areas equipped with wireless Internet technology, permitting New Yorkers to relax on the Great Lawn while surfing the Web. The roster of events was diversified from the traditional fare of dance performances and holiday celebrations to include, for example, a gala celebration for couples who had met or married in Bryant Park. Bryant Park's private managers even developed innovative tactics for combating any urban park's perennial nemesis, the pigeon. Those tactics ranged from scattering corn kernels laced with avian birth-control drugs to hiring a falconer to patrol the park with his birds of prey.[50]

Daniel Biederman did not rest on his laurels. He parlayed his success as executive director of the Bryant Park Restoration Corporation into simultaneous leadership roles in two more business improvement districts in Midtown. The 34th Street Partnership, founded in 1992, focused on a commercial stretch of mid-Manhattan a few blocks south of Bryant Park, and followed a similar model: special taxes on neighborhood businesses—enforced by state law—were used to fund extra sanitation and security programs to promote business and tourism,

[48] "Our Mission" section of the BPRC Web site at http://www.bryantpark.org/park-management/mission.php, accessed February 2004.

[49] Glenn Collins, "All the Pretty Horses, and a 6-Ton Gear Drive," *New York Times,* June 1, 2002, p. B-5.

[50] Eleanor Blau, "Pigeons on the Pill Bring Cleaner Bryant Park," *New York Times,* May 28, 1994, p. 23; Robert F. Worth, "In Bryant Park, Hawks Are Circling and the Pigeons Are Nervous," *New York Times,* April 17, 2003, p. D-1. In 1994 Parks Commissioner Henry Stern conceded defeat in the struggle against pigeons in the public park network, saying his department had fought a "long twilight struggle with pigeons, and it's coming out in favor of the pigeons" (quoted in Blau, "Pigeons on the Pill Bring Cleaner Bryant Park").

and other services to raise the tone of the area.[51] The Grand Central Partnership carried out a similar mission for a sprawling area surrounding New York's premier land transportation hub.[52]

Biederman deftly deployed the money and leverage that came with joint control of these three organizations into an integrated and business-led renewal strategy for midtown Manhattan. The strategy worked, as anyone who visited that sector of the city could see, and Biederman prospered in pace. His combined pay package of more than a third of a million dollars raised some eyebrows, though few denied his drive and initiative, or gainsaid his results. But in the late 1990s, Biederman quite publicly ran afoul of Mayor Rudy Giuliani—a man with his own ample quotients of drive and initiative. Giuliani was apparently uneasy about the concentration of so much quasi-public power in one man, possibly concerned about reports of heavy-handed tactics against the homeless by the Grand Central Partnership, and almost surely irritated at frequent press references to Biederman as "the mayor of Midtown." Three years later, the administration of Mayor Michael Bloomberg was considering a rule to bar simultaneous leadership of multiple BIDs, a debate that everyone knew focused on Biederman. "This is something we need to discuss as a city," said the Bloomberg aide in charge of BIDs, adding, in reference to Biederman, that "it would be a lot easier if he weren't doing a good job."[53]

The New York City Department of Parks & Recreation—while formally Bryant Park's owner—was a mostly silent and, indeed, nearly invisible partner in the enterprise. This rankled some folks at the department's headquarters. Compared to the Central Park Conservancy, for example, the corporation's interaction with city officials tended to be limited and at arm's length, and the parks department did not figure at all prominently on Bryant Park's signs, Web site, or promotional material. Yet Bryant Park remained a public park. It neither charged admission nor required membership. It was locked for security at night, but open to the public for twelve to sixteen hours each

---

[51] http://www.34thstreet.org/partnership/index.php.

[52] http://www.grandcentralpartnership.org/home.asp.

[53] Quoted in Terry Pristin, "For Improvement Districts, Restored Alliance with City," *New York Times,* February 18, 2002, p. B-1.

day, depending on the season. (New Yorkers who donated $10,000 to the corporation for a concrete bench could get security to unlock the gates for private access after hours, though Biederman said, "We started that benefit tongue-in-cheek.")[54] At times a terrace, plaza, or the Great Lawn was reserved for private events paying market-rate fees. But generally all were welcome to enjoy the park so long as they observed the rules, which barred drugs and panhandling, putting on performances without a permit, sitting on the balustrades, unleashing dogs, "organized ballgames," wading in the fountain, feeding the pigeons, or the "use of plastic on the lawn."[55] Thousands of New Yorkers and visitors each day were happy to use Bryant Park on these terms.

A park that used to depend on meager shares of tight government budgets, meanwhile, turned out to be able to generate a strengthening stream of its own resources. Paid events had always been part of Biederman's plan, but they became a runaway success after the restoration was completed in the mid-1990s. An early hint of Bryant Park's potential prestige as a cultural venue came in 1995 when MTV televised its Music Video Awards program from the park, featuring the unlikely duo of Michael Jackson and Rudy Giuliani on the same stage.[56] Each year thereafter the roster of performances, fairs, holiday celebrations, weddings, corporate parties, and other events grew longer and more lavish. Bryant Park's weeklong fashion show quickly developed into an annual highlight of the international couture scene. The Restoration Corporation prepared an eight-page brochure for groups wanting to hold private events in Bryant Park, explaining that fees depended on, among other things, how much of the park would be closed off and for how long.[57]

The commercial potential of Bryant Park made the parks department's quarter-million-dollar contribution a secondary and ultimately a superfluous part of the park's budget; the annual payments were

[54] Elaine Louie, "Chronicle," *New York Times*, August 26, 1995, p. 20.

[55] Bryant Park Web site rules page, http://www.bryantpark.org/park-rules.php, accessed February 2004.

[56] Weber, "Town Square of Midtown."

[57] The brochure also mentioned, on p. 3, that not only the Restoration Corporation but also the parks department had to approve the event. *Bryant Park: The Events Guide* (Bryant Park Restoration Corporation, 2003).

reduced in 1998 and stopped altogether the next year. By 2003 annual fees from private events reached $1.85 million. Rents from the restaurants and other concessions, plus revenues from private sponsorships for park amenities, provided another $1.3 million. Assessments through the BID had actually been reduced from their original level and, at $750,000, covered less than one-fifth of the annual budget.[58] The Restoration Corporation's total revenues, at nearly $4 million, dwarfed the $1.2 million Biederman had deemed necessary when the refurbished park opened. The flood of money from rents and events had freed the corporation to realize and then exceed what had seemed a quixotic vision when the master plan was unveiled two decades earlier.

In perhaps the surest sign of success in image-conscious New York, other players began poaching on the Bryant Park brand. "It has become a beautiful word," said a leading businesswoman in the real-estate industry. "Bryant Park is known internationally because of functions like the fashion shows. It's a global address."[59] The upscale Bryant Park Hotel opened in 2000. On a once-tawdry corner adjacent to the park, work was soon underway on a fifty-story office tower to be called One Bryant Park; the land alone had changed hands for $12.5 million. In 2003, after the New York City Transit Authority relabeled the nearest subway stop as 42nd Street–Bryant Park, a reporter asked Daniel Biederman about future plans for extending the franchise. The "Bryant Park Library," perhaps? "That would be nice," Biederman deadpanned. "What's it called now?"[60]

A critic could note that Bryant Park represents a relatively large investment of public funds to create an asset with quite focused private benefits—a "semiprivate" or "directed" good, to use the terminology we introduced earlier. The example could even be characterized as collaboration in reverse, with government maneuvered into using one of its most precious assets—the power to tax—in the service of rather

---

[58] "Bryant Park Restoration Corporation, Proposed Operating Budget with Comparison to Current Year Operations, for the Year Ending June 30, 2004," provided by the New York City Department of Parks & Recreation.

[59] Faith Hope Consolo, quoted in Denny Lee, "You're a Hot Park When Everyone Wants Your Name," *New York Times*, April 27, 2003, p. 14-6.

[60] Biederman is quoted in ibid.

narrow private benefits. Yet the inescapable fact remains that a seedy and sometimes dangerous tract has been transformed into a small jewel of a park that most people, most of the time, for most purposes, are free to use. It is hard to argue that the outcome would have been as good without private involvement.

In each of these New York park examples there were benefits for the public that went beyond the incremental resources that the partnerships poured into the parks. The private organizations enjoyed major advantages in operational flexibility. Like any city agency, the parks department had to hew to formal procedures whenever it issued a contract for building a swimming pool or painting a fence, set a worker's salary, or fired a poor performer. Each rule had its own logic and usually had roots in some long-ago scandal. But collectively they robbed government of flexibility. The partnerships, by contrast, could hire, fire, and pay as they saw fit.

Similarly, the partnerships could procure goods and services with far fewer constraints than could the parks department. The boards of the Conservancy, the Bryant Park Restoration Corporation, and the other major partnerships were studded with powerful business leaders, which conveyed a subtle but by no means insignificant economic advantage: a caterer, construction company, or other contractor had reason to hope that excellent service to one of these partnerships could boost the odds of winning business with a board member's company. Shoddy performance, conversely, could damage a firm's reputation in influential business circles.

Beyond infusing money and labor into New York's parks and making operations more businesslike, in both direct and indirect ways, advocates for these arrangements saw more diffuse but fundamental benefits from the partnerships. They helped to create a coherent constituency for the parks department, which had an inherently diffuse set of beneficiaries. Unlike the Education Department (which could count on parents to defend its interests in budgetary struggles), or departments with strong labor unions, the parks department had too few institutional focal points around which supporters could coalesce. The network of partnerships partly filled this deficit in organized political support.

Would New York's most influential citizens fight more fiercely for public dollars once their personal dollars were flowing to the parks? The answer is not obvious up front. They might become strong advocates for a public mission to which they had concretely signaled their commitment. But they might also feel that the quality of parks in general, and especially the quality of parks adopted by themselves and people like them, had come to depend far less on public resources, undercutting the incentive to lobby for parks to get their share of scarce city budgets.

The behavior of city budget officials is less difficult to foresee. They can be predicted to reason that parks can raise their own money, while cops and firefighters (at least without fairly radical changes in funding conventions) cannot. Given that, parks will tend to get short shrift when funding is tight, and tight funding is the norm in government. Basic conflicts between the nonprofit donor organizations and the internal parks department personnel extend beyond budgetary matters to preferences and questions of control. The executive director of one organization that funneled private money to a Manhattan park noted that "deep down some of the parks department people think that the ideal partner is someone who writes a check and then shuts up. . . . When somebody makes a significant contribution to the parks, they expect to be listened to in a special sort of way."[61] Priorities and preferences differ, and something is lost as well as gained when politics is displaced as the mechanism for resolving these differences. Referring to another organization, parks commissioner Adrian Benepe himself observed: "There are people on the board who don't like the scruffy element and would like to chase them out. That's why the bottom line has to be policy control by the mayor and the commissioner."[62] Even this sophisticated enthusiast of the collaborative approach to governance recognized that private discretion must be subject to limits.

The three parks examples profiled here include one spectacularly successful case of private stewardship, one in which the creation of a

[61] Interview with Donahue, October 16, 2003.
[62] Interview with Donahue, September 4, 2003.

magnificent park produced great public benefits amid a sharp tilt toward private priorities, and one in which a lovely park arose from a trash heap, but private collaborators—however public-spirited— prescribed a world-class boathouse for a neighborhood that probably had many higher priorities. For all three instances it is clear that the public as a whole is much better off, on balance, than it would have been without the private involvement. If these parks are a representative sample of the broader campaign—and most indications are that results with other park partnerships tend to reach the generally impressive range of these three cases—then Adrian Benepe's solution to the resource crisis for New York's parks represents a triumphant application of collaboration. By 2002, private partners were raising a total of about $50 million annually to improve, maintain, and run programs in New York's parks.[63] Volunteers supplied over a million hours in support of the parks—labor that it would have cost the parks department $40 million or more to provide with civil-service staffers. Moreover, some of the volunteer labor came from highly skilled individuals —high-profile lawyers, A-list business leaders, well-connected consultants, and prominent fund-raisers—the department could never hope to hire.[64]

The Partnership for a New Generation of Vehicles

During his 1992 campaign for president, Bill Clinton called for increasing federal fuel economy standards from about twenty-eight to forty miles per gallon within a mere eight years. Clinton's election— and that of his running mate, Al Gore, whose best-selling book *Earth in the Balance* had called the conventional car "a moral threat to the security of every nation"—was greatly regretted, therefore, by American automakers. In the previous Congress, they had narrowly managed to block legislation raising mileage standards, which they feared

[63] Estimate by Benepe, interview with Donahue, September 4, 2003.
[64] This is a rough estimate, based on the assumption that fully loaded personnel costs account for around 80 percent of the parks department's expense budget.

would help their Japanese and European competitors (who fielded fleets of smaller and more efficient cars) at their expense.

The industry braced for tougher rules under Clinton. The new administration, however, wanted to avoid a head-on confrontation with the auto industry. Entering office with a long list of ambitious goals and scant reserves of political capital, Clinton had to pick his fights. Moreover, once in office Clinton and Gore realized that reducing climate-damaging emissions (rather than just slowing their growth) would require mileage improvements far beyond what government could force upon an unwilling industry. Only if the automakers could be induced to devote their own resources and expertise to the goal was there much hope of success.

A series of overtures by technical experts in government and business led to high-level discussions over how to structure a cross-sectoral campaign to reinvent the automobile. A collaborative plan emerged. Early in the Clinton administration, the president and vice president, along with the CEOs of the three major U.S. automakers, formally unveiled the Partnership for the Next Generation of Vehicles (PNGV). The mission was to put into production, within a decade, cars getting up to triple the fuel economy of 1993 models, with no sacrifice in performance or increase in cost.[65] An undersecretary of the Department of Commerce and senior vice presidents from Ford, GM, and Chrysler were assigned to cochair the initiative's steering group. Working teams of government and industry scientists and technicians, with full access to the national laboratories and research facilities of the departments of Energy and Defense, the National Aeronautics and Space Administration, and other federal agencies, would push for breakthroughs in engine design, new materials, emissions control, and alternative fuels. A new unit in the Commerce Department, with a direct line to the White House, was given the mandate to work closely with industry. Three hundred million dollars annually in federal research and development monies would lubricate the arrangement, but a far greater flood of private money was expected.[66]

---

[65] "Partnership for a New Generation of Vehicles: A Declaration of Intent," joint press release of September 1993.

[66] Details from Kennedy School of Government Case "From Confrontation to Cooperation: How Detroit and Washington Became Partners" (Harvard University, 1997).

The Clinton administration did not promise to forgo mandated increases in mileage standards, and that threat hovered over the partnership. But through its money and its high-level participation, the administration strongly signaled that the Partnership was its preferred strategy for accelerating the development of cleaner, more efficient cars. So long as industry upheld its end of the deal, the administration was prepared to entice, rather than compel, the carmakers to devote their resources to the goal.

By mid-2000 Washington had invested about $800 million in the PNGV, and the auto industry added nearly $1 billion more. Ford, Chrysler, and GM had each developed, as a custom-made "concept car," a family sedan that approached the goal of eighty miles per gallon. None of these cars, unfortunately, was close to being ready for mass production, and each would have been prohibitively expensive to make and market.[67] Honda and Toyota—which were not participants in the PNGV—were already far ahead. Each of them was preparing to market its own "hybrid" vehicle boasting major mileage improvements at a modest price premium over conventional cars. And while not explicitly renouncing the Partnership, American auto executives were taking it far less seriously than they had at the start, dragging their heels on spending for items that would not benefit individual companies with reasonable certainty and a reasonably short time frame. It was not in automakers' interests to make new-generation cars a priority unless market demand warranted—or unless government was able and willing to preempt the priorities of the market.

The latter would not happen. The Democrats lost control of Congress in 1994. It appeared that Al Gore might *not* be the next president, as scandal and fatigue sapped the Clinton administration's political capital. Draconian car-mileage regulation was no longer a credible threat. The PNGV encountered a fierce headwind when George W. Bush became president in 2001 and the new administration announced its skepticism toward the Partnership. The administration's first budget proposal cut its funding sharply.[68] Within a year

[67] Justin Hyde, "GM Says Precept Concept Car Achieves 80 mpg in Tests," *Associated Press State and Regional Wire Service*, Business News section, October 20, 2000.

[68] Nedra Pickler, "Partnership May Not Reach Goals for Affordable 'Super Car' by 2004," *Associated Press State and Regional Wire Service*, Business News section, August 13, 2001.

the Bush administration canceled the PNGV altogether, calling instead for an effort to develop hydrogen-fueled cars—conceivably the automobile technology of the future, but certainly of a future rather far distant.[69]

The Partnership for a New Generation of Vehicles cannot be chalked up as a winning collaboration. But the problem was less a matter of conception or management than of timing. The PNGV might well have gained more traction and traveled further and faster had it been launched in 2009, when both Congress and the new administration concurred (at least compared to their counterparts of 1993) on the urgency of environmental action, and when a broader public constituency was aware of and alarmed by the dangers of climate change.

Contemplating the reasons such a seemingly sensible venture ended up in the ditch reminds us that successful collaboration requires three sets of perceptions and motivations—those of the government, of the private collaborator, and (in most cases) of the relevant public—to be reasonably well aligned. Here the private collaborators were somewhere between skeptical and antagonistic to the government's goals, and the public was apathetic.

Perfect alignment is almost never possible, but rarely is it necessary. Good-enough alignment among all three can suffice to forge a sturdy triangle, and strength on one or two sides can substitute (up to a point) for strength on the others. If government and its private collaborators are ardent enough in their shared enthusiasm for an undertaking, the partnership might prosper even if the public's support is lukewarm. If government and the public are in rock-solid agreement on an enterprise requiring private collaboration, they may well find a way to induce private actors to play their required role. And common commitment between the public at large and private collaborators can often bring along a reluctant government. With the PNGV, only the government—and within the government, only a few senior elected and appointed officials in the executive branch—had passion for the undertaking. Industry was willing to collaborate only

---

[69] Ed Garsten, "Bush Abandons High-Mileage Program for Hydrogen Fuel-Cell," *Associated Press State and Regional Wire Service*, Business News section, January 9, 2002.

in order to forestall the even less welcome option of regulation. And the public at large was basically indifferent. The triangle collapsed; a new generation of vehicles would have to wait.

Funding Safety Review for New Drugs

The Food and Drug Administration (FDA) regulates commerce that accounts for roughly twenty-five cents out of every dollar American consumers spend.[70] The FDA, with its roots in the Progressive Era, saw its mandate expand incrementally in reaction to a sequence of tragedies and scandals in the early and mid-twentieth century: the abysmal food-industry conditions documented in Upton Sinclair's *The Jungle*; the indiscriminate sale of alcohol-and-opium nostrums; children killed by defective diphtheria antitoxin during the Theodore Roosevelt administration; scores of fatalities from an early antibiotic compounded with ethyl alcohol; and the thousands of children born maimed by thalidomide in Europe. (The United States was saved from the thalidomide tragedy by a suspicious and stubborn bureaucrat at the FDA who held up approval of the drug long enough for its dread consequences to become known.) Each tragic episode triggered new or toughened legislation for the FDA, widened its authority, and slowed its approval process.

A pivotal part of the FDA's mandate is the regulation of prescription drugs. No drug can be introduced, altered, or extended to new uses before the FDA certifies both its safety and efficacy. The administration thus serves as gatekeeper between enormous product development investments and comparably massive sales opportunities. And since other countries often piggyback on U.S. regulation, the FDA is the indirect portal for many overseas markets as well.

New drugs poured out of pharmaceutical companies' laboratories in the 1970s and 1980s. Over the same period, budget cuts constrained

---

[70] One of the authors was the "site visitor" sent by the Innovations in American Government award program in the course of the FDA's successful candidacy for one of the Innovations in American Government awards issued in 1996. Some material in this section draws on the site report.

the FDA's staffing, and its reviewing capacity became increasingly stretched. The share of federal spending devoted to health and safety regulation, a budget category whose biggest component is the FDA, dropped by over a third between 1975 and 1985.[71] Given increased demand, diminished capacity, and heightened concerns over safety, the natural result was lengthening queues for approvals. By 1992 the average new drug review took more than two years. Patient advocacy groups joined drug companies in a chorus of protest against the laggardly FDA. Periodic public relations offensives offered the image of poky bureaucrats denying drugs to dying children.

Resources are rarely the only barrier to good performance, but it was clear that shortages of money and personnel were first-order impediments preventing the FDA from meeting its mandate of conscientious but expeditious review. Legislation dating to 1962 had set a six-month standard for drug approval times, but the target was seen as preposterous within the FDA. Staff, computers, and other resources couldn't possibly keep pace with the growing scale and complexity of its mission. The backlog meant that work rarely even *began* on an application within a year of submission. FDA scientists and physicians viewed themselves as the overstretched line of defense between profit-hungry drug companies and "another thalidomide." They felt a defiant sense of honor in resisting pressures for faster approvals, which with current budgets would inevitably mean sketchier scrutiny. More resources were needed if the drug reviews were to be fast but not sloppy.

A confluence of factors shook up this dysfunctional equilibrium. First, David Kessler was appointed as FDA administrator in 1990. Kessler's considerable ambitions were constrained both by funding gaps and by the bunker mentality that had developed within the FDA. Second, a convincing demonstration that more money for drug review could indeed make a difference emerged within the FDA itself. The units responsible for approving cancer and especially AIDS drugs received extra resources for several years and markedly outpaced

---

[71] Calculated from Office of Management and Budget, *Budget of the United States, Fiscal Year 2006*, historical table 3.2, "Outlays by Function and Subfunction, 1962-2010."

other divisions in shortening approval times. Internal and external reformers noticed.

But this was a time of exceptional anxiety about federal deficits. Where could the extra money be found? One innovative possibility would be to charge the companies whose drugs were being reviewed for some of the costs of the review process. The idea of collecting user fees to expand the FDA's capacity was not new. But earlier proposals had been opposed, both by legislators concerned that fees would erode the FDA's independence, and by the drug companies themselves, who were not eager to shoulder a new burden. Prior user-fee initiatives had originated with the Office of Management and Budget, not to augment resources but simply to shift costs toward the drug companies. Industry was on guard against moves to reduce the deficit at its expense. But the user-fee idea seemed the only solution, and long rounds of negotiation among industry, Congress, and the FDA groped toward a workable deal.

The Prescription Drug User Fee Act (PDUFA) of 1992 encodes the basic bargain that emerged. Drug companies pay user fees and commit themselves to a set of procedural rules, and the FDA commits to performance goals of twelve months for the review of "standard" new drug applications and six months for "priority" applications.[72] PDUFA required the goals to be met 55 percent of the time in FY1994, with the standard ratcheting up to 90 percent by FY 1997. And in a detail that would turn out to be crucial, the FDA and Congress agreed to maintain drug-review appropriations at their 1992 level, in nominal dollars, to assuage industry fears that private money would simply substitute for public money.

Money mattered. Within a few years, user fees had bolstered the resources available for drug reviews by roughly 50 percent. New hires financed by the incremental funds added six hundred full-time equivalents to the FDA's staff, with comparable increases in equipment and facilities. Management reforms instituted by Kessler complemented this infusion of private resources, including formal procedures for

---

[72] "Priority" status goes to drugs that promise new therapeutic possibilities, while "standard" is for new competitors to drugs on the market. The time lines listed are for new products; there are comparable performance goals for reviews of new facilities or new uses for existing drugs.

establishing review priorities, a system for setting time lines and tracking progress, and more intensive interaction with the drug companies at all levels.

To virtually everyone's astonishment and delight the FDA vaulted beyond the final-year performance goals in the first year of performance tracking: instead of 90 percent reviewed on time by FY 1997, 95 percent of new-drug applications were reviewed on time in FY 1994. The speed of FDA review more than doubled in the first few years of the new system, even as the number of new-drug applications rose. The most dramatic medical payoff was a stream of new AIDS drugs, and its accompaniment, sharply falling death rates from HIV. Other early fruits of PDUFA included Infanrix, an improved infant vaccine for diphtheria, tetanus, and whooping cough that was approved after twelve months of review; Pulmozym, the first treatment for cystic fibrosis, reached the market after a nine-month review, and Activase, the first drug to treat stroke victims, hit pharmacy shelves in 1997 after just three months of review. PDUFA was judged a success from both the public and private perspectives, by advocates for both corporations and consumers. It easily won reenactment in 1997 and again in 2002, with mostly minor amendments. Average approval times fell by more than 40 percent in less than a decade. By 2004 the FDA was processing well over two hundred applications a year, with clearance times systematically exceeding performance goals.[73] Not just in its early laps, but for a decade or more, PDUFA looked to be a triumph of collaborative governance.

Both industry and the FDA accept obligations under PDUFA, and both endorse arrangements that anchor those obligations. The FDA

[73] Performance reports for FY 2004 can be found at http://www.fda.gov/ope/pdufa/report 2004/default.htm. It is important to note that other factors may also explain the acceleration in review. The health economist Ernst Berndt and his colleagues attribute only around two-thirds of the speedup to PDUFA. Ernst R. Berndt et al., "Assessing the Impact of the Prescription Drug User Fee Act on the FDA Approval Process," National Bureau of Economic Research Working Paper No. 10822 (October 2004). Two other scholars note that FDA resources were already rising prior to PDUFA, and attribute much of the increase in approval speed to pressure from patients and their advocates. Daniel Carpenter and A. Mark Fendrick, "Accelerating Approval Times for New Drugs in the U.S.," *Regulatory Affairs Journal* 15, no. 6 (June 2004): 411–417.

commits itself to explicit standards for the speed of drug review, and pledges to devote specified levels of appropriated funds to the mission. Drug companies not only accept a legally binding requirement to pay for a governmental function that they formerly got for free—and in their ideal world might prefer to forgo in favor of some more malleable kind of private certification—but also commit to compliance with demanding standards regarding the timing, format, and other aspects of review applications.

The deal also grants discretion to each party. The FDA retains the right and the duty to interpret safety requirements by its own lights. It is obliged to apply the standards more rapidly, but no more loosely, than it did prior to PDUFA. It can reject a drug application, or demand more information, at any point in the process should its public mandate so require. And a drug company can determine whether and when to seek approval to market a new compound, retains significant control over what kind of evidence to submit, and (under the original version of PDUFA) could make and market a drug with little regulation once it was cleared for sale.

The central issues—as with any example in which collaboration leverages private resources to promote a public goal—concern how well private motives align with public goals, and government's legal, political, and managerial capacity to harvest the benefits and limit the risks associated with private discretion. We can highlight these issues by drawing a distinction between premarket and postmarket safety regulation. Up to the date when the FDA grants approval to market a drug, the interests of government and business are substantially aligned. Both parties want effective new drugs to reach patients quickly, and both want drugs to be safe.

Even on the common grounds of speed and safety, of course, the parties have slightly divergent priorities. Drug firms, with their intense and focused stake in revenues from new drugs, will always put more weight than does the FDA on speed to market. If a new drug is only modestly superior to medicines already on the market, the FDA (if it is doing its job) will be in no great hurry to approve, while pharmaceutical executives (if they are doing *their* jobs) will be seeking speedy approval. It is also natural for the public and private parties to have different perspectives on the relative values of blocking risky drugs versus approving safe ones.

If a drug that turns out to be dangerous is approved for sale, that is terrible news for both the pharmaceutical company and the FDA, and more so for the injured patients. In seeking to avoid that possibility, the company and FDA interests are reasonably well aligned. Nevertheless, trade-off rates might differ between the parties. The FDA—thanks to the culture produced by its mandate and history—may feel it is better for twenty safe drugs to get delayed than for one risky drug to get approved; the drug companies might feel a better number is five or ten. There is thus some disparity in priorities—but also substantial alignment. Motives are somewhat less aligned on the specific issue of "drug lag," the sluggish transit from laboratory to market that PDUFA was meant to remedy. If a drug that turns out to be safe spends extra weeks or months in review, the FDA suffers some from the slippage on its mission and consequent public criticism—but the potential sales the company loses during the lag are gone forever.

Yet the divergence in public and private priorities with respect to premarket review—its stringency, and even its speed—is minor relative to the yawning gap in preferences on the relative importance of new-drug approval versus everything else the FDA does. Drug companies have an entirely understandable desire that the FDA focus on reviewing drugs and clearing them for sale, even at the expense of other parts of the agency's mission, such as assuring the safety of the food supply. In an integral aspect of the PDUFA bargain, industry was able to codify that preference into law with the provision that government funding for drug review would not slip below its 1992 level. This provision had teeth. If the FDA failed to spend enough of its appropriations on drug review, it could not legally collect new user fees or spend any money from fees it had already received.[74] This binding agreement on how government monies could be spent was

[74] General Accounting Office, "Food and Drug Administration: Effect of User Fees on Drug Approval Times, Withdrawals, and Other Agency Activities," GAO-02-958 (September 2002), p. 16.

the final component of a bargain that put the FDA in a position to secure vast new revenues from user fees.

By 2005, more than half of the resources for new-drug review came from industry rather than taxpayers.[75] Yet as the FDA's dependence on user fees grew, the imperative to spend its own money on pre-market drug review intensified lest it lose those dollars. The structure of the collaboration, in short, widened FDA access to private resources but narrowed its discretion over how its public resources would be allocated. Under PDUFA, drug companies made significant commitments regarding premarket safety review, but PDUFA imposed no new obligations on industry once a drug received FDA approval.

One competing claim on the FDA's appropriated resources was safety review for drugs that were *already* on the market. Both before and after PDUFA, the FDA was considered the global gold standard for premarket safety review, requiring companies to demonstrate through painstaking clinical trials the safety and effectiveness of any proposed new medicine. But some risks inevitably elude even the most rigorous premarket review. Adverse side effects may emerge only after a patient has been using a drug for years, and hence may not show up in clinical trials. Other risks may hinge on patients' behavior, such as using alcohol or other drugs concurrently with a new pharmaceutical. They, too, may elude premarket safety reviews. And some side effects are quite rare: they may not occur in clinical trials with dozens or hundreds of patients, but still prove to be significant problems once hundreds or thousands or millions of patients begin taking a new drug. It is in a drug company's financial interest, of course, to fix safety problems that emerge once a drug hits the market. Tort liability and loss of reputation are costly punishments. But the advantage in being early to market, particularly with a new class of drug, can attenuate industry's stakes in postmarket safety review, making the FDA an especially important bastion for this phase of patient protection. And PDUFA imported into the FDA a subtle but significant bias toward premarket and away from postmarket review.

---

[75] Susan Okie, "What Ails the FDA?" *New England Journal of Medicine* 354, no. 11 (March 17, 2005): 1063–1066.

This tilt in emphasis came amid an intensification of the long-term trend of tight budgets for most regulatory agencies, including the FDA. Total federal spending on health and safety regulation crept up slowly in the decade after that benchmark year of 1992—indeed, at only half the rate of the prior decade.[76] Largely because of PDUFA's strictures, the *share* of the FDA's tightening appropriations spent on premarket review grew from 17 percent in 1992 to 29 percent in 2000. Staff devoted to premarket drug review doubled, to around 2,300, while staff available for everything else shrank not just in relative terms but absolutely, from about 7,700 to about 6,500.[77]

In part because of concerns about an unintended distortion of spending, the 2002 amendments to PDUFA permitted some user-fee resources to be spent on postmarket safety review. But shortly thereafter a series of grave safety problems damaged the FDA's reputation. Whatever was the true explanation for such problems, they inevitably raised questions about whether the FDA's dependence on industry for part of its resources had warped its priorities. Bad outcomes breed suspicions, whether merited or not.

The most spectacular incident concerned Vioxx, a powerful painkiller that was made by Merck, perhaps America's preeminent pharmaceutical company. Vioxx had sailed through premarket approval in 1999 and quickly became popular with doctors and patients as a buffer against arthritis pain. By 2004 it reached blockbuster status, with sales over $2.5 billion annually.[78] But evidence was accumulating that Vioxx had side effects of precisely the sort that slip past premarket clinical trials—cardiovascular risks that emerged only after patients had been taking the drug for a year and a half, and only once the number of patients grew large enough for the statistically low risk to manifest itself with noticeable numbers of victims.

Merck scientists completed an in-house study revealing that long-term Vioxx use was linked with elevated rates of heart attack and

---

[76] Calculated from Office of Management and Budget, *Budget of the United States, Fiscal Year 2005*.

[77] General Accounting Office, "Food and Drug Administration: Effect of User Fees on Drug Approval Times, Withdrawals, and Other Agency Activities," GAO-02-958 (September 2002), p. 15, fig. 5, and p. 16, fig. 6.

[78] John Carey and Amy Barrett, "Lessons from the Vioxx Fiasco," *Business Week*, November 29, 2004.

stroke, and the company withdrew the drug in September of 2004. Merck braced for an avalanche of lawsuits. And the FDA came under withering criticism from the press and Congress for failing to spot problems with Vioxx and other drugs once they were on the market. The *New England Journal of Medicine* charged that the FDA was approving drugs with undue haste and failing to monitor existing drugs. It alleged further that the FDA's dependence on user fees had made the once-respected agency "timid and toothless."[79] The equally prestigious *Journal of the American Medical Association*, a health-care publication noted for its caution, called for consideration of a major regulatory restructuring that would establish a postmarket safety organization not only separate from industry funding, but independent of the FDA itself.[80] David Graham, a senior scientist within the FDA's Office of Drug Safety, told a Senate panel that "the FDA as currently configured is incapable of protecting America against another Vioxx."[81]

The next iteration of PDUFA, debated and revised in the wake of Vioxx and other safety breakdowns, dragged discretion back from industry and toward the FDA. Revisions enacted in 2007 enabled the agency, and required pharmaceutical companies, to place far more emphasis on safety surveillance for medicines already on the market. New legislative provisions increased user fees but, much more importantly, let the FDA deploy resources garnered from industry not just to screen applications for new drugs, but also to monitor the safety of drugs once they were in widespread use.[82] Industry recognized that even with the tightened terms the user-fee arrangement remained

[79] According to the FDA's inspector general, nearly a fifth of staffers reported pressure to approve drugs despite concerns. Office of Inspector General, "FDA's Review Process for New Drug Applications: A Management Review," OEI-01-00590 (March 2003). And an internal FDA study cited by the *New England Journal of Medicine* found that 65 percent of the postmarket studies firms promised to do as a condition of approval were never undertaken. Okie, "What Ails the FDA?"

[80] Ricardo Alonso-Zalzibar, "Congress Weighs New Restraints on FDA to Improve Drug Safety," *Boston Globe*, November 29, 2004.

[81] Graham is quoted in Simon Frantz, "How to Avoid Another Vioxx," *Nature* online (December 4, 2004), at http://www.nature.com/news/2004/041220/pf/nrd1629_pf.html, accessed October 2005.

[82] Gardiner Harris, "House Passes Bill Giving More Power to the F.D.A.," *New York Times*, September 20, 2007, p. A-18.

beneficial, on balance, and also recognized the need to cope with scandal. Industry broadly supported the revised legislation.

There is no hard evidence that reliance on private resources, or the need to favor new-drug review in spending priorities, really did lead the FDA to stint on safety. Indeed, the probability that a drug would be withdrawn for safety problems that emerged subsequent to the FDA's initial imprimatur did not differ significantly for products introduced before and after PDUFA was enacted.[83] But the widespread perception that PDUFA triggered a safety breakdown—and the inherent plausibility of such a charge, given the incentives and constraints embodied in the pre-2007 versions of the legislation—put a black mark on the otherwise positive performance of PDUFA's first fifteen years. If adequate public funding for drug-safety regulation was out of the question, the quest for private resources was a reasonable resort. David Kessler and the other architects of the PDUFA system were well intentioned, well informed, and sophisticated. But they failed to fully anticipate what forces the structure of incentives and the allocation of discretion embodied in the legislation would set in motion, how they would affect public and private choices, what bad outcomes might result, and what perceptions might emerge. When one is regulating risk, the probabilities of loss can be tamped down, but they can be driven to zero only if the activity is stopped, an impossible course for drug approval. It is therefore important to anticipate what losses represent the greatest risks, and what will happen when big losses are incurred. PDUFA, as originally enacted, gave insufficient attention to postmarket surveillance. Subsequent rounds of amendment fixed this flaw. Today's PDUFA is far from perfect—like any collaboration, indeed any arrangement for pursuing public goals—but it is a positive innovation.

Ann Landers on Collaboration for Resources

A sound resource-based collaboration might be likened to a modern marriage, where both partners accept responsibility and wield power.

---

[83] FDA data referenced in Okie, "What Ails the FDA?"

If they both bring resources to the relationship—as with so many marriages today, and as with all of the cases considered in this chapter—it is unthinkable for one party to monopolize discretion. Sharing is the only way.

Ann Landers, the famed advice columnist, was often asked about troubled marriages, where one partner (usually the husband) falls short. Her invariable question of the correspondent attempting to decide whether to put up with the erring spouse's laziness, selfishness, or worse was "Are you better off with him or without him?" If the answer was "With him," she would offer her thoughts on how to go about improving the relationship.

The three examples of this chapter—New York City parks, the Partnership for a New Generation of Vehicles, and PDUFA—all represent situations where the sensible response to the Ann Landers question is "With him." Aggravations and missteps aside, these collaborations advanced the public's agenda. Two of the parks examples are stunning successes; the third, still successful, featured an expensive present—the boathouse—that did not jibe well with the intended recipients' needs. The PNGV was a marriage now seen to have been entered into too early. The progeny fiercely hoped for by one partner —fuel-efficient vehicles—were not forthcoming. Had political tectonics or petroleum prices or both moved differently, the outcome could have been different. The outcome was unfortunate, but not disastrous. Some resources were wasted, yet it is hard to see how a go-it-alone approach by government would have fared any better in 1993. The parties appear ready to have another go, with the same intentions, roughly a decade after their breakup. PDUFA has been broadly successful, shortening the transit from lab to medicine cabinet for many valuable drugs. The relationship was blemished in its first phase because the private partner exercised undue control to downplay postmarket surveillance. But after a few bad outcomes, leading to public outcry and political response, the most important problems in this relationship have been fixed. Not all resource-based collaborations will pass the Ann Landers test, but these surely do.

PART III

The Art of Collaboration

Chapter 8

◇◇◇

Tasks and Tools

The workaday term "tools" in this chapter's title signals the primacy of the practical aspects of collaboration. Good practice—getting public work done well—is the whole point. The tools metaphor, though, should not suggest that collaboration requires only rote competencies akin to driving a screw or finishing wood on a lathe. Such skills are readily honed because feedback is immediate, results are readily apparent, and the task is often repeated. In those sorts of contexts, tools are quickly mastered.

The skills required for public-private collaboration are a different matter entirely. Many collaborations are one-time-only undertakings for the public party, the private party, or both, so that experience offers little guidance. Results of a collaboration often remain indeterminate for months or years. And even when the parties pick up wisdom along the way, the learning often comes too late to permit fundamental revision of an established collaboration's structure. A more pertinent tool metaphor could be a sculptor's chisel applied to a piece of rare marble. The challenge is to work with the grain in the stone while simultaneously changing its shape. Only a skilled sculptor will be up to the task. She is able to anticipate how the grain will develop beneath the surface, to recognize how a gentle bend here can echo or anticipate a stronger curve there, to foresee the form that skill will ultimately coax from the stone. Only then is the chisel applied to the stone. Yet this analogy does not capture the richness of the concept, either, since in collaboration the stone has its own agenda and can rap back. We'll eventually propose our favored metaphor for the skilled craft of collaboration, but first let's explore a bit more the nature of the work.

Thinking Forward and Backward

As our image of the sculptor suggests, it is useful—indeed, it is essential—for the mental trip to go both ways, from the abstract to the concrete, from conception to implementation, and then back again, since a vision of a journey's end informs its first step. One cannot assess whether collaboration is more promising than direct governmental production or simple contracting or any other alternative approach without predicting how it will be carried out. Just as it's hard to decide between New York and Miami as a vacation venue without envisioning what you would do in each locale, a clear view of implementation helps one choose the right delivery model. Many an effort to create public value through leverage has foundered because it failed to look ahead to predict whether and how it would actually work.

Looking ahead means not just worrying in general terms about the prospect of damage from payoff and preference discretion, but also considering the concrete details that shape the odds that such problems will materialize—the structure of contracts, the terms on which money will change hands, procedures for making decisions, when and on what basis the collaboration can be declared a success. The prudent analyst ponders such practical matters before settling on any approach for pursuing public value, just as a wise architect considers the equipment available to the builders before finalizing her choice of design.

Formal Tools of Analysis

Government often relies on formal analytical tools to select and assess the progress of any delivery model, collaboration included. Two common tools—cost-benefit analysis and cost-effectiveness analysis—are objective and dispassionate approaches that are employed to ensure that the government gets maximum bang for its buck. They fall under the general heading of systems analysis, or (its frequent alias in this particular setting) policy analysis. The terms *systems* and *policy* indicate the object of the analyst's scrutiny—a new weapons system, for example, or a proposed policy change to alter reimbursement rules for nursing-home care. Whatever the label, the hallmark of this sort of analysis is disciplined attention to the interconnected impacts that ripple out from almost any action. These methods are applicable to the study of instances of collaboration, such as a park under private management, or an entire collaborative policy, such as subsidizing R&D in the biotech field.

Systems analysis tended in its early days—and to some degree it still tends—to be dominated by economists, in part because such analysis often hinges on the value of things with no price. Dealing with what's priceless, perhaps paradoxically, is a strong suit for economists. If the purpose of some project is to lower citizens' risk of exposure to a toxic chemical, analysts can cast about for clever ways to approximate the value of that risk reduction—perhaps by measuring how much more workers had to be paid to entice them to take a job that involved exposure to the toxin, or the price difference between otherwise-similar houses that differed in their proximity to a chemical factory. Similarly, to determine the worth of a new public park—open to all and charging no admission—analysts might measure how far people had traveled to enjoy it, and then attach a value to their travel time. It is reasonable to presume that the lower bound for how much value people got from visiting the park was how much they paid (in money, and the money equivalent of their time) to get there.

Since few policy problems come with ready-made metrics that tell how much they produce or cost, those magnitudes must be inferred, estimated, or otherwise summoned into being by the analyst's creativity and resourcefulness. The fields of statistical estimation and econometric analysis have grown up to support, with reasonable empirical assessments, inquiries into the net merits of some envisaged public undertaking. Such assessments often employ large bodies of data to trace out, for example, what health benefits one might reasonably attribute to a new network of clinics.

Cost-benefit analysis and cost-effectiveness analysis can seem forbiddingly technical and off-puttingly artificial. But we all use them routinely—albeit informally—when, for example, we ponder whether to fix the broken water heater ourselves or call a plumber, weighing the plumber's bill against the certainty of a busy afternoon, the high probability of sore knees and skinned knuckles, and educated guesses about the odds of a flooded basement or a troublesome explosion. For the purposes of this book, both cost-benefit and cost-effectiveness analysis begin by identifying as many as possible of the pluses and minuses associated with a policy. Often, the minuses will merely be the financial costs, but there may be other negative aspects as well. A new park may not only cost money, but also bring traffic congestion. Benefits, likewise, may flow not just to the people who use the park, but to those who walk past it, live nearby, or merely have the option of using it should they someday feel like retreating for an hour from the city streets. Cost-benefit analysis ultimately tallies all the pluses and minuses—cast in the best estimates of monetary terms that the analyst's art can achieve—to arrive at a net sum. When projects must compete against one another, say, because they use the same building, or, as with the park, they use the same land, the one with the greatest sum is chosen. If a project is judged on a freestanding basis, it is adopted if it yields positive benefits on net.

Cost-effectiveness analysis is employed when the prime output is safely presumed to be valuable but is especially resistant to being measured in dollar terms. For example, if the goal is to maximize educational quality, the investigation will see how much output is produced for the same cost using a variety of approaches. A cost-effectiveness analysis might show that when given the same dollar amounts, charter schools produce more educational benefits than do traditional public schools. Cost-effectiveness analysis seeks to sidestep any unattainable requirement to equate the output, in this case educational benefits, with the dollars it takes to produce them.[1]

The Challenge of Uncertainty

What we would all like, of course, is a set of shiny new analytical tools that (when properly deployed) give us a soothing sense of certainty

[1] See Edith Stokey and Richard Zeckhauser, *A Primer for Policy Analysis* (W. W. Norton & Company, 1978), which is generally considered to be the pioneering text in the arena of policy analysis.

about how the collaboration will play out. But an element of imprecision surrounds any prediction, and the uncertainties multiply when predictions concern something as complex and as densely populated with capricious human beings as a collaboration between public and private institutions. Predicting the outcome from a collaboration will always be an exercise in assessing uncertainties. Will the private party—to continue the example, say, an educational organization promoting a pathbreaking model of charter schools—perform as promised? Even assuming the *intent* to deliver on pledges, will the private party's curricular model work as well in our city as it has elsewhere? Will parents here embrace the level of involvement that has underpinned the success of the charter school in other settings? The honest answer to each of these questions will always be maybe. But that does not mean that the analyst has to hang a big question mark on his analysis. Policy analysis actually *is* like rocket science, in that scrupulous care and incremental improvements in technique can drive uncertainty down, while never eliminating it entirely. Through the use of techniques like computer simulation, Delphi methods (which aggregate the opinions of experts), statistical assessments of such efforts elsewhere, and just plain sweating the details, what might look like a fifty-fifty proposition for success at first glance might be revealed as 90 percent likely, or perhaps as only 20 percent likely.

Collaborations take place in a dynamic context, and implementation is not a once-and-for-all decision. As later sections of this chapter relate, the reduction of uncertainty has implications for action. Each time experience reveals a new card, the fresh information affects how—and how much—the wise public official is willing to bet on a collaboration. Poorly performing collaborations should be scaled back, shut down, or radically revised. To allow for such flexibility, project designers must contemplate changes in operation, depending on what is found.

Uncertainty brings an upside as well: when the news about a collaboration is good, it can be solidified, scaled up, or replicated. Government agencies contemplating collaboration and small high-tech firms cherish the same magic word: *scalability*. If an experiment is scalable—that is, if it can be made bigger without breaking, should it prove to be a winner—it is much more attractive *ex ante*. Thus even if a district suspects that four of its first five charter schools will turn out to be disappointments, it will still want to launch the charter experiment if that one-in-five winner can quickly inspire a dozen high-achieving look-alikes.

Uncertainty will always be with us, and especially so in an enterprise that features complexity, novelty, or both—as is usually the case with collaborative governance. The right response is not to wish uncertainty would magically go away, but (first) to learn and apply techniques for dealing with it in a disciplined way and (second) to make uncertainty an ally rather than an enemy by keeping plans fluid and adjusting them to make the most of each bit of information as experience unveils it.

Suppose you work in a government agency charged with responsibility for some important public goal. You are convinced, by and large, by the logic we have laid out here. You believe that using leverage, capitalizing on the capabilities of private entities, can enable you to produce more and better output in your domain. And you recognize that to do so effectively, you will have to cede some discretion to your partners. You are alert to the twin pitfalls outlined in chapter 3, payoff discretion and preference discretion, and you seek to design arrangements to minimize their cost. How do you proceed?

The Principal's Twin Tasks: Monitor and Motivate

Recall our discussion in chapter 1 of the "agency relationship" that lies at the heart of governmental efforts to get work done through leverage. Whether it is regulating drug approvals or rating hospitals, issuing school charters or recruiting park volunteers, the government seeking leverage is trying to elicit good performance from a private agent. The major challenge, as we remarked before, is information, or, more precisely, the lack of information. The government often does not know what the private collaborator knows, what actions he has taken, what actions he *could* have taken instead. Government has two generic responses to this information shortfall, relative to its private agent—it can *monitor*, and it can *motivate.* Usually it can, and should, do both.

Monitoring

A public official tasked with getting some collective mission accomplished can attempt to monitor what her private-sector agent does, what the agent fails to do, sometimes even what the agent knows. Such monitoring efforts can take many forms: inspections and evaluations, assessments by outside parties, and self-reports by the agent under pain of severe sanctions for deception or negligence.

To the extent that government relies on collaboration to get its work accomplished, monitoring must be an integral, instinctive, incessant aspect of its management process. The first decision, of course, is who should do the monitoring. There are several possibilities: (1) Each organization responsible for some public mission monitors for itself; (2) Overarching departments use central monitoring units responsible for all the bureaus within the department; (3) Broad-spectrum monitoring operations oversee the agents of the entire federal government or a comparably broad swath of a state or local government; (4) Outside contractors are hired to do the monitoring.

In-house monitoring. Most bureaus—the conventional term for a specialized unit within a larger governmental organization—monitor the work of their contractors, grantees, and other private agents, at least to some extent. This approach has several advantages. Bureaus are closest to the problem at hand, are more likely to spot problems early enough that course corrections are possible, and are in the best position to exert incentives relative to future collaborations.

Beyond-the-bureau monitoring. For various reasons governments will frequently seek to have monitoring carried out beyond the boundaries of the bureau that is responsible for the collaboration. Monitoring "beyond the bureau" was the approach most federal departments undertook in the 1960s and 1970s when reforms such as systems analysis, inspectors general, and program evaluation came into vogue. Systems analysis was pioneered by the Whiz Kids in Robert McNamara's Defense Department in the early 1960s. The mission was to review departmental programs to determine what was working, what was not, and what choices should be made. As other departments followed the Defense Department's lead, specialized analytic units sprouted across the federal government.

Broad-spectrum monitoring. Carrying the principle of beyond-the-bureau monitoring to a higher level, this approach creates bureaus that work across the government specifically to monitor and improve performance or ensure that government funds are spent efficiently. At the federal level in the United States there are a number of entities with such cross-departmental responsibilities. They include the Government Accountability Office (GAO; formerly the General Accounting Office), the Office of Management and Budget (OMB), and administration-specific units such as the National Performance Review in the Clinton White House. Pushing the concept of external oversight one step further away from the operators and toward the authorizers, the Congressional Budget Office (CBO) was created in 1974, with the charge of giving the legislature objective information about the performance of government programs to guide its budgetary decisions. Comparable organizations—such as California's Legislative Analysts' Office—perform similar functions at other levels of government.

This is not the place to assess the performance of the government's monitoring agencies, though we will note that the GAO, the OMB, and the CBO are widely considered to be well led and well staffed, and their studies are generally respected. This is particularly impressive given that they are tiny relative to the requirements of operating an entire government. The combined head count of these three organizations is about four thousand, or roughly 0.2 percent of the total for the federal government.

Third-party monitoring. Government has regularly relied on outside entities to supplement the monitoring work of internal analytic units. Some of this third-party monitoring is so integrated into standard procedures that it draws little attention. At the state or local level, for example, environmental impact statements are regularly required for significant new construction projects, be they public or private. A whole industry of specialized consulting firms provides such analyses.

Government contractors are often required to submit accounting statements, an arrangement that brings a third party—the contractor's auditor—into the loop. Conventional accounting statements ensure that a governmental principal is informed about at least some aspects of the performance of a nonprofit that is delivering welfare services, a data-processing firm handling a city's payroll chores, or a charter school that is instructing students. Accounting reports are useful for telling whether and where dollars have been spent, but that is only half the equation. Such reports say little about what has been accomplished. It is reassuring to learn that the charter school has not been pilfering dollars, or even that its budget has been spent mostly on instruction rather than overhead. But knowing that tells little about what or whether children have learned. Similarly, however comforting it may be to learn that the payroll-management contractor keeps executive pay within industry norms, such measures leave us blind to the quality of the actual work.

To investigate quality and performance issues, given that government does not have legions of educational assessors or process-quality experts, it frequently turns the evaluation task over to private contractors. Some of this outside monitoring work is done well, some just adequately, and some quite poorly indeed.

Selecting the monitor. None of these four approaches can be declared the right answer across the board. Which monitoring model makes the most sense will depend on the collaborative task, the nature of the private collaborators, the capabilities within the bureau, the skills required for monitoring, and so on. If special engineering expertise is required, for example, of the sort that governmental organizations are unlikely to have on hand, then third-party monitoring is likely to be attractive. If the task lies outside a single bureau's bailiwick, but within the domain of its parent agency, beyond-the-bureau monitoring may be promising. If the bureau engages many different agents to pursue similar tasks, it probably has—or should build—strong in-house monitoring skills. A bureau responsible for a reasonably rich array of tasks and well-disposed toward leverage is likely to use two, three, or all four of these monitoring approaches simultaneously.

Deficiencies that subvert monitoring. Monitoring is a fundamental challenge of collaboration. When the challenge is not met, government is unable to detect deviance, deter opportunism, or block abuses. In the case of in-house monitoring there are two clear dangers. Monitoring skills for some tasks are relatively specialized—involving advanced financial vocabulary and concepts, for example, or arcane realms of engineering—and often quite different from a bureau's core operating capacity. There may be no one who can adequately fulfill the monitor's task. And the bureau's leadership may decide that avoiding embarrassment outweighs the benefits of improved performance, and simply ignore deficiencies.

Third-party monitoring can pose similar problems since most government bureaus have neither the manpower nor the expertise to monitor the monitors. To be sure, when scandals erupt and whistle-blowers blow, the small cadre of true government experts in this area may swing into action. But much outside monitoring is carried on with little oversight.

The spectacular financial collapses of 2008 provide a salient illustration of the dangers of unwatched outside monitors. The major bond-rating services—handsomely paid for keeping close tabs on risk—fell somewhere on the spectrum from comatose to corrupt. Neither private actors nor government regulators were watching the raters.

Often bureaus outsource monitoring less because they lack the specialized capacities it requires than because they view monitoring less as a central imperative for strategic management than as a tedious chore the rules impose. The frequent result is that the monitors are slack, sloppy, or even "captured" by the interests they ostensibly oversee. The bureau, sadly, may be perfectly content with shoddy monitoring, since it is unlikely to surface bad news. Worse, even in the large majority of cases when monitoring is conscientious, poor performance does not reliably lead to sanctions against or replacement of the erring agents. Private players come to anticipate that, and inertia shields their shortcomings; the problems of payoff discretion and preference discretion flourish in the shadows.

Any monitoring system, even if well built at the start, may decay over time, until it becomes little more than "alarm-bell monitoring," in which government attends closely to its agents' behavior only when a catastrophe comes to light. Everyday shortfalls, routine divergences of value, are missed. The private agent knows he can get away with such everyday episodes of opportunism, and the episodes expand and multiply. To be sure, occasionally the behavior that leads to modest shortfalls will produce a big loss, or an alert reporter or blogger will chronicle the agent's self-serving behavior. But that is a risk that the agent can run if the probability of detection is small, the gains from self-serving are significant, and the penalties, if the misbehavior is caught, are mostly mild.

The Big Dig in Boston, the largest recent public-works project in the United States, provides a good example of the prime deficiency of alarm-bell monitoring: the bell often rings too late. After the project was virtually complete, it was discovered that a prime provider of concrete had supplied some five thousand truckloads of substandard product—often watering down a truckload of slurry that had started to harden during delays at the work site, restoring its fluidity but diluting its strength. Cement procurement was meant to be a simple contract, not collaboration as we use the term, but an unintended sliver of discretion was exploited to pernicious effect. In contrast to most instances of opportunism on an agent's part, this misbehavior was definitely illegal, seriously so since it imposed physical risk on the public. The company was found out by and by, and eventually paid $50 million to settle the matter.[2] But the discovery did not come before uncounted tons of unknowably weakened concrete had been laced through Boston's transportation infrastructure. The company knew that it had a good chance of getting away with cutting corners, and that there was a ceiling on the penalty it would pay if it were caught. Even if it were to be sued to the point of bankruptcy—and the actual penalty was far milder, with no ban on future business with the state—incorporation limited investors' liability to their stakes in

---

[2] Details of the settlement with Aggregate Industries can be found on the *Boston Globe*'s Web site at http://www.boston.com/news/local/massachusetts/articles/2007/07/28/big_dig_payment _for_fraud_at_50m/. See also the official Transportation Department report at http://www.oig .dot.gov/StreamFile?file=/data/pdfdocs/Aggregate_Plea_PRjuly27.pdf, accessed in November 2007.

the firm. The ironic tragedy of such chiseling is that it saves the company so little, although it potentially costs the public so much. The waste is egregious.

Motivate

The information provided by monitoring must be complemented by well-targeted reward structures if private agents are to be induced to behave in ways that advance public missions. Thoughtfully calibrated incentives will usually be required to focus agents' energies on the production of public value. The most common form of incentive is a simple arrangement that gives greater rewards for better performance. The arrangement could be as specific as a schedule of payoffs administered by the government or—shifting along the spectrum from contract to collaboration— as vague as the general expectation that agents who deliver value tend to get more contracts and higher payments.

The nature of rewards. Incentives can come in many forms. In a market economy monetary rewards may be most familiar, but many other forms are imaginable and, indeed, quite extensively in operation, such as expanded authority, an enhanced reputation, or control over resources. We divide rewards into *direct* and *indirect*.

Direct rewards are given by the government on the basis of some aspect of performance. Beyond money itself, the government may grant the private entity something that will produce money in the future, such as a follow-on contract. Or it may offer an award yielding prestige, which may be an end in itself, or possibly a source of money from others. For example, while National Endowment for the Arts grants are far from munificent, they provide a seal of approval that makes private benefactors more willing to donate dollars. For a nonprofit, a significant government reward may be the grant of control over a greater area of responsibility. Frequently mere government endorsement will enable an organization to rise in the esteem of fellow citizens, which can bring all manner of benefits.

In many instances, governmental organizations take action that enables private actors to secure benefits from elsewhere. We label these indirect rewards. Thus when the Department of Health and Human Services grants hospitals accreditation through the Joint Commission, it unleashes rewards well beyond direct government payments by inducing the broader public to patronize the hospital. Drug companies require FDA approval before they can put their products on the market, but most of the payoff comes from individuals or private insurers rather than the government. When a state or local education agency grants approval to a charter school, it is offering a license to compete for students in a market that is far from the textbook model but still economically consequential.

When rewards are indirect, government may have a more difficult time calibrating its incentives scheme. To predict output and quality levels it must anticipate not only how its private collaborator will respond, but the behavior of other market participants as well. These challenges of prediction and assessment are unlikely to be completely mastered, since government does not feel the full financial effects of its actions. Accountability is exercised at arm's length. Even though the public sector accredits hospitals and pays the bills for a significant share of patients, government can deflect some blame for low-quality care by observing that patients and their families are closer to the action and endowed with choice over where to go for care. No such buffer, conversely, would shield government from blame for shortcomings at a Veterans Administration hospital.

Well- or moderately aligned interests. In some fortunate cases, the interests of the governmental principal and the private-sector agent align well. The Central Park Conservancy is a nonprofit group whose prime concern is to present citizens and visitors with a high-quality park. Its leadership and membership are deeply committed to the park or (almost as good from the government's perspective) to the social standing they earn through being perceived as committed to the park. Thus neither the mayor nor the parks department need lose much sleep over the prospect that the Conservancy will skimp on maintenance in order to offer a fatter benefits package to its staff or ritzier refreshments at the board meetings. Similarly, given that the boards of most charter schools are substantially composed of parents, community leaders, or other citizens with a lively interest in the welfare of the students, school authorities need have little concern that a charter school will shortchange mathematics instruction in order to provide lavish furnishings for the faculty lounge. When principal and agent preferences align well, the motivation problem mostly takes care of itself.

However, even with general alignment, some divergences of preference or interest are somewhere between likely and inevitable. Since board members of the Conservancy tend to be substantially older than the typical user of Central Park, for example, it would be surprising if the Conservancy were not somewhat more partial to scenic plantings, and somewhat less devoted to swing sets, than the average New Yorker. If so, the parks department might find it desirable to nudge the Conservancy leaders toward a package of services closer to typical citizen preferences. Even if those two groups had identical preferences concerning the park's amenities, Conservancy members, but not the typical users, are contributing resources to construct and maintain facilities. That creates its own divergence in preferences. To overcome it, the parks department could create some beneficial incentives. It might assure the Conservancy a prime place for a concert pavilion if and only if $10 million dollars were raised to build it. Alternatively, or in addition, it might—and indeed does—pledge city funds to supplement incremental private revenues as a means to better align incentives.

The charter school may be marked by similar divergences, which could lead public education authorities to worry about reward structures. Differences in interests could be particularly sharp on admissions criteria. Charter-school managers and the parents of existing students would often prefer to admit on the basis of academic qualification, while city or state education authorities might desire a broad mix from the community. To manage such disparities in priorities, public officials responsible for running charter-school systems often impose explicit requirements, such as mandating that all or most students must be admitted by lottery. School authorities and board members may also be divided on features of a school's curriculum and culture. The charter school may be told it cannot operate if it proselytizes in favor of a particular religion, for example.

Strongly divergent interests. The motivation task is doubly difficult if the government's private partner has interests that diverge strongly from what it wants to accomplish. The corporate contractor wants to ramp up revenues, but one party's revenue is the other's cost, and the government wants to hold down expenses. The nonprofit wants to have some mission—welfare-to-work services for Latinas in Lowell, say—all to itself; the government wants to maintain a healthy rivalry among competing nonprofits. And even when the nonprofit has a well-defined area of responsibility, with little aspiration for more, there are some aspects of its charge that it welcomes more than it does others. Thus a museum may prefer catering to genteel grownups rather than to scruffy schoolchildren, but the city may prefer to culti-vate the culture of the coming generation. Precisely this kind of clash has been at the center of the recent debate over how much charity care hospitals must deliver if they are to keep their tax-free status. Munici-palities argue for more, whereas hospitals have little interest in up-ping their intake of nonpaying patients.

When interests do part ways, the government's key task is to iden-tify where the frictions are worst, where public and private interests are most sharply out of alignment. It should then direct incentives toward those issues. It needs to impose penalties for behavior that serves the agent at the expense of the principal, and should provide explicit rewards for serving public needs at private cost. A charter school, for example, might be penalized through a payment reduc-tion if it is discovered indoctrinating students with religion. Dollars are likely to trump moral suasion ("don't proselytize") in preventing inappropriate activities. A chemical firm considered at risk of terror-ist attack should get subsidies for work assessing how chemical plants in general—not just its own facilities—might be targeted, and sharing that information with authorities. Absent such incentives, much too little private effort would go into the task.

Even the best-targeted incentive system, alas, is no panacea. Some-times the outputs are extraordinarily difficult to assess, perhaps be-cause the objectives are multiple, spread out over time, and imper-fectly measurable. Under such circumstances, incentives are not likely to work. If a collaborator is rewarded for what is readily observed and measured, energies will shift to the measured and rewarded aspects of the undertaking and other objectives will be neglected. In some professional organizations, employees are given bonuses based on the subjective impression of their supervisors, in recognition of the impracticality of basing rewards on strictly objective metrics. But such subjective reward schemes can be used only when there is an ongoing relationship, when the agent is confident of the goodwill of the principal. Situations where the government is the principal often do not lend themselves to such informal incentive schemes. Forces that work against them are the need for accountability beyond the bureau's walls, the frequency of one-time-only collaborations, and prohibitions against open-ended arrangements with private partners, implying that a relationship may not continue. In short, well-tailored incentives are an extraordinarily valuable tool for collaborative relationships, but they will be available to do the job only in some circumstances.

The first lesson when interests diverge is that accountable collaboration must be intentionally engineered. The path of least resistance, in other words, generally leads to a bad place. The second lesson is to monitor with alacrity any unexpectedly good *or* bad behavior. Surprise implies that the relationship isn't well understood, and that is always bad news. The third lesson applies when monitoring is likely to be too costly (if robust enough to keep agents in line) or too feeble (if costs are held to a reasonable level), and where incentives are not likely to be effective substitutes: Don't collaborate. It will likely come to grief. Choose another model for getting the government's work done. If appropriate monitoring *is* feasible, the fourth lesson applies: Proceed with the collaborative approach. Use meaningful monitoring and well-tailored incentives as your lever to promote good behavior and discourage bad.

The Cycle of Collaboration

You are a government official charged with a particular mission. You have determined that collaboration may be the most effective way to advance that mission. You are under no illusions that collaboration yields a simple sort of relationship, and understand that the goal is to maximize the benefits while minimizing the risks and costs that flow from private discretion. You know your objectives; your strategy is in place. So now what should you *do* to make it succeed?

The principal lesson we wish to convey here is that effective collaboration is not a one-time-through process. You can't just define a once-and-for-all solution, and "let 'er rip." Collaborative governance requires a continuing cycle of analytical and managerial work; as you learn, as events take their course, as priorities evolve, the structure of the collaboration must be revised. To impart this lesson, we separate out specific aspects of this work, using illustrations from some of our case studies. Then we take a single spin around the whole cycle as it relates to two attempts to pursue public goals—workforce development and drug safety—by collaborative means.

The analytic and managerial work required for effective collaboration can be classed under four headings: analyze, assign, design, and assess. They are arrayed not in a one-time, linear sequence, but rather in an ongoing cycle, with attention to the four kinds of tasks varying over time. There are multiple considerations that make repeat spins imperative. First, external conditions change. Second, the priorities of the government—or, more precisely, the priorities of the citizenry the government is pledged to serve—evolve over time. Third, a static structure invites opportunism. If private players know that they are immune from course correction, they may indulge in escalating levels of self-serving behavior. Fourth, more generally, you learn as the collaboration moves forward about what works well and what does not. For all these reasons, what worked well in 2011 may not in 2021. The cycle needs to keep on turning, and each go-round requires fine tuning.

The Four Components of the Cycle

Figure 8.1 shows the four-step cycle, beginning at the top.

Analyze. The first step in the process is to analyze the situation. Analysis begins with an understanding of what the governmental organization is seeking to accomplish. The grand collective goal may be set—say, "promoting human health"—but too abstract to be a

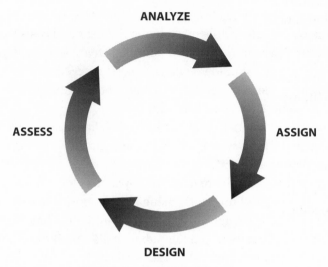

Fig. 8.1 The Cycle of Collaboration

helpful touchstone for structuring collaboration. Accountable action calls for concreteness. The FDA might perceive its goal as assuring that drugs brought to market are both *effective* and *safe*. But even this goal is too broad-brush. In reviewing new drugs, the bureau must recognize that a trade-off is inevitable between efficacy (getting beneficial drugs on the market) and safety (running one more study to check for serious side effects).

Sound analysis starts with a careful examination of the status quo in light of the central question: in what ways can we hope to do better? Sometimes bureaus learn by looking at practices in somewhat similar organizations. The charter-school movement, for example, was inspired in part by observations that parochial schools and other donor-supported private schools seemed to be doing a better job than conventional public schools at serving challenging populations.

Some problems, of course, have few analogues. Consider the Megatons to Megawatts program discussed on pages 74–79. Continent-scale empires bristling with weapons of mass destruction only infrequently come unglued. No weighty analysis was required to determine that having fissile material up for grabs in and around the former

Soviet Union was not a good thing. The challenge was figuring out a place to start the analysis of what to do about it. And the critical insight was recognizing the affinities between the military issues embedded in crumbling communism and the organizational default for peacetime capitalism—the market. While the implementation of the insight left something to be desired, it remains true that creating a lucrative commercial outlet for Russian bomb materials was a much more promising long-term strategy than was trying to bottle them up.

The analysis must also assess who the private players might be. In many cases, the usual suspects will be readily known. In others, the collaborative arrangement itself will create new potential partners, or rearrange the rosters of old ones. Once the model of the Central Park Conservancy became established, other groups began to coalesce to care for other specific parks. Once a few charter schools get established, nonprofit groups that never played in the education field may consider starting one, and parents may get together to form a new nonprofit to run a school.

Imitation of success, far from mere flattery, is the path of progress in the natural world, of prosperity in the economic sphere, and of value-creation in the common realm. A critical role for analysis is to predict how new partners will spring into existence if various alternatives are pursued. The answer is at the core of the potential for scalability, the ability to turn an experiment into a way of life. Such predictions lay the groundwork for the next two tasks, which are usually (and appropriately) considered together: assign and design.

Assign is the critical matter of getting the right player in the right position. Even in the assignment process discretion is shared with private collaborators. Drug-safety regulation shows the government in a minor role at the first stage, but in the predominant one at the second stage. Any pharmaceutical company can designate itself as a partner to the FDA. All it needs to do is step forward with a drug to sell. However, the FDA determines the role private companies have in the approval process. They run drug trials under the oversight of the agency and then submit applications for ultimate approval. If the trials are not conducted according to prescribed form, the drug has no chance for approval.

The assignment of partners for New York City presents a somewhat different story. The parks department negotiated an explicit agreement with each of these organizations. Adrian Benepe, the commissioner who oversaw many of these arrangements, sometimes signed up the first group that raised its hand for a park, but sometimes he selected the most promising or tractable from among multiple contenders, and on occasion he nurtured the development of a private group from the start.

Design is the complementary role to assigning responsibility. It tells what each assignee will be allowed and expected to do, how he will be monitored and rewarded, how long he will retain his responsibilities, and so on. If the task were merely contracting, with production for and payment by the government, these matters would be straightforward. Each private party would have a separate contract spelling out its duties. But our concern is collaboration, not contracting, which means sharply stepped-up complexity. In many instances, as with charter schools, there will be competition among potential collaborators. The "design" stage thus overlaps with the "analyze" and "assign" stages, as government must contemplate how the different potential players will interact with one another, including players yet to be identified. A second complexity is that rewards beyond money are frequently involved, including the pure satisfaction of advancing the public good, or the status and bragging rights that come with being the government's chosen partner, or a privileged perch for influencing public policy.

The design task—like almost everything else connected with collaboration—is easier if the interests of the governmental organization and its private collaborator are closely aligned. This lesson is a general one, far from restricted to collaborative governance or even government in general. Family businesses suffer the disadvantages of nepotism, but they can thrive because aligned interests permit streamlined management with modest monitoring and few formalities. The president of the United States recognizes this when he appoints people from his wing of his party to serve as cabinet officers, and gives a big edge in appointments to people who were with his campaign from the beginning. He is securing people whose fidelity is unquestioned.[3]

Alas, for many tasks, the interests of the public organization and the private provider part ways. The design task then becomes to provide incentives that work to counteract these tendencies, as we outlined in our discussion of motivation above. Thus—please indulge our rhyme—we underscore that a central underlying objective of the *assign* and *design* tasks is to *align* goals as closely as possible.

Once the process has been designed, and the private collaborators assigned (or a process that allows for assignment has been created), collaboration swings into action. Drug approvals get financed; parks groups get organized and begin to plant trees and pick up litter; hospitals get accredited. That brings us to the third task in the cycle.

Assess. Most collaborations, including virtually all those studied in this book, are enduring arrangements rather than one-shot affairs. Many are put in place with no effective date or termination; sunset provisions are rare. Unfortunately, initial designs are sometimes flawed; processes that are desirable today may decay by tomorrow; new circumstances arise that make yesterday's brilliant design today's dreadful blunder. That means that the governmental bureau, and perhaps the legislative or executive branch overseeing it, has to assess how the collaboration is going. Assessment means determining whether the collaboration is performing as intended, and (if so) whether that performance is in fact advancing public goals as had been envisaged at the start. Sometimes only minor tweaks will be needed. At other times, major revisions in design, or significant changes in who does what, will be required.

The cycle of analyze, assign and design, then assess may turn swiftly or slowly, but it should never stop as long as the collaborative process remains in operation. The cycle is important not only to improve matters through the choices made by the government, but also

---

[3] This theme of selecting for prealigned interests, a mainstay of agency theory in economics, has been extended into the political science literature by our colleague Jane Mansbridge: "A 'Selection' Model of Political Representation," *Journal of Political Philosophy* 17, no. 4 (December 2009): 369–398.

to maintain incentives for the private collaborators to produce public value.

Around the Cycle with Drug-Safety Regulation

Earlier sections of this chapter illustrated the application of analytic tools to America's leveraged approach to drug-safety regulation. Here we take an additional lap around our cycle. Thus far the Prescription Drug User Fee Act has had four incarnations: PDUFA II and III modestly modified the original. For the most part they tweaked the rights and obligations of public and private collaborators without revising the architecture of the relationship in any radical way. PDUFA IV, passed in 2007, was more ambitious. It revised the previous models substantially and thus illustrates our cycle of tasks at work. The cycle started in the *assessment* phase, with a growing and spreading dissatisfaction concerning some key elements of PDUFA. Most troubling was the FDA's comparatively weak incentive and constrained ability to act on safety problems that arise after a drug has been approved for sale to the public, as opposed to premarket approval. Over a period of years, in a process involving a wide range of actors, the process looped around to *analysis*. This crucial stage explored the relative capacities of the FDA, the drug companies, patients, physicians, and other players in the health-care industry to identify and act on safety problems that arose with drugs already on the market.

As the five-year time line for renewing, revising, or abandoning PDUFA approached, legislators and their advisers revisited the *assignment* of responsibilities. Revised assignments in the new legislation expanded the role of the FDA in determining how user-fee resources should be deployed, and granted the agency new discretion to use those resources for safety surveillance once drugs are on the market. Drug companies were also assigned new responsibilities. Most importantly, they were now required to gather and pass on information about bad outcomes. (Lawmakers considered, but rejected, assigning doctors the duty of reporting any adverse effects their patients had from prescription drugs.) Finally this fourth and latest iteration of PDUFA altered the *design* of the collaborative relationship in significant ways. It boosted the level of user fees for most applications for review. It let the FDA insist upon altered labels in response to new information—for example, about safety problems—and it tightened rules on conflicts of interest for the experts who advise the government on drug approvals.[4]

Around the Cycle with Job Training

The history of federal efforts to promote the development of human capital in adult workers also involved several turns around the cycle of collaboration. The basic notion of a collaborative approach is nothing new in federal job-training policy, which goes back at least to the Manpower Development and Training Act of 1962.[5]

The nation had an unsatisfying dalliance with direct government production of job training in the 1970s. The Comprehensive Employment and Training Act of 1973 (CETA) began as an effort to consolidate the clutter of separate job and workforce development programs that had accumulated at least since the New Deal. As the decade closed, its most visible—and often derided—component was the massive public employment program that gave states and localities federal money to hire the unemployed. The media churned out exposés of make-work and inefficiency. Widespread revulsion against wasteful public-works employment under CETA, and the general presumption that private businesses—with their privileged access to information, as we discussed in chapter 5—would produce job training more efficiently, ensured that the next iteration of workforce policy would feature a larger role for the private sector.

President Ronald Reagan savaged CETA during his campaign and called for a more businesslike approach to job training. Congress complied. Legislation pioneered by the improbable senatorial team of

---

[4] Gardiner Harris, "House Passes Bill Giving More Power to the F.D.A.," *New York Times*, September 20, 2007, p. A-18. Some skeptics still questioned the basic logic of PDUFA. For example, see Jerry Avorn, "Paying for Drug Approvals: Who's Using Whom?" *New England Journal of Medicine*, 356, no. 17 (April 26, 2007).

[5] This section on federal job-training policy prior to the Workforce Investment Act draws on John D. Donahue, *The Privatization Decision: Public Ends, Private Means* (Basic Books, 1989), chap. 9.

Edward Kennedy and Dan Quayle realized that strategy with the Job Training Partnership Act of 1982 (JTPA). The new law emphasized the collaborative approach by requiring a results-oriented contractual accountability model for all training funded with federal money. JTPA matured from an abstract legislative framework to a nationwide training system over the course of the 1980s and early 1990s. Funds flowed out for cities and states to spend in accord with a complex formula based on prevailing levels of employment and unemployment. Thousands of Private Industry Councils were assembled, and tens of thousands of business people at all levels sampled the satisfactions and frustrations of PIC membership. Private training programs proliferated. Many were nonprofit, though for-profit businesses had an important role to play. They figured prominently in a sharp expansion of subsidized on-the-job training. In the language of this chapter, assessment and analysis led to a sharp reassignment of functions away from government and toward private players.

Collaborative job training in most respects represented an improvement over government's go-it-alone approach under CETA. But ongoing assessment in the light of experience revealed that JTPA had its own, quite different, set of gaps and flaws, and the cycle of collaboration continued to turn. JTPA's hallmark governance provisions, which required large but loosely specified roles for businesses, led to occasional instances of corruption and self-dealing, blatant forms of payoff discretion.

More serious than these egregious lapses—because they were subtler and harder to spot—were the common gaps between agents' priorities and those of the government, and the feeble means JTPA provided for narrowing those gaps. JTPA in practice featured a pattern of sweeping preference for business principles and institutions—a reflexive and undiscriminating reaction against CETA—uninformed by much analysis about the relative advantages of public and private models. And JTPA's vaunted system of results-based accountability frequently failed to motivate private actors to direct their discretion toward creating public value. (For a general overview of channeling discretion in this policy domain, see our discussion of the dilemmas entangled with training Betty on pages 105–107 of chapter 5.) Assessment of the evidence from JTPA's first decade or so revealed that its design was too loose to steer training funds reliably to that relatively narrow niche where public value should be sought.[6] The problem was not that the well-off were burnishing their skills at public expense; eligibility rules limited subsidized training to the disadvantaged. Rather, it was that the pool of eligible trainees was sufficiently deep and diverse, and the menu of acceptable training programs was so broad, that firms could frequently claim public money for training that they would have undertaken on their own. Blunt corruption was apparently rare in JTPA, but the venial forms of payoff discretion—collecting rewards without being constrained to deliver public value; using public money to pay for skill investments with mostly private payoffs—were routine.

As with its predecessor, CETA, experience revealed the defects of JTPA, and it was time to trek around the cycle of collaboration again. The next generation of training policy created a more nuanced division of labor between public and private entities. Perhaps the biggest shift in assignment was to expand the role for *individuals,* the people who were being trained, as opposed to that of either government or private employers. Some within the Clinton administration called for a massive reassignment of discretion toward individuals.[7] This approach would have remade job training along the lines of post-secondary education. Most federal funds would go not to training institutions, public or private, but rather to individuals in the form of "scholarships" that they could spend as they saw fit. Government's role would be to provide purchasing power, and plenty of information on the track records of alternative training providers as well. It would then step aside. The actual assignment of the work across governmental, for-profit, and nonprofit training institutions would depend not on governmental decisions but on the choices of individuals. A

---

[6] The most important evidence on JTPA was assembled in a massive study funded by the U.S. Department of Labor, conducted by a team of researchers assembled by Abt Associates, and published by the Urban Institute. Larry Orr et al., *Does Training for the Disadvantaged Work? Evidence from the National JTPA Study* (Urban Institute Press, 1996).

[7] Donahue was a Labor Department policy official as these debates played out, and broadly favored tilting discretion in the job-training arena toward individuals rather than either public or private institutions.

full shift to the voucher model was too big a design change for Congress to swallow, but what eventually emerged as the Workforce Investment Act of 1998 did move somewhat toward individual discretion, with more scope for individuals to promote accountability through the choices they made.

The collaborative approach makes excellent sense for job training. Yet the ideal structure for focusing private discretion on the production of public value is not only elusive but evolving. The appropriate approach changes as the economy transits from manufacturing to services, from national to global, and from concentrated to distributed technologies. We must continue to assess, analyze, and alter both the assignment of tasks and the design of the collaborative system. Trips around the cycle of collaboration will continue as long as government is ambitious enough to attempt to boost citizens' earning power through training, honest enough to concede when the status quo is not working as well as it should, and smart enough to adapt its approach to changing conditions.[8]

Our simple cycle—with just four major stages, each an apparent no-brainer imperative of collaboration—may strike some readers as too rudimentary and self-evident to improve actual practice. The evidence, sadly enough, suggests otherwise. Most government programs, whether collaborative or not, escape serious evaluation of any form. Where there is collaboration, assignments generally stick where they start, with little thought as to whether different collaborators might generate more public value. In this sense business has it easy, in that the market delivers automatic feedback: did the product make money? But government serves multiple masters with complex objectives, most of which are not priced. Without any automatic external gauge of success, the simple checklist suggested by our cycle should be helpful in keeping collaborative strategies on track.[9]

---

[8] For one sample of the reassessment as the Workforce Investment Act became ripe for reauthorization or replacement, see U.S. Government Accountability Office, "One-Stop Infrastructure Continues to Evolve," report GAO-07-1096 (September 2007).

[9] Atul Gawande, the famed surgeon, academic, and *New Yorker* essayist, has chronicled the improbable impact of simple checklists. Looking across endeavors ranging from operating an airplane to operating on a patient, he observes that most mistakes are those of ineptitude—not making proper use of what we know—rather than ignorance, and he finds that checklists can

Lest our readers infer from the simplicity of our cycle that we be-lieve the work it involves is child's play, let us explicitly raise a caution-ary note. Every stage of the cycle is likely to require heavy lifting, in managerial, intellectual, and political terms. In particular—and in con-trast to collaborative relationships between friends or acquaintances, and also unlike most alliances between private firms—collaborative governance can be very difficult to revise. The reasons are many, including the elemental inertia that even healthy governments tend to display and the eagerness of private players to retain roles that they find agreeable. Even when assessment signals problems and analysis identifies alternatives, assignments can turn out to be deeply an-chored, and designs virtually etched in stone. Why did we give private players so large a role in making student loans (for many long years, and a great many dollars, prior to the 2010 reforms) and so small a role in providing transportation, food services, and other readily del-egated functions within public schools? The explanation, we believe, is that politics and vested interests have made initial assignments from long ago very hard to change. Collaborations, once established, prove sticky. This reinforces the importance of hard, clear thinking up front.

Government's Role in Collaboration

As the government runs through this cycle, how should it construe its own role? In searching for a satisfying response to this sweeping question, we start by observing that metaphors matter. The words we choose to signal *what sort* of thing is at issue exercise a subtle but powerful force over our perception. They guide the focus of our at-tention, and signal the features that are essential and those that are second-order. To declare "war on drugs" privileges some imaginable

---

dramatically reduce such errors. Simply by making sure everyone in the operating room knows each other by name—through a checklisted protocol for introductions before the procedure starts—operating room personnel can cut surgical complications by 35 percent, mostly because team members become more likely to speak up when they spot a problem during the operation. http://www.leanblog.org/2010/01/dr-gawande-checklists-featured-on-npr/. More generally see *The Checklist Manifesto* (Metropolitan Books, 2009).

policies with respect to certain citizens' tendency to ingest illegal substances, and rules out (or at least imposes a stiff burden of proof upon) alternative policies. When George W. Bush dubbed himself "the Decider," he revealed a conception of the president's role very different from that of the wily FDR or the avuncular Reagan (and rather inconsistent with the famous dictum of our late colleague Richard Neustadt that presidential power is chiefly "the power to persuade"). Louis Brandeis characterized America's separate states as "laboratories," and in so doing affected how governors, legislators, and ordinary citizens viewed states' distinctive function within America's public sector. The point can be overdone, of course. When the poet Robert Burns declares that "my love is like a red, red rose," he is not predicting how she will respond to daily soakings or the regular application of manure. But the general point holds true: given how our image-hungry minds operate, metaphors, similes, and allegories influence how we think.

Governments have decades, in a few instances centuries, of experience in designing collaborative arrangements. But it is only in recent years that collaborative governance has become such a widespread phenomenon. It seems on course to find important application in new areas, and with forethought and experience our collective capacity to collaborate well should advance apace. If we are right about this—or even in the neighborhood of right—the gradual growth in the prevalence, sophistication, and success of collaboration will alter how we *ought to* think about governmental action. So it would be handy to have an appropriate image of how government operates in the age of collaboration.

For a long time, the conventional image of public management was a simple civilian analogue of military command: the bureaucrat takes orders from above and issues them downward. The chain of authority is both unambiguous and complete, with little confusion about who is calling the shots. Any deviation from legitimate command —any second-guessing or freelancing on the part of subordinates— constitutes pathology. The military command metaphor is vividly present, explicitly or implicitly, in Max Weber's *Bureaucracy*, Wood-

row Wilson's writings on American government, and other classics of
public administration. And in some settings, of course, it remains
a perfectly appropriate model for how government does and should
operate.

But as the practical realities of governance continue to evolve—
and as scholars began to notice, a little later, that the practical realities
of governance are in flux—the command model became a less plausible depiction of the typical governmental task. Modern scholars
have developed different metaphors to capture more complex models
of indirect and delegated governmental action. We started this chapter analogizing the official structuring of a collaboration to the work
of a technician choosing from a set of tools; we then dropped in the
slightly fancier image of a sculptor—a craftsman and an artist at
once—studying the stone and contemplating the desired result before
applying that first stroke of the chisel. Lester Salamon, in his magis-
terial five-pound edited volume *The Tools of Governance*, takes a similar tack, arraying the various conceptual and institutional gadgets
that can come in handy for getting the public's work accomplished.

Our colleague Mark Moore enriches the metaphor—and imparts
some Gallic sophistication to the conversation—by comparing modern public managers to the archetypal improviser that the famed an-
thropologist Claude Lévi-Strauss calls the *bricoleur*. (The term, used
not merely by celebrated anthropologists but also in ads for French
hardware stores, is pretty much synonymous with our own "handyman.") The *bricoleur*'s role certainly includes mastery of a diverse tool
kit but goes beyond technical proficiency. The key characteristic
stressed by both Lévi-Strauss and Moore is imaginative opportunism
with respect to materials. Some handyman ancestor thirty thousand
years ago, when the Ice Age made big straight trees scarce in most of
Europe, figured out that mastodon tusks could form a dandy frame
for a hide-covered dwelling. His modern descendant might survey
the shed and realize that an old barn door, trimmed to shape and
braced underneath with two crisscrossed skis, would do just fine as a
ping-pong table. Likewise, in Moore's conception, a little tinkering
with rules and budgets and personnel can transform an underused

local library into a safe drop-in center for latchkey kids. The *brico-leur's* genius is imagining valuable new uses for the materials at hand, whatever their origins or intended application. For present purposes, though, the *bricoleur* metaphor obscures the crucial fact that in collaborative governance the tools and materials are not just acted upon, but act on their own.

Donald Kettl, in *The Next Government of the United States*, engages many of the themes of delegation and interorganizational action that concern us here. His distinctive image of the public manager is that of mission controller for a spacecraft launch. The controller is the unflappable veteran of mission after mission, at each go-round scrutinizing and directing the complex network of public and private players required for a safe round trip to and from space. Kettl's evocative image offers much to admire, and indeed it (like Moore's) is spot-on for calling to mind the essentials of some governmental undertakings. But it is not quite right for what we've been calling collaborative governance, since the very term "mission *control*" brings with it a misleading sense of one-way authority.

The essence of collaboration is shared discretion. Government explicitly yields some control to its private agents to promote efficiency in the creation of public value. We suspect, for that matter, that the best and shrewdest of NASA's mission controllers know this perfectly well, and yield some discretion now and then. But the I'm-in-charge image is somewhat at odds with the role we have in mind. Reliance on private collaborators endowed with a degree of discretion imposes risks and challenges, but it also lays the predicate for efficiency, innovation, and the creation of unanticipated forms of public value.

The Ringmaster's Repertoire

A different metaphor is required to capture the role of the governmental official in a collaborative relationship. We nominate the circus ringmaster, and our shorthand for the tradecraft of collaboration is the *ringmaster's repertoire*. The calmly multitasking presence of the ringmaster under the big top, by tradition resplendent in top hat and tails, orchestrating a diverse tangle of activities, captures what we view as government's key role in a world of collaboration.[10] Here is how Fred Badna, the legendary ringmaster for Ringling Brothers, Barnum and Bailey from before World War I until well into the Cold War era, described his role. The ringmaster

> keeps performers on their toes, insisting that they give their best. He meets each moment as it comes, adjusting the displays to the urgencies of weather, illness and temperament with minute attention to detail....
>
> ... He must be at once a showman, a stage director, a martinet, a diplomat, a family counselor, a musician, a psychologist, an animal keeper and a weather prophet.[11]

The ringmaster certainly possesses a degree of formal authority. No Ringling Brothers performer was long left in doubt about what Fred Badna considered the right kind of performance, or could remain with the circus while ignoring Badna's priorities. But the ringmaster must advance those priorities without any illusion that his control is complete. Rather than issuing blunt commands and counting on precise compliance, he employs a portfolio of subtler skills to steer the behavior of performers in the most valuable direction. This involves knowing what the performers are apt to do of their own accord, absent any intervention from the ringmaster, and knowing as well which interventions will be effective in altering each individual's behavior. The ringmaster must possess a sophisticated understanding not just of horses, not just of Arabian horses as a class, but of Emir—and not just of Emir on average but of Emir specifically during a show on a hot August evening after an earlier matinee. He must appreciate not just acrobats, not just Chinese acrobats, but how Wen Chou is apt to perform on the day he got a disturbing letter from his family back home.

Such fine-grained intelligence can be useful in any context, of course, but its importance mounts as control diminishes—as the manager

---

[10] We are convinced of the metaphor's objective merits but feel bound to disclose that both authors enjoy attending the circus, sometimes together, while one is married to a descendent of P. T. Barnum.

[11] Fred Badna (as told to Hartzell Spence) *The Big Top* (Simon and Schuster, 1952), pp. 101–102.

deals less with machines or servile subordinates and more with will-ful animals or discretion-wielding collaborators. Indeed, the very verb "to manage" shares roots with "menagerie."[12] The ringmaster man-ages, but does not fully control, what happens under the big top. He shares discretion. He leaves the performers room—as he must—to work out how best to add their own bit of luster to the collective gleam of the circus.

The public manager who seeks to advance her mission through collaborative arrangements, similarly, needs to combine disciplined mastery of the general characteristics of a class of collaborators—a local nonprofit, a for-profit franchise of a national chain, a global corporation, an international charity—with close attention to the particulars of the specific people and organizations across the table. The requisite skills, analogous to those of the circus ringmaster, range from conducting financial analyses and structuring agreements, to gauging the political clout or managerial soundness of partner orga-nizations, to reading body language in a meeting. Our ringmaster's repertoire, in short, requires an extraordinary blend of analytic acu-men with empathy, interpersonal instincts, and emotional intelli-gence. This, we realize, can be a tall order. But it is increasingly what the work of the governmental manager requires today.

The history of heroic figures in American government tends to-ward leaders who launched bold programs, and skillful managers riding herd over agencies churning out vital public services—think of Robert Moses in New York City, or David Lilienthal (who headed the Tennessee Valley Authority during its crucial early days) or Ad-miral Hyman Rickover, who dragged the U.S. Navy into the nuclear age. When the history of twenty-first-century government is told, we are confident that the pantheon of public leaders will be comple-mented by individuals who were great collaborators. They will be the figures who drew on a deep, diverse tool kit of hard and soft skills to analyze, assign, design, and assess—again and again, iterating through

---

[12] Martin Landau and Russell Stout, Jr., "To Manage Is Not to Control: Or the Folly of Type II Errors," *Public Administration Review*, March/April 1979.

the cycles as circumstances change—to create public value through collaboration with private parties. Whether standing in the spotlight's glare or working from the shadows to orchestrate the action, through the din of politics and despite the muffling layers of bureaucracy, the voice of the ringmaster can be heard.

Chapter 9

<><><><><><><><><><><><><><><><><><><><><><><><><>

Getting Collaboration Right

The performance of America's government depends on its ability to engage private players to accomplish public work. The motivating theme for this volume is not unique to the contemporary United States. But it applies more vividly to our market-friendly country than it does to most other polities. And it is likely to hold with special force over the next few decades as the nature and scale of foreseeable public problems preclude solution by government acting alone. Government's reliance on private collaborators affects its odds for success on any given issue, conditions the ways it is prone to fail, and implies major revisions to the list of pivotal skills that government officials must possess.

Collaboration has the potential to unleash the energies of people and organizations across the sectoral spectrum. Successful collaboration generates payoffs on several levels. The most obvious—and the level that drew most of our attention in prior chapters—is solving public problems more completely, satisfyingly, and efficiently than government could on its own. A turn to the collaborative approach should reflect neither ideological romance nor empty aspiration, but an accurate reckoning that collaboration will beat alternative models. Utilizing private capacity, as we have observed, is often the most effective way to get public tasks accomplished.

The use of collaboration to create public value, at one level, simply exemplifies the division of labor. Here, though, the division is not among individual workers, but among organizational models. Government retains the ultimate responsibility for getting the job done, but parcels out to private players some, or even all, of the work required to deliver on that duty. Adam Smith, in his epochal *Wealth of*

Nations, sketched the enduring metaphor of a pin factory to illustrate the division of labor among workers specialized in particular tasks. Smith's metaphor ignored the pivotal role of the manager who, among other things, had to determine who did what. With collaboration, the government plays this crucial managerial role. It sorts out functions across and within sectors, keeping for itself those tasks suited to direct governmental performance and assigning other tasks to private-sector organizations that possess skills, knowledge, and assets that government lacks, and that it cannot—or can only at prohibitive cost —acquire itself. It would seem that governments ought to figure out over time which tasks are best suited to collaboration, and that those tasks would, most of the time in most of the places, be pursued collaboratively. A closer look at how collaborative efforts have played out in the real world tells a more nuanced story.

Tales from Six Cities

In the summer of 2007 we mustered a team of graduate students to undertake some fieldwork into delivery models for local public services. The plan was to see how the same set of four governmental services was handled in different locales. The services to be examined —park maintenance, emergency medical transport, job training, and preschool services delivered under the Head Start program— were chosen to be amenable to a variety of delivery models, from direct governmental action to a range of different kinds of delegation. Study sites—Boston, Raleigh, Miami, Louisville, Colorado Springs, and Oakland—were chosen to be comparable in size (ranging from around a quarter million to around a half million in population) but geographically and demographically diverse.

We were curious to learn whether and how city officials tapped private capacity in pursuit of these missions, and to see whether there were any patterns in how the work got done. The project was exploratory rather than definitive—you'd need a much bigger sample to generate the kind of evidence you can take to the bank—but still planned and carried out with some care. A two-stage process determined where we would look. The first stage was systematic: we drew up a short list of midsize cities in each major region—Northeast, Midwest, South, Mid-Atlantic, Mountain, and West. The second stage was less so: we picked from each regional list the city where we could recruit a grad student with enough local knowledge and connections to have good odds of collecting some decent data. We had no strong expectations one way or the other about how the cities would end up handling the services, and gave no hint to our researchers that we were predicting or rooting for any particular pattern of findings. Apart from anecdotal observation in Boston, we had no prior knowledge of the use of collaboration in these locales. Our team of students scattered across the country in July, checking in with us periodically by phone or e-mail, and regrouping for periodic meetings back at Harvard. With only two exceptions—Head Start services in Oakland and job training in Louisville—we were able to assemble sufficiently detailed operational and financing data to classify the delivery model as *direct*, *contractual*, or *collaborative*.

We learned that collaboration at the local level wasn't just a figment of our imagination, or reckless generalization from a few unrepresentative examples we had encountered by chance. For each of the four services, at least one city used the collaborative approach. Private organizations figure prominently in Louisville's campaign to upgrade and raise the profile of its city parks. Most ambulance service in the Raleigh area is provided by six nonprofit organizations whose operations are orchestrated by a county agency. A sophisticated network of public and private organizations, decades in the making, delivers job-training services in Boston. Raleigh delegates most of its Head Start responsibilities, and the associated funding, to a large multistate nonprofit, while Colorado Springs relies to a similar degree on a local organization with roots in a religious charity. These "existence proofs" by no means establish that the collaborative approach is the right answer for every service in every locale. What works for Boston might do poorly for Oakland, and Raleigh and Miami might have good reasons for doing the same thing differently. But we had a hunch that a service that was chosen for a collaborative approach in one city would tend to be selected for collaboration elsewhere as well.

That hunch was wrong. The fact that one city opted for a collaborative approach to a particular service didn't come close to indicating that other cities would do the same. Consider parks management, a service particularly rich with opportunities for collaboration. Private actors' interests are fairly clear and visible; many of the tasks involved can be carried out in multiple ways; the stakes are low enough to permit experimentation. But while collaboration was at the heart of Louisville's parks strategy, comparable arrangements in Boston and Colorado Springs were much smaller. Two small parks in Miami were managed in collaboration with private trusts, but city employees were responsible for the bulk of the system. While some volunteer work goes on in Raleigh's parks, it is dwarfed by direct governmental effort. And city workers have essentially exclusive responsibility for Oakland's parks.

Ambulance services were delivered through collaboration in Raleigh in the archetypal manner described in this volume: government orchestrated the activities of a network of private providers, none of which was wholly under the public sector's control. By contrast, such services were delivered by straightforward contracts in Colorado Springs and Oakland, and by public employees in Boston, Louisville, and Miami. Even though federal law comes close to mandating a collaborative structure for job training—requiring a major private role in governance, for example—none of the other cities came close to Boston's extensive reliance on private capacity for targeting and delivering training. And the private sector's preeminent role in Raleigh and Colorado Springs' Head Start efforts is not mirrored by the government-centered model on display in other cities. Even when collaboration was theoretically possible, and even when at least one city showed it was feasible in practice, the pattern of delivery models actually employed was all over the map. Nor could local political proclivities explain the patterns—one town collaboration-phobic across the board, another avid to collaborate—since cities that were unusually collaborative on one activity were unusually oriented toward full public production on others.

Table 9.1 summarizes what our grad-student researchers found. Cells containing italic type indicate arrangements that we consider

TABLE 9.1
A Tale of Six Cities

Service	Park Management	Emergency Medical Services	Worker Training	Preschool Education
Boston	Significant private roles, but mostly through contracts controlled by city agency. Public resources swamp spending by private voluntary groups.	City ambulance fleet and employees handle most emergency calls, with small amount of overflow delegated by contract.	*Extensive network of public, private, and nonprofit organizations collaborate to deliver training.*	*All services delegated to a single nonprofit.*
Colorado Springs	Some private grants for capital projects, some organized volunteer work, but city department with budget of roughly $20 million dominates park management.	All EMS services contracted out to a single private provider.	Most training delivered by public workforce-development center; a few specialized training services contracted out.	*All services delegated to a single nonprofit.*
Louisville	*Explicit and strategic use of collaborative model to upgrade city's parks and ensure long-term support for maintenance.*	As in Boston, city ambulance fleet and employees handle most emergency calls, with small amount of overflow delegated by contract.	Not enough data	All services delivered by public school system.

Miami	City employees do most park management work; trusts with joint public-private governance manage two parks.	Emergency medical services almost entirely handled directly by government.	*Extensive reliance on for-profit and nonprofit private organizations to run training centers.*	Roughly half of services delivered by public agency, the other half by a mix of nonprofit and faith-based organizations.
Oakland	City employees do most park management work; small amount of delegation by simple contract, not collaboration.	As in Colorado Springs, EMS contracted out to single private provider.	*Mix of direct governmental delivery and contracts with nonprofits.*	Not enough data
Raleigh	City employees do most park management work, supplemented by limited organized volunteering.	*A network of nonprofits under agreement with government provides ambulance services.*	*Training centers operated by board with public funding and mixed public-private governance.*	*All services delegated to a single nonprofit.*

collaborative. Every city but Oakland employed collaborative governance for some service, but none took a collaborative approach to all
four services. Every service was carried out collaboratively *somewhere*,
but no service was collaborative *everywhere*. The table reflects two
somewhat surprising findings: first, no service displays much more of
a trend toward collaboration than the others; and, second, no city in
our sample relied on collaboration dramatically more than the others.

Our six-city summer research study is just a small pilot for the
kind of systematic investigation that needs to be done before anyone
can make confident generalizations about the extent, intensity, or motivations of collaborative governance at the local level. There might be
excellent reasons for cities to do the same thing differently, and we by
no means want to suggest that collaboration is the right answer for
any of these services. But we find the pattern—or rather the lack of a
pattern—an interesting hint that we shouldn't expect public officials
elsewhere to converge on a particular model either because it so obviously lends itself to collaboration, or because it's been tried successfully in other locales. The evolution of public service delivery models
isn't like biology, in which natural selection relentlessly weeds out un-
successful options and leaves standing only the versions that are well
suited to their context. Neither is it like a densely interconnected industry where what works at one firm is quickly imitated at another.
When it comes to getting public work accomplished, we see a major
role for intelligent design—the search for a good fit between the characteristics of a task and the capabilities of the institutions assigned to
perform it—of the sort this book aims to encourage.

Goldilocks on Collaboration

If Goldilocks were to review the evidence on collaboration—in our
six cities and beyond—she would observe it was sometimes used too
little, sometimes too much, sometimes just right, and sometimes,
alas, just wrong. Multiple factors can lead collaboration to be under-
utilized, misapplied, or abused. *A failure of imagination* prevents
government from looking beyond the status quo when considering

options for discharging its duties. *Information gaps*—a dearth of data about collaborative alternatives to direct government delivery or cut-and-dried contracting—may prevent a government that thinks about collaborating from pursuing it beyond the thought.

Opposed interests represent a bigger challenge, since they may not yield even to inspired leadership, the spread of ideas, and fuller information. In the context of our six cities, and for those functions now carried out directly by government, potential opposed interests include the city workers already doing the jobs that could be better accomplished through collaboration. Their interests, and the political efforts those interests inspire, go far in explaining why direct governmental delivery dominates park maintenance in Oakland or emergency medical service in Boston. Government work is more attractive than private-sector work for some categories of workers who hold government jobs. It is only human for these government workers to resist the delegation of those tasks.[1] If the current framework for production is contractual outsourcing, conversely, the interests opposing collaboration will be private. The current private producers, not wanting to lose the returns from their contracts, will develop political allies to defend their interests. If the private interests lobby effectively, they will block the progression from simple contracting to subtler collaboration, even when the latter is the preferable delivery model. Dwight Eisenhower warned us against such a powerful opposed interest in his presidential farewell address, which gave rise to the term "military-industrial complex." Cozy contracts can be much more profitable to the entrenched private party than a well-crafted collaboration, particularly if some other party may be the government's partner in that collaboration.

A lack of governmental management capacity can stifle collaboration even if a governmental organization would welcome a collaborative approach as the best way of accomplishing a public purpose, and even if political challenges to collaboration could be met. A traditional public-sector institution may lack the talented personnel,

---

[1] See John D. Donahue, *The Warping of Government Work* (Harvard University Press, 2008), for evidence and arguments on this theme.

management systems, or other assets essential to orchestrating collaboration effectively. Of course, this produces a chicken-and-egg problem. If collaboration is never used in an area, the government will likely lack the resources to implement it effectively; but lacking those resources, it will not choose collaboration. Two alternatives suggest themselves: one option is to let capabilities and the use of collaboration grow concurrently; the other is to build our capacity to collaborate in the expectation of growing future use of the collaborative model. Part of the latter approach would require giving current and future public workers training in such areas as contracting, negotiation, evaluation, and finance, which are much more important in a collaborative world.[2]

Thus far we have discussed various reasons governments may fail to opt for collaboration when collaboration makes sense. A different set of pathologies is associated with the erroneous embrace of collaboration. The potential downside of the collaborative approach—wrongly selected, or badly implemented—spans a range from narrowly specific to sweepingly systemic. We discussed some of these dangers in chapter 3, "The Delegator's Dilemma," but a second pass is warranted here. Collaboration gone wrong, most obviously, can yield bad results for the task at hand. Costs can be high, quality low, innovation slow, and other metrics of service quality can disappoint, relative to expectations and to what could have been achieved through alternative approaches. More subtly, but perhaps more important, public priorities can be distorted as options are chosen for enactment not in order of their collective benefit but in order of their parochial appeal to private collaborators. Broader still is the risk that vital public institutions will atrophy or warp as private roles expand to occupy societal terrain better left to government.

Even when we pick the right missions to pursue through collaboration, and sign up the right private parties with whom to collaborate, success is far from assured. Three broad categories of problems can, and do, cause collaborative ventures to end in tears.

---

[2] Both of us, for many years, have been doing what we can to nudge the curriculum of Harvard's Kennedy School toward training in the skills most central to collaboration, for precareer, midcareer, and executive-education students alike.

Errors of conception. Government may simply play the wrong game. It may fumble on the form of delegation—choosing complex collaboration for a task well-suited to a simple contract, constraining private discretion when loose reins promise greater public value, or, conversely, granting ill-advised broad latitude to its private collaborator and suffering the consequences from discretion abused.

Errors of construction. Though the arena may be right, the design or implementation may be wrong. These errors feature missteps with respect to incentives, information, or assignment. Incentives may channel private energies in the wrong direction; if charter schools are paid on the basis of test scores for subjects covering a narrow subset of the curriculum, they may neglect to teach unmeasured dimensions of learning, however central they may be to intellectual growth. Information flows may be distorted, blocked, or uselessly slow. Tasks may be assigned to the wrong private collaborators, or the wrong government agency—one lacking the capacity or motive, or both, to labor toward success—may be charged with orchestrating the collaboration.

Errors of performance. Flaws are inevitable even in well-conceived, well-designed collaborations. There is an eternal proclivity for human endeavors to turn out worse, from time to time, than theory predicts that they should; Murphy's Law has not been repealed. Errors of performance are particularly likely when collaborative arrangements are put in place for the first time, for there has been no opportunity to adjust to realities. Put any new machine in operation, particularly in new surroundings, and some adjustments or modifications may be required, however effectively the machine has been designed. Even well-established arrangements must be monitored and altered as conditions change, including the identities and behaviors of the people involved. An ace manager may become complacent and lazy, an incentive scheme may drift out of alignment with a changing mission, or a heretofore honest employee may give in to temptation.

Poor management of a collaborative arrangement lies not in avoiding all errors, but in failing to catch errors in time to remedy them. The goal should not be to achieve perfection—avoiding any hint of any of these types of errors—but to strike some achievable balance that inevitably falls short of perfection. Errors of conception should be rare, those of construction only occasional, and those of performance inevitably common, but swiftly corrected. If such standards are met, a governmental repertoire that includes collaboration will produce results vastly superior to those of the traditional models involving only pure government production, on the one hand, or conventional contractual outsourcing, on the other. And Goldilocks will pronounce her verdict: "Just right."

Reaching the Right Pattern

In collaboration as in golf, the critical question for those calibrating what counts as par concerns the number and toughness of the obstacles. The odds for success or failure in collaboration in any particular case, and the relative prevalence of commendable versus regrettable outcomes in cross-sectoral undertakings, depend on a set of conditions that are easy to summarize but sometimes hard to measure, and usually far harder still to engineer in practice.

Alignment of interests. Perhaps the most fundamental condition for success is a reasonably close alignment of interest between the public at large and the private actors engaged in a collaborative enterprise. At one extreme, where public and private interests sharply diverge, shared discretion poses grave dangers. In such circumstances, blunter relationships—cut-and-dried contracts, classic regulation—are better bets for engaging private capacity. And in such circumstances the case can be compelling for government to act on its own. Consider the formulation of foreign policy. Most of us, whatever our political leanings, will concede that it's possible for government to make a mess of foreign affairs. Yet virtually no one would propose giving discretion over foreign-policy choices to private players, however shrewd or well informed, lest they hijack diplomacy to serve their own purposes.

At the other extreme, where public and private interests are perfectly aligned, there is no need for the managerial complexities of collaboration. Government can stand aside as private capacity creates public value of its own accord, perhaps providing some subsidies, if

appropriate, to ramp up the scale of activities with the happy property of systematically and simultaneously generating public and private benefits.

It is when interests are somewhat, but not fully, aligned that collaboration gets interesting. It is too useful a tool, after all, to reserve for
the rare occasions when it's a cinch to apply. Further considerations
come into play.

Consensus about the nature of public value. Collaboration has the
best chance to flourish when all agree that it serves a worthy goal.
Nobody disputes that higher scores on math tests are a good thing, or
that higher rates of HIV infection are a bad thing. This should lessen
concern about discretionary private involvement in efforts to raise
math scores or lower HIV prevalence. But when goals are contested,
private roles can summon unease. Conservatives might be uncomfortable having Planned Parenthood involved in USAID's population-
control programs, while liberals might be uneasy about accepting
advertising firms' offers to help shape elementary school curricula.
And even if there were full agreement on which direction counts as
forward on each dimension—"more" for test scores, "less" for HIV—
there might be controversy on how much weight to accord different
dimensions. For example, while all might agree that high math scores
are better than low math scores, all things being equal, some might
feel rather strongly that all things are *not* necessarily equal since
schools might boost math scores by draining time and attention from
other, even more valuable aspects of the curriculum. Other groups
might feel that HIV is getting too many resources relative to Alz-
heimer's or alcoholism or cancer. Ambiguity or controversy about
relative priorities, or simply dramatically different weighting of alternative goals, can preclude the open-minded ecumenism about means
that is a hallmark of collaborative governance.

Readily measured performance. Even when ends are contested, collaboration can remain a feasible prospect when all aspects of performance are readily measured and monitored. For example, a business
group bidding for the right to manage a city park may be primarily
interested in the park's contribution to retail sales and real estate values. But if it's easy for government to determine whether the park is

accessible to all users, open and well-maintained on weekends and evenings as well as during business hours, and so on, then the agent's narrow interests present no impediment to effective collaboration. If some business-oriented foreign-policy organization were managing our trade relationships, conversely, it would be much harder to know whether it had bargained in the public interest when striking the balance between defending intellectual property and defending human rights. This ability to monitor makes it sensible to collaborate on park management, but not on tariff policy.

Collaboration and Comparative Advantage

A broad-spectrum prerequisite to successful collaborative governance is a clear-eyed view of collaboration as one model within a wider repertoire of ways to get public work accomplished. Conceptual snares can cause confusion on this score, and a few merit special attention.

Preferences about delivery models, often quite fiercely defended preferences, are commonplace in discussions about government. For-profit contractors, classic public agencies, secular nonprofits, faith-based organizations, local grassroots operations, and all manner of partnerships and alliances: each has its champions. Despite their ubiquity, such preferences strike us as neither logical nor helpful for the policy debate. It is understandable, if not particularly admirable, for a governmental employee, or an investor in a government contracting firm—with concrete stakes in the choice—to care about the means by which government pursues its goals. But observers with seemingly little to gain or lose frequently feel strongly about the merits and defects of particular collective action models.

Sometimes such preferences represent sensible generalizations anchored on inferences from experience. If you have encountered a dozen independent public authorities, each pursuing several different kinds of public missions, and all of them operate inefficiently and with little regard for citizens' priorities, you might be predisposed to reject the public-authority model proposed for a thirteenth case. More frequently, we suspect, delivery-model preferences have a sort of symbolic value to those who embrace them. Readiness to assign public tasks to public agencies or private contractors or informal neighborhood groups often reflects deep, not entirely conscious, not entirely rational convictions about how the world ought to work.[3]

We recognize that we are not immune to this sort of ideological tropism toward particular organizational forms. The two of us probably lean in opposite directions as often as not, however, which acts to curb any joint bias. More to the point, we try hard to treat delivery models as instrumentally, not intrinsically, valuable. (Even those who care about institutions based on the relationships and norms they breed are taking an instrumental view of the case.) We also recognize, though, that not everyone is going to be indifferent about choices among alternative mechanisms, which are, after all, constructed primarily of human beings and propelled in large part by human appetites, emotions, and convictions.

Biases in perception further complicate the preference for particular delivery mechanisms. The term "availability bias" refers to the tendency to judge the frequency of an event by how easily an example can be brought to mind.[4] Someone who has witnessed a dramatic success by some faith-based organization or a neighborhood group carrying out some public task is likely to believe—perhaps without even being conscious of the sources or even the existence of this belief— that such successes are common, or even inevitable. Someone else who has encountered a calamitous collaboration, conversely, will be inclined to assume that failure is the norm—with neither recognizing how a vivid instance can trump systematic efforts to assess likelihood.

An analytic approach to the matching of missions and means, in its strongest form, would assign tasks to delivery models (agencies, contractors, volunteers, collaborations, and so on) in terms of the absolute goodness-of-fit between the task to be pursued and each

---

[3] They are not entirely irrational, either, of course. If you care a lot about the norms and relationships and habits of mind that faith-based organizations or for-profit firms or whatever tend to inculcate, you will want there to be a lot of your preferred organizational form, and you might quite logically incorporate this desire into the schedule of preferences that you deploy as a citizen.

[4] Amos Tversky and Daniel Kahneman, "Judgment under Uncertainty: Heuristics and Biases," *Science*, n.s., 185, no. 4157 (September 27, 1974): 1127–1128.

organizational option. Whatever collective-action model is most conducive to the efficient and accountable accomplishment of a task should be chosen, function by function, irrespective of the organizational ecology these choices produce in the aggregate. But suppose that you happen to be confident that most private organizations are capable and public spirited, and that most of the things the government does are clear and straightforward and easily delegated. And suppose I worry a lot about government's complicated goals and the links among functions and the ways that ill-informed or sleazy private players might pervert them. Whether we think that the collaborative realm should constitute a big or small share of what government does, we may well be able to agree on which functions are *comparatively* better and worse suited to the collaborative approach. In other words, we can come together to gauge a delivery model's fitness for a particular task, not on an absolute basis, but in relative terms.

Observers with wildly divergent views about the overall worth of an institutional form can often see eye-to-eye on its ranking across different applications. Consider three tasks that a city must undertake: pick up the garbage, install and operate a new light railway, and administer the tax department. If given his druthers, A would like to see city workers handle all three tasks, whereas B would put private entities in charge of everything. But we suspect that if both were told that one service had to be contracted, one had to be subject to a collaborative approach, and the third had to be city run, they both would agree that garbage would do well with contract, the light rail with collaboration, and the tax department with municipal employees.[5]

Even if one prefers more corporations and fewer agencies (or vice versa), more local initiatives and fewer federal standards (or vice versa), more secular institutions and fewer religious ones (or vice versa)— indeed, even if one has fierce convictions about the share some particular institutional form should claim across society's organizational

---

[5] The comparative advantage approach was first developed for international trade, assessing which countries had a relative advantage in producing different goods. In the original example, England could gain by trading wool to Portugal for wine as long as it had a relative advantage in wool, even though it could produce either good using less labor than Portugal used.

Tax Administration	Garbage Collection	Light-Rail Transport System
City Agency	Contract	Collaboration

Fig. 9.1 Comparative Advantage across Tasks

repertoire—one can still embrace the analytic approach, so long as it is tuned to the logic of comparative advantage. I might believe that faith-based organizations affirm bedrock American values and incubate primal virtues, and so should be encouraged to flourish. You might believe that they stifle reason, stir up faction, and pervert public services. But we could still consult the same prudential considerations and concur that the advantages of faith-based organizations are more valuable, and the disadvantages less troubling, in treating drug addiction than in forecasting the weather. Similarly, you might celebrate private enterprise as the wellspring of free culture, and I might fear the profit motive as a corrosive influence once it escapes the narrow commercial realm. But we may nonetheless be able to reach agreement that a voucher program relying on for-profit providers is a better idea for adult worker training than it is for primary education for young children. The overall size of government is something none of us can control. So let's embrace the principle of comparative advantage in the service of a civil, pragmatic conversation about means.

Alternative Ways to Engage Private Players in Public Missions

We are far from the first observers to notice that private actors are heavily involved in efforts to create public value. For a wide range of reasons, many of them explored in earlier chapters, it is unrealistic today—if it was ever an option—to relegate all collective missions to government alone. Resource imbalances, shortfalls in key competencies, information gaps, legitimacy concerns, and a vast array of other considerations motivate the involvement of private organizations. And we readily concede that our way is not the only way. Two different approaches that may be seen as alternatives to what we describe as collaborative governance warrant some attention here.

Public-private partnerships. This approach has been associated with both fine scholarship and admirable practical action. Our complaint against the concept, however, is its imprecision. On occasion, partnership—with its connotation that the two parties are in roughly parallel situations, as with business partners who align their efforts to pursue the commercial goals that motivate them both—is an apt description for the relationship between public and private actors. However, among both academics and practitioners public-private partnership has become a perniciously broad category, spanning the whole spectrum of delegation from cut-and-dried contractual outsourcing to the loftiest forms of philanthropy. At either of those extremes, the concept of partnership misrepresents the nature of the relationship. And in between, the crucial domain of collaboration, the roles of government and private party are rarely even roughly parallel. Thus the term "partnership" misses the essence of the situation all along the spectrum of public and private engagement.

Asking, "Do public-private partnerships work?" is as unhelpful as asking, "Do animals belong inside?" The answer depends so much on particulars (gerbil or orca or cow? aquarium or barn or rec room?) that no categorical response makes sense. Thus our practice, which we commend to your attention, is to disaggregate forms of delegation, discriminating among categories according to the allocation of discretion, and to deal separately with contracting, voluntarism, and the broad middle ground we label collaborative governance. Think of it as public-private partnership, if you prefer, but beware the dangers of getting mired in that conceptual swamp.

Corporate social responsibility. An admirably well-defined but (we believe) mistaken conception of the private corporation's public role generates another impediment to clear thinking about collaboration. Public-private collaboration and corporate social responsibility present competing visions for how to unleash corporate capacity to create public value, and these models differ more profoundly than is commonly realized.

The first model, the collaborative approach we have described, clearly envisages deploying private expertise, energy, and resources to augment government's effectiveness. Driven by whatever blend of motives—pure commercial considerations, the benefits it receives from improved public performance in an area, the urge to burnish its image, the convictions of senior leaders or rank-and-file employees, or self-aggrandizement by the firm's executives—a firm commits itself to maintain a street, support a school, or combat a disease. The firm's discretion is substantial—but it is still circumscribed. Some unit of formal government, ultimately answerable to the electorate, defines public value, determines priorities, and gauges success or failure. It is this constrained range of private discretion, and ultimate deference to the electorate for the definition of value, that is the hallmark of collaborative governance. The collaborative model combines humility about government's operational capacity with an insistence that government cannot abdicate its primordial role in designating legitimate collective missions.

Corporate social responsibility represents a quite different approach to harnessing private capacity to public goals. Proponents of this approach concur with collaboration advocates that government is frequently at an operational disadvantage relative to private organizations. But it discounts the notion that government has any privileged role with respect to defining value, setting priorities, or assessing outcomes. By this view government's disabilities—stemming from cluttered and contested agendas and the lack of clear accountability—undercut its capacity to specify, not just to accomplish, key collective missions. Socially responsible corporations thus can, and indeed must, act on their own to advance the public interest without waiting for government's imprimatur. Missions suggested by employees, customers, or other constituencies; or developed as priorities by community-relations departments; or distilled from chief executives' consciences—all these are presumed to be at least as valid as those that emerge from some surely tangled and possibly corrupted legislative process.

The Conference Board commissioned a survey of some twenty-five thousand people in twenty-three countries about the scope and nature of corporate responsibilities. Respondents were asked whether corporations' roles should be defined as "making a profit, paying taxes, employing people, and obeying all laws," or whether firms should be expected to "exceed all laws, set a higher ethical standard, and help build a better society." In every developed industrial country, significant majorities opted for the second, more ambitious, definition of corporate responsibilities.[6]

Even if we were to stipulate that such behavior is desirable, the question remains whether it will be reliably forthcoming. Corporations that espouse such responsibilities tend to be quite strategic about the domains in which responsibilities are exercised. Public visibility, relatively low cost, and potential commercial advantage are primary considerations.[7] Within some range, and with respect to some sorts of behavior, it makes eminent sense for corporations to strive to meet society's expectations for responsibility. It is certainly prudent to refrain from actions that offend your employees or repel your customers. A chain of pet-grooming salons would be unwise to launch a fur-coat subsidiary, for instance. Beyond this negative imperative, activities that burnish a corporation's reputation may increase net revenues by attracting customers or justifying a price premium relative to less-admired producers. A company presumably will be able to attract better workers, at lower cost, if joining its payroll brings prestige rather than shame. To the extent that lenders and investors are concerned about the kinds of activities their resources enable— and are equipped and inclined to make trade-offs between corporate behavior and financial returns—responsibility can lower the cost of capital. And in any legitimate democracy, of course, firms should obey the law and pay the taxes they owe.

---

[6] Millennium Poll on Corporate Social Responsibility (Environics International, Ltd; Prince of Wales Foundation; The Conference Board, Toronto, 1999).

[7] Google's strong support for hybrid cars comes to mind. The corporation buys only such vehicles, subsidizes its employees when they buy them, and is subsidizing research in this area. Admirable. But it is also the case that Google owns trivially few cars relative to its $150 billion market capitalization, while the firm has received extraordinary favorable publicity for this move. It has made contributions in the $1 and $10 million range, not much for a company worth as much as Google. If the company committed to an effort to diminish by, say, 20 percent the electricity it uses to run its operations, that would represent a major environmental benefit, but it would also be extremely expensive and less newsworthy.

When the proposed agenda is costly, and extends beyond reputational polish and a decent respect for the opinions of customers, workers, neighbors, and other constituencies, the logic of corporate social responsibility comes into question. As missions move closer to the core functions we traditionally assign to governments—to borrow from the Constitution's preamble, "establishing justice, insuring domestic tranquility, providing for the common defense, promoting the general welfare, and securing the blessings of liberty"—then assigning the work to corporate managers, no matter how enlightened, becomes problematic. There are two broad objections, each sufficient on its own to cast doubt on ambitious variants of corporate social responsibility.

First, corporate managers tend not to be the most appropriate parties to define, evaluate, and rank public priorities. This is not so much because they lack relevant training, experience, or temperament—though frequently they do—as because they are not embedded in the machinery of representation that separates true republics from every other sort of society. They are not entangled in the intricate networks by which the public at large conveys its concerns, its priorities, its permission, and its resources to those who would act in its name. This freedom from political feedback and encumbrance, which keeps corporate social initiatives nimble and focused, radically circumscribes their claim to legitimacy.

Second, to the extent that managers devote their own time and energy, and the resources of their firms, to the pursuit of the broad public good undiluted by commercial motivation, they risk neglecting —indeed, they almost certainly *do* neglect—the fiduciary duties that define their mission, and that enable our capitalist economy to keep on delivering the goods. This is not the case, to be clear, when there is a link between beneficence and the bottom line. If the expectation is that corporate virtue will be rewarded in the currency of shareholder value, this objection loses force. We don't dispute the justification for corporate philanthropy in the home community, as a goodwill gesture, or for installing equipment that exceeds current regulatory requirements in the expectation that current standards are too timid and will eventually be tightened. But without a reasonably direct, reasonably certain link to shareholder value, managers' claims to be serving the greater good can become convenient excuses for glorifying CEOs while shirking on fiduciary duties.

The current enthusiasm for corporate social responsibility displays some striking parallels with a policy debate from the 1980s. Distressed by the erosion of industrial mainstays like steel and autos, dissatisfied with America's slipping position in television and other mature electronics industries, and alarmed that Japan and Europe seemed poised to seize the lead in high-tech, some academics and politicians called for more direct government influence over key corporate investment decisions. America's private sector, it was alleged, was blundering at its core task of optimal capital allocation and missing the boat on promising new industries. Proposals for unleashing the public sector to compensate for private-sector failings were clustered under the omnibus term "industrial policy."

Some advocates called for government to undertake major investments on its own, with an eye to rescuing cities in decline and shoring up the middle class, while others endorsed preferential tax rates or alternative devices to tilt resources toward favored categories of investment. Some opponents, meanwhile, charged that industrial policy was just a newfangled label for old-fashioned socialism. Other skeptics framed a less ideological, more analytical critique. They conceded that the trajectory of industrial change was doing considerable damage to some American cities and regions, and more broadly to the middle-class economy of the early postwar decades. It did not follow, however, that the trajectories marked economic wrong turns—rather than the creative (but uncomfortable) destruction inherent in the capitalist system—or even if they were wrong turns, that government would be very good at getting the economy back on track. Targeting investment, particularly in opposition to market forces, requires skills and norms and institutional structures that American government did not possess and—for deep-rooted reasons—could not readily acquire.

Industrial policy enthusiasts, in other words, were asking the public sector to perform tasks for which it was inherently ill suited. Many advocates eventually concurred with this assessment and called for a different strategy. Rather than attempting to pick winning industries, government should concentrate on improving infrastructure, promoting basic science, and (especially) ensuring widespread, ongoing access to high-quality education and training. By investing in the prerequisites for productivity, government could improve the odds that the pattern of investments yielded by private capital markets would support widespread prosperity.

To be sure, that strategy, too, posed significant challenges in implementation. Few would argue that results over the past generation have been entirely satisfying—as advocates warned, the middle class has eroded and income inequality has increased. But the strategy of investing in infrastructure and human capital, rather than trying to fine-tune industrial investment, capitalized on a more realistic conception of what our governmental organizations could do well. Making the right investments in highways, basic research, and education—while by no means a sure thing—is a much more appropriate domain for government than making the right investments in high-definition television, biotechnology, or next-generation automobiles. It is understandable that advocates wished government had a more direct way to shore up the middle-class economy, but wishing wouldn't make it so.

Mirroring the industrial-policy boom and bust of a generation back, today's widespread enthusiasm for responsible corporations to compensate for feckless government rests on a core confusion about sectoral strengths and weaknesses. Some very real problems would have been averted, back in the 1980s, had American government been capable of choosing wisely and dispassionately among industrial investment alternatives. Similarly it would be an excellent thing if corporations today were systematically capable of defining, and willing to address, vital public missions. Both aspirations, alas, assume more versatility than either sector of the economy can be expected to display in a large, complex, and democratic nation.

Conceptual confusion, of the sort this book aims to combat, is one major cause of society's failure to allocate tasks optimally across alternative organizational models. Another, subtler, barrier arises from the distortions in America's economy that make government a

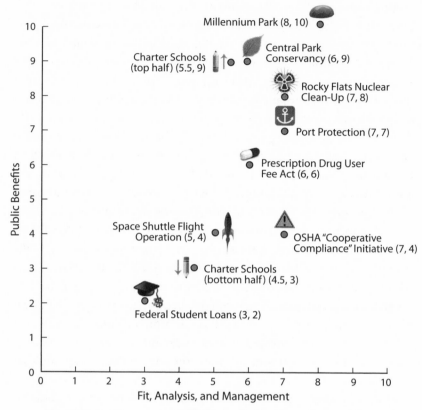

Fig. 9.2 Better Governance Yields Better Performance: Concrete Cases

particularly attractive employer for less-fortunate workers but the last choice for the sorts of talented and lucky workers whose private-sector prospects have soared in recent decades. As we suggested earlier in this chapter, many failures to seize what are otherwise excellent opportunities to employ collaboration come from resistance by public workers who fear, often quite rationally, that if delegation renders their government jobs redundant, they will never find equally desirable work. At the other end of the scale, there is an understandable reluctance of elite workers to accept public employment. The chronic talent drought within government does much to explain why the public sector uses collaborative governance—a notably talent-intensive way of getting things done—less frequently and less adroitly than it might. And elite workers' aversion to governmental careers does much to explain why so many of them yearn to believe that well-paid, high-status corporate jobs offer a perfectly valid perch for public service. The desire is understandable, but, once again, wishing doesn't make it so.

We conclude this chapter with a reprise of the theme that getting collaboration right is fundamentally a matter of *governance*. The quality of outcomes hinges on how well those on the public side of the relationship carry out the work summarized in the prior chapter's cycle of collaboration—an iterative process of analysis, assignment, design, and assessment. Figure 9.2 arrays some of the concrete cases we've discussed on two dimensions. The horizontal axis tracks (on a 0-to-10 scale) our sense of whether government appropriately chose the collaborative model, correctly analyzed the situation, and adroitly managed its relationship with the private sector. The vertical axis tracks (also on a subjective but carefully applied 0-to-10 scale) our bottom-line judgment of the public value created. There is no simple, straight-line relationship. Sometimes fate frowns on the best-laid plans, and sometimes luck smiles on careless conceptions. But the general trend is a strong one: the more diligent, honest, and skillful are the leadership and management on the public side, the more successful, on average, have been efforts at collaborative governance.

Chapter 10

◇◇◇

Forging the Future: Payoffs and Perils

We began chapter 1 marveling at the transformation of New York's Central Park, and the emergence of Chicago's festive Millennium Park out of a tattered tract of abandoned rail yard. You already know now how savvy public managers and an inspired private conservancy rescued Central Park from the blight that had descended upon it. How Chicago collaborated to create Millennium Park is a different tale and one worth telling.

The Creation of Millennium Park

Chicago, that most pragmatic and least sentimental of great American cities, has a soft spot for scenery. Citizens especially cherish the Lake Michigan shoreline. Downtown's dense forest of skyscrapers stops dead at Michigan Avenue to make way for some three hundred acres of lakefront parkland. Preserving lakeside green space goes way back to Chicago's earliest days, formalized as long ago as 1835 with a resolution to maintain the stretch east of Michigan Avenue "forever free of buildings."[1] As the city grew and downtown space turned scarce and valuable, however, the tradition came under pressure. Aaron Montgomery Ward, the mail-order mogul, dedicated much of his fortune to a series of lawsuits around the turn of the last century blocking development within what came to be known as Grant Park.

---

[1] Chicago Park District Web site, Grant Park history, at http://www.chicagoparkdistrict.com/index.cfm/fuseaction/parks.detail/object_id/83AA6305-ADBE-4D8A-B333-004449057EA9, accessed September 2007, and "Say No to Museum in Park" (editorial), *Chicago Sun-Times*, September 21, 2007, p. 35.

In 1909 the tradition was codified as the "Chicago Plan," which permitted a handful of decorous public structures—eventually to include Chicago's famous Art Institute, Shedd Aquarium, Adler Planetarium, and Field Museum of Natural History—but otherwise barred development on a broad swath of shoreline.[2]

For well over a century, however, a ragged tract at Grant Park's northwestern edge stood as an exception. In the mid-1800s the city had ceded the twenty-four-acre lot to the Illinois Central Railroad for its downtown terminus complex, largely as recompense for the railroad's extensive lakefront landfill and erosion-control projects. Rail transit and related industries dominated Chicago's economy for decades more, but by the last fifth of the twentieth century the industry's economic significance had faded drastically. The muddy gap in the lakefront parkland deteriorated from a bustling maintenance and switching yard, to a storage space for damaged or redundant rolling stock, and finally to an improvised parking lot for Illinois Central employees, with just a mothballed boxcar or two and a wisp of rusty track attesting to its original purpose.

The Mayor's Teeth and the Lawyer's Bike

Richard M. Daley, first elected in 1989, has been mayor of Chicago longer than anybody, including his fabled father, "Hizzoner" Richard J. Daley.[3] Prominent among Daley's abiding ambitions is to burnish Chicago's aesthetics, especially downtown. He instinctively resented the "eyesore on the city's front lawn" represented by the Illinois Central

[2] This historical background draws on Timothy J. Gilfoyle, *Millennium Park: Creating a Chicago Landmark* (University of Chicago Press, 2006), pp. 5–30. It is worth starting with a bit of history and noting what did not happen. When Frederick Law Olmsted created Central Park in New York in the second half of the nineteenth century, he worked on commission to the city's government. When Robert Moses reshaped New York's park system—and much of the rest of the city—in the mid-twentieth century, he was a municipal employee. But the startling transformation of that Chicago tract, as the twentieth century gave way to the twenty-first, took place in an era when resources for vast public undertakings were scarce, and expansive minds were more frequently found in the private sector. Different times required a different model.

[3] The mayor—who shocked Chicago by declaring that he would not run for reelection in 2011, instead of dying in office like his father—exceeded his father's tenure shortly before this book was published.

parcel, and his irritation was regularly reinforced by the fact that the waiting-room window at his dentist's office overlooked the site.[4] Subjected to doubly painful twice-yearly views of the gravel-strewn lot—the mayor was meticulous about his six-month dental checkups—he finally ordered his staff to find out whether there was any way to wrest the parcel away from the railroad and put it to better use.

As it happened, the lead attorney of the Chicago Park District, Randall Mehrberg, had been thinking along the same lines. A few years earlier, Mehrberg had been in private practice, specializing in railroad law. He was young and vigorous, and liked to get his exercise on long mountain-bike explorations of Chicago's urban byways. Both on the job and on the bike he had encountered the Illinois Central's parking lot, and thought that the piece of land made much more sense as a park. That opinion stayed with him as he became the top lawyer for the Chicago park system.

Mehrberg reviewed old legal documents. What he found was that, contrary to almost universal belief, Chicago had not *given* the parcel to the railroad back in the 1850s. Rather, it had granted it the right of use, indefinitely, for "railroad purposes." Free parking for office workers at the Illinois Central and its affiliates, Merhberg reasoned, hardly counted, and in 1996 he filed suit to force the railroad to return the parcel to the city.[5] Then a lucky break—quickly recognized and deftly exploited by Chicago officials—let the city achieve the same result by milder means. Canadian National Railway announced its intention to acquire the Illinois Central. Park District lawyers realized that if the Illinois Central *gave* the city its now-disputed rights to the twenty-four-acre parcel, it could claim a hefty tax deduction. Such a tax break, in the year prior to a merger, would sharply boost after-tax earnings and justify a higher acquisition price. When the city lawyers explained that a donation could benefit both Chicago and the Illinois Central—at the expense of federal taxpayers and Canadian National—the rail-

---

[4] Andrew Martin and Laurie Cohen, "Millennium Park Flounders as Deadlines, Budget Blown; Poor Plans, Constant Changes Slow Progress, Drive Up Price—and City Taxpayers May Have to Help Make Up Difference," *Chicago Tribune*, August 5, 2001.

[5] Gilfoyle, *Millennium Park*, pp. 82 and 364.

road agreed to the deal. Toward the end of 1997 the twenty-four acres were returned to public hands.[6]

Shaping the Plan

The city's initial plan centered on transforming the parcel from a wasteful private parking lot to an efficient public parking structure— a twenty-five-hundred-space underground garage for office workers and visitors to Grant Park cultural facilities. An aide to Daley summarized the city's goal thus: to "build the parking structure and maybe put grass on top."[7] The plan was soon revised, however, to make the garage rooftop a park in its own right, featuring cultural attractions, to name it for the impending millennium, and to dedicate it in 2000. A proper park, however, especially if it included facilities beyond green space, would require funding beyond the $120 million needed for the garage itself. Initial estimates were that $30 million would be required. Chicagoans in the late 1990s, like the citizens of most cities most of the time, tended to make high culture a low priority for tax dollars. So Mayor Daley decided to seek private financing for the park. He approached John Bryan, the chairman of food-products giant Sara Lee, to head a campaign to raise the $30 million for "enhancements on top of the garage."[8]

The mayor was pushing on an open door. Bryan quickly persuaded Daley to raise his sights. Bryan had already chaired a record-breaking capital campaign for Chicago's Lyric Opera House and Orchestra Hall, and felt $30 million was too timid a target to set for private contributions to an arts-oriented downtown park. He proposed going for $60 million, with an explicit proviso for private discretion: donors must be given an opportunity to shape the vision. Bryan and Daley considered and rejected the conventional fund-raising approach of multiple tiers encompassing many contributors—from small-ticket "supporters" on up. They favored instead a strategy targeting only

[6] Ibid., p. 82.
[7] Ibid., p. 83.
[8] Ibid., pp. 94–97.

heavy hitters. There would be two categories of contributions. A handful of wealthy individuals, families, and firms would be invited to donate at least $3 million to develop a particular segment of the park or cultural asset within it, in exchange for naming rights and "participation in the development of that space." Other contributors would provide support to the overall park project and would be recognized on an appropriately visible monument. To join even the lower tier would require a minimum donation of $1 million.[9]

Raising the Money and Building the Park

The strategy of seeking private money only in big chunks, which an admirer and aspiring copier would later call "clever and courageous," paid off for Millennium Park.[10] Bryan recalled the fund-raising campaign as "the easiest sell" of his career.[11] By the time the park opened, ninety-two donors had contributed at least $1 million; and eight individuals or organizations had contributed more—often much more —than the $3 million entry ticket for naming and shaping an attraction. The Pritzker family—Chicago's wealthiest, with a vast fortune flowing from a portfolio of businesses including the Hyatt hotel chain— put up $15 million for a performance hall to honor Jay Pritzker, its recently deceased patriarch.[12] The Crown family, with stakes in Maytag, the Chicago Bulls, and the New York Yankees, put up a similar sum for a landmark fountain.[13] A consortium of donors put up an initial $6 million, and eventually far more, for a large-scale sculpture by Anish Kapoor to anchor AT&T Plaza. Check after check poured in to create Wrigley Square, Bank One Promenade, the BP Bridge, the McCormick Tribune Plaza, and on through the list of civic-minded,

[9] Martin and Cohen, "Millennium Park Flounders."

[10] Noreen S. Ahmed-Ullah, "Millennium Park Wows VIP Visitors: President of Czech Republic, Entourage, Get Whirlwind Tour, *Chicago Tribune*, April 28, 2006.

[11] Martin and Cohen, "Millennium Park Flounders."

[12] Andrew Herrmann, "$475 Million Millennium Park Set to Open July 16," *Chicago Sun-Times*, March 11, 2004, p. 8.

[13] http://www.forbes.com/lists/2005/54/58EE.html, accessed September 2007.

image-conscious Chicago institutions.[14] Bryan's fund-raising campaign soared beyond its initial targets of $30 million and then $60 million. Eventually $205 million of private money poured in to build, adorn, and maintain Millennium Park.

The financial bounty did not assure success. Actually creating the park took longer and cost more than anyone had anticipated. The target of mid-2000 came and went with no opening in sight. As delays stretched into 2003, then 2004, wisecrackers referred to the construction site as "Next-Millennium Park." As the schedule lengthened, the cost ballooned. What the city had originally envisioned as $30 million worth of "enhancements on top of the garage" ultimately grew into a cluster of cultural jewels costing more than ten times as much. But when a target of mid-2004 was finally set for a grand opening, the project director promised that Millennium Park would be worth both the wait and the price tag: "I think Chicago is going to be frankly blown away by it."[15]

He was right.

An Instant Icon

Millennium Park opened in the summer of 2004 to the sort of nearly unanimous acclaim all but unheard of in tough-minded, contentious Chicago.[16] The Pritzker Pavilion, the park's cultural anchor, was the latest masterpiece by superstar architect Frank Gehry—surely the only living architect to have appeared, in cartoon form, on both *The Simpsons* and the children's show *Arthur*. Like his other landmark buildings in Bilbao, Prague, and Los Angeles, Gehry's Chicago band shell featured bold planes of polished metal. Swirling ribbons of stainless steel framed the warm wood tones of the stage, and an intricate

---

[14] Tara Burqhart, "4 Years Late, Chicago Gets Millennium Park," Associated Press Online, May 15, 2004.

[15] Project director Ed Uhlir, quoted in ibid.

[16] Where no specific source is given, general information on Millennium Park comes from one author's experience with the park and the other's perusal of the detailed Web site at http://www.millenniumpark.org/.

lattice of metal tubes packed with hidden speakers swooped out over the Pavilion's four thousand seats and the lawn space that accommodated seven thousand additional listeners. Musicians swooned over the Pavilion's acoustics and its artist-friendly array of studios and practice space, and lovers of music and dance swarmed the venue for the free evening concerts and daytime open rehearsals, which were offered several times a week all summer long. The repertoire stretched from classical to hip-hop, from ballet to flamenco. The city's leading cultural institutions performed there; so did its youth and community groups.

If, as it sometimes seemed in the early twenty-first century, any city on Earth needed a Gehry construction to count as a serious cultural center, then Millennium Park alone qualified Chicago twice over. The BP Bridge was a second Gehry original, stainless steel banks framing a river of wooden planks meandering from the Pritzker Pavilion to the Daley Bicentennial Plaza. The bridge was sited to offer spectacular vistas of the skyline and the lake, gently graded to accommodate wheelchairs and fragile pedestrians, and carefully designed with sufficient bumps to deter skateboarders.

The Crown Fountain, anchoring another stretch of the park, managed simultaneously to exude cosmopolitanism and to celebrate, quite literally, the face of Chicago. Eager to avoid a boring pool of water surmounted by static stone, the Crown family had auditioned the world's top sculptors before hiring the up-and-coming Catalan artist Jaume Plensa to design something new and different. Plensa sought to radically reinvent the iconic urban fountain that mounted figures from history or mythology atop a bubbling pool. The new-millennium version he designed for the Crowns featured a placid rectangular pool mere millimeters deep, flanked by what looked at first like paired stone monoliths. But the slabs turned out to be fifty-foot towers of glass bricks laced with light-emitting diodes that turned them into giant television screens. To find the images to project on the screens, Plensa dispatched students from the Art Institute of Chicago to film the close-up faces of a thousand Chicagoans from all walks of life. The glass towers were programmed to cycle randomly among the faces, projecting them at monumental scale for five minutes or so, including a moment when each giant face purses its digital lips and a real-life spray of water arcs across the reflecting pool in a high-tech echo of old-world gargoyles.[17]

Perhaps the most improbable popular favorite was the Kapoor sculpture on AT&T Plaza. The sixty-six-foot-long dollop of gleaming steel reminded some of a giant bead of liquid mercury. The artist reported his intent to "engage the Chicago skyline so that one will see the clouds kind of floating in, with those very tall buildings reflected" —hence the official title of "Cloud Gate."[18] But to most Chicagoans, despite its gargantuan scale and metallic surface, the elliptical, asymmetric Kapoor sculpture quite obviously represented a bean. And to the artist's initial dismay, but with his eventual acceptance, the sculpture was known and loved from the start, by both the cultural elite and the hoi polloi, as "The Bean."

Beyond the high-profile cultural and artistic attractions, Millennium Park boasted manicured gardens; elegant paths; a skating rink; the McDonald's Cycle Center offering bike rentals, showers for cyclists, tours, maps, and pro-bike proselytizing; and the high-end Park Grill restaurant, where the food, by most accounts, was nothing special but the spectacular setting made tourists and locals willing to pay the price.[19] The park instantly found a place in Chicagoans' hearts. An unanticipated problem in the first few weeks showed its popularity; the dense crowds wore away the grass surrounding the art.[20] Well before the second anniversary of the park's opening, it had attracted more than five million visitors, and had drawn delegations of foreign visitors hoping to uncover the secret of how Chicago had built so thoroughly and suddenly successful a park.[21]

---

[17] The technological and logistical challenges behind this artistic feat are discussed in Emily Nunn, "Millennium Park's Spouting Faces," *Chicago Tribune*, January 27, 2005.

[18] Anish Kapoor quote from Millennium Park Web site.

[19] Zagat Survey online, at http://www.zagat.com/, accessed October 2007.

[20] Gilfoyle, *Millennium Park*, pp. 291–292.

[21] Ahmed-Ullah, "Millennium Park Wows VIP Visitors."

A Muffed Collaboration: American Health Care

Let's shift up several multiples of scope, complexity, and consequentiality, and down quite a few notches on the success scale, for our other concluding tale of collaboration. America's health-care system notoriously costs too much, delivers too little, and covers too few. We pay more, both absolutely and as a percentage of GNP, than do other developed nations, yet trail many of them in major indicators of health, such as life expectancy, infant mortality, and morbidity rates. Across a broad range of areas, it is obvious that American health care falls far short of potential.

Consider the use of information technology. We are the nation that invented the Internet, Google, and Facebook. We make the iPad a virtual home office and library, tap the online experience of thousands of people to learn about the quality of dozens of places to buy a camera or the reliability of tens of thousands of eBay sellers, and use Facebook to orchestrate our social life. Yet we make virtually no use of information technology to computerize medical records, to help formulate diagnoses, to learn from the observations of millions of Americans who have experienced particular procedures, prescriptions, and treatment plans,[22] or to assess the quality of medical-care institutions.

Some collaborative stumbles can be excused in part because America is well behind the frontier. Thus the Partnership for a New Generation of Vehicles had a monumental task getting American manufacturers to push high-mileage vehicles, given that the Japanese had such a lead in making fuel-sipping autos. The same excuse cannot be made for medical care. America leads the world in the production of new medical knowledge and products, and in the quality of our best delivery institutions. We have stumbled because we failed to capitalize on that advantage, to spread our superior capabilities to typical medical care delivery. Our problem is not ignorance but ineptitude.

---

[22] We recognize that privacy is important, but it should not be an overriding trump card, and existing encryption technologies should be sufficient to adequately protect the privacy of medical records while researchers learn from them.

Moreover, when we *have* reformed our health-care system, we have done it piecemeal, usually offering a patch in a politically appealing way. Medicare Part D, which subsidizes prescription coverage for the elderly, is a salient example. Though quite expensive, it did nothing to deal with the critical problems of our system: improving the average quality of care, controlling costs, and extending coverage to the un-insured. Excuse us a medical metaphor to make our point: the American medical care system is like a patient afflicted with a raft of grave chronic maladies, but whose doctor's past efforts first tackled his eczema, and then addressed his ingrown toenails. No doubt a benefit, on balance, and a balm against discomfort, but rather missing the most important problems.

The symptoms of poor performance in our health-care system are easy to see, but that tells us little about the underlying diagnosis. A major source of the problem is that the health-care system is pervasively collaborative, but we have not faced that central truth head-on. A lack of diagnosis is no more likely to lead to good results in the pursuit of public goals than it does in the practice of medicine.[23] Look at the evidence for our assertion. Government is responsible for financing a great deal of American health care both directly (primarily through Medicaid and Medicare) and indirectly through tax subsidies for health insurance premiums, favorable tax treatment for the nonprofit institutions that deliver so much care, and support for biomedical research and medical education. Yet government delivers but a sliver of care itself, delegating most of the work to private actors who operate with a range of discretion that is generally substantial but seldom crafted with insight. In short, in health care we chronically mismanage the public-private relationship. We ignore areas—such as promoting the widespread use of information technology to keep records, grade institutions, and learn from experience—that are appropriately a government responsibility.

[23] A poorly functioning system, like a patient with many maladies, is hard to diagnose. Minor problems may be thought to be major, and vice versa. What is required, but extremely difficult to conduct in the highly charged political atmosphere surrounding U.S. health care and health insurance, is a dispassionate examination of what is wrong. See Katherine Baicker and Amitabh Chandra, "Myths and Misconceptions about Health Insurance," *Health Affairs* 27, no. 6 (September/October 2008).

Similarly, we create insurance arrangements, such as Medicare Part D and Medigap, that violate central principles of effective insurance. Medicare Part D covers small prescription expenditures for an individual, and then has a hole where it covers none of them till expenditures get massive. Medigap, whose structure is strictly dictated by the government though coverage is provided through private insurers, reinsures the coinsurance and deductible payments that were designed to control Medicare expenditures. The government is thus orchestrating a program that defeats its own cost-control measures.

In some sense these are hopeful findings. Once we adequately recognize and focus on the prime game at hand, we can significantly improve the performance of a sector that takes up one-sixth of our economy. To be fair, the failures of analysis and management of the sort this book aims to remedy are but part of the explanation for the lamentable state of American health care. But they are an important part of the story.

In 2009, the nation struggled through a painful political process that led to passage of the Patient Protection and Affordable Care Act (PPACA). The overwhelming benefit of the act will be to lower the cost of coverage to a significant number of individuals by extending Medicaid and subsidizing insurance directly and through businesses. It also severely restricts the ability of insurers to raise rates on or restrict coverage for people with particular conditions, and expands some forms of coverage. The law supports the required expenditures by raising Medicare taxes on high earners, and cutting expenditures on high-cost Medicare Advantage plans.

However, the basic challenge of coping with the collaborative relationship between government and the private health-care sector is hardly addressed by these reforms. The only consequential measure to promote competition or cost-effective care was a requirement for state-level health insurance exchanges, starting in 2014. Medicare and Medicaid, the prime areas of direct expenditure by the government, were not touched. The tax deductibility of insurance premiums, a major tax subsidy that helps to enable all manner of inefficiencies, escaped nearly unscathed.

To be fair, the Obama administration has advocated measures to improve medical procedures and health outcomes apart from this legislation, and is spending nearly $20 billion dollars of the fiscal stimulus package to foster health information technology.[24] The PPACA also contains provisions for health system modernization. These include payment innovations, such as higher payment for preventive services, along with "bundled" payments for hospital, physician, and other services for single episodes. Moreover, they establish an Innovation Center to streamline the testing and subsequent expansion of demonstration and pilot programs within Medicare and Medicaid. The reform legislation also features provisions for rating medical care providers on cost and quality, and making that information broadly available, along with increased comparative effectiveness research. Whether this effort will be more like the proverbial mustard seed and eventually yield a bountiful harvest of cost-effectiveness, or more like the likewise-proverbial hill of beans, is far from clear.[25] But the supposedly earthshaking health insurance reform package—which may have drained the well of political will for many years to come—only lightly engaged the pivotal task of restructuring the collaborative relationship between the government and the private sector in health care.

To close this discussion of health care, we should mention a third critical collaborator, the citizen. Her health-conscious behavior could dramatically improve outcomes. But far too often Americans get their nutrition at McDonald's and their exercise punching the TV remote. Moreover, large numbers of us fail to take our medicines for chronic conditions,[26] or to eat well and get checkups during pregnancy. Too

---

[24] Additional spending will come from the Health Information Technology for Economics and Clinical Health (HITECH) Act, which went into effect in February 2010. It provides bonuses be paid to hospitals and physicians who adopt and use qualifying health IT. Letter from Robert A. Sunshine, acting director, CBO, to Charles B. Rangel, chairman, Committee on Ways and Means, U.S. House of Representatives, January 21, 2009.

[25] For a thoughtful and optimistic analysis from the progressive point of view, see David M. Cutler, Karen Davis, and Kristof Stremikis, "The Impact of Health Reform on Health System Spending," The Commonwealth Fund, the Center for American Progress, Issue Brief (May 21, 2010), vol. 88.

[26] Recent estimates are that as many as half of all patients do not faithfully follow their prescription medication regimens, leading to more than $100 billion spent on avoidable hospitalizations. Better adherence to antihypertensive treatment alone could prevent eighty-nine thousand premature deaths annually. See David M. Cutler and Wendy Everett, "Thinking Outside the Pillbox—Medication Adherence as a Priority for Healthcare Reform," New England Journal of Medicine, April 7, 2010, 10.1056.

many of us are underweight at birth and overweight in life. Health suffers. We require people to get twelve or thirteen years of schooling, but let them eat and exercise as they want. Here we tip our hats to Michelle Obama, who has made curbing the nation's obesity a central goal of her role as First Lady. Citizens are also poor stewards for health expenditures, primarily because we insure them so heavily against low-level expenditures. Thus we get much less health benefit than we should out of the dollars we spend.[27]

The Two Exemplars of Collaboration

Millennium Park displays in microcosm most of the major advantages, and just a few of the risks, of the collaborative approach to governance. Its origins reflect, in varying degrees, all of the motives for government to pursue its missions with the aid of private associates. The goal of augmenting resources was both obvious and amply achieved. Fund-raising efforts led by John Bryan brought in more money for the Pritzker Pavilion alone—and nearly as much money for just the Bean—as Mayor Daley had at first envisioned for the entire park. What had originally been seen as $30 million worth of prettification for the top of a parking garage eventually garnered more than ten times that investment, most of it from the private sector. And the payoff from that investment elevated Chicago a few notches

---

[27] See David Cutler and Richard Zeckhauser, "Extending the Theory to Meet the Practice of Insurance," in *Brookings-Wharton Papers on Financial Services*, ed. Robert E. Litan and Richard Herring (2004), pp. 1–53, which argues that extensive coverage for small expenditures means that what is labeled health insurance is not really insurance at all.

We could extend this line of reasoning to the U.S. financial system, and its regulation, and identify ways that wrongheaded approaches to collaborative governance contributed to the meltdown of 2008–2009. While different observers allocate blame for the calamity in different directions, we suspect most would agree that the government and the private sector did not have an effective collaborative relationship for managing systemwide risks. Indeed, the relationship was so poorly structured that neither party could even recognize its inadequacy. The view of the meltdown espoused by one author of the present volume is reflected in Richard Zeckhauser, "Causes of the Financial Crisis: Many Responsible Parties," in *New Directions in Financial Services Regulation*, ed. Robert Glauber, Thomas Healey, and Roger Porter (MIT Press, forthcoming).

in the global hierarchy of cultural centers while boosting property values (and tax revenues) in the park's vicinity.

Productivity is a somewhat imprecise concept when art and culture are the outputs. But it is clear that private donors—enabled to shape the products by the terms of their collaboration with the city, and motivated to excellence by linking their reputations to the outcomes—were able to induce performances from Gehry, Kapoor, Plensa, and the networks of other artists, craftsmen, and prosaic gravel, concrete, and HVAC contractors in ways that city procurement officers never could. Private donors, particularly those whose backgrounds and interests made Millennium Park an appealing place to mark their legacies, often had information about and relationships with artists, art, and construction that gave them an edge in getting the work done well.[28] And finally, in Chicago—as in most cities—it would have been politically unacceptable for government to place such priority, and spend so heavily, on world-class art. Even if government had possessed the resources, information, and capacity to produce Millennium Park on its own, and even if stepped-up future tax revenues would have justified the expenditure, it is all but inconceivable that the venture would have been seen as legitimate. For Millennium Park to take shape as it did, rather than as "enhancement on top of the garage," it had to involve private collaborators. Moreover, they had to be endowed with discretion for two reasons: to induce them to give the money, and to get the job done right.

This match between Millennium Park and the motives for collaboration does not on its face prove that this kind of park, delivered this way, was in every way the right answer for Chicago. There were serious glitches, setbacks, and instances of waste in the way the park was designed, funded, and built. And a plausible case, at least with the wisdom of hindsight, can be made that important aspects of the enterprise were fundamentally ill considered. The basic strategy of

---

[28] See Gilfoyle, *Millennium Park*, pp. 278–279, for relevant observations on the Crown family's interaction with Plensa. This practice of marking legacies through public structures was well known in Renaissance Italy. See Jonathan K. Nelson and Richard J. Zeckhauser, *The Patron's Payoff: Conspicuous Commissions and Italian Renaissance Art* (Princeton University Press, 2008).

inducing private collaborators to contribute their capacity and resources by granting them substantial control over their piece of the
park almost guaranteed costly, time-consuming coordination problems. The Pritzker Pavilion and the Bean, for example, turned out to
be so heavy that they would have crushed the parking garage as originally designed. As plans for the artworks and performance spaces
evolved, the garage had to be reworked and retrofitted multiple times
to accommodate the shifting plans for the surface.[29] The disparate
pieces of the park, each representing its own evolving equilibrium of
substantive plans and willingness to pay, did not mesh neatly with
each other, and time lines lengthened. A purely public effort, with one
master monopolizing discretion, might have avoided some of these
problems. But this imagined governmental model for creating Millennium Park would have encountered many of its own characteristic
problems, and on balance we suspect they would have been more
serious in this setting.

For the Millennium Park story as it actually played out, the nastiest
surprise concerned escalating costs. A *Sun-Times* editorial invoked
Cloud Gate as a case in point to question the park's fiscal sense: "If
you had asked us whether $9 million would be enough to build a
giant mirrored bean, we'd have guessed it would be plenty." The sculpture, originally budgeted at $6 million to pay the artist, construct the
piece at an Oakland precision foundry, ship it to Chicago, and assemble and finish it on-site, ultimately cost about $23 million.[30] The
price tag for the Pritzker Pavilion soared even more sharply, from an
initial estimate of around $10 million to an eventual total of around
$60 million.

These were not, for the most part, conventional cost overruns—
increasing payments for an essentially unchanged task, caused by
some combination of corruption, private opportunism, and public
managerial shortfalls. (There was a bit of corruption, to be sure, but
despite their best efforts journalists could never establish that graft
or cronyism explained much of Millennium Park's surge in costs.)[31]

[29] Gilfoyle, *Millennium Park*, pp. 164–165.

[30] "Our Sky High Cloud Gate," *Chicago Sun-Times*, May 27, 2005.

[31] Mike Robinson, "Former Chicago Park Official Pleads to Fraud at Millennium Park," Associated Press State and Local Wire, September 1, 2005.

Rather, the collaborative approach, and the substantial discretion that private players enjoyed, meant that the park ended up being dramatically different from what government originally had in mind. The money was not frittered away, but went to fund highly ambitious, innovative, and correspondingly expensive art, architecture, landscaping, construction, and so on. Overall the cost of the park, exclusive of the parking garage on which it rested, reached about $355 million, or more than an order of magnitude greater than Daley's original budget. The majority of this—about $205 million—came from private donors. But the government's share, $150 million for the park alone, was five times the original estimate of $30 million that Daley had seen as too big a burden for taxpayers, a burden that led him to seek private resources.[32]

The collaborative approach, and its imperative to accommodate private actors' priorities, also led to some sacrifices on dimensions that Chicago's government should and did value. Reinforcements to take the weight of the statues and structures above pared away space in the public parking garage. More parking spaces disappeared to accommodate the electrical and hydraulic infrastructure of the Crown Fountain. And the need to make way for the Harris Theater for Music and Dance, a late addition to the plan, meant losing another three hundred parking spaces. Since the city's share of the investment was financed largely by bonds, to be serviced by parking revenues, the ever shrinking garage—it ended up with just over twenty-one hundred slots—was a serious matter.[33]

The Pritzker family's design priorities meant that seating capacity for the main music pavilion, which the city targeted at thirty thousand to replace an aging public band shell nearby, was reduced to eleven thousand.[34] A controversy erupted when security guards evicted a professional photographer taking pictures of the Bean, and gallery owners were warned to stop selling postcards of Millennium Park structures. Restrictions on commercial use of copyrighted images were well established, and no tourists were arrested for taking snapshots,

[32] Figures are from Herrmann, "$475 Million Millennium Park Set to Open July 16," p. 8.
[33] Gary Washburn, "Garage at Downtown Chicago Park Failing to Pay Its Way," *Chicago Tribune*, January 19, 2005.
[34] Martin and Cohen, "Millennium Park Flounders."

but the control over images of public art grated on some Chicago-ans.[35] There were grumbles that private guards kept the park sealed tight from eleven in the evening to six in the morning, and occasion-ally roped off some facilities for private rentals.

And there are perfectly respectable arguments, from both the right and the left, that Chicago had no business sinking $150 million of public money into a predominantly high-end cultural and arts center, whether or not private resources supplemented public funds. If that money had been left in citizens' hands, they could have saved it, in-vested it, or spent it on something higher in their personal hierarchy of desires than a giant metallic bean or a world-class concert hall. From the other end of the political spectrum, one could lament the fact that government devoted $150 million to artistic frivolities in-stead of putting more police on the streets, better teachers in the classrooms, or even, indeed, more swing sets in the humble public parks in poorer neighborhoods. Both these views strike us, on bal-ance, as reflecting an unduly cramped and timid conception of pub-lic value.

However one judges the final project—and in our view the plausible range runs from polite to exuberant acclaim—it is crucial to recog-nize the central role that Chicago's government played in the creation of Millennium Park. Mayor Daley exercised ultimate authority over every important decision—even when the decision was to cede some authority in exchange for private resources and expertise.[36] Heavy private involvement did not represent an abdication of governmental responsibility. It was the way government chose to exercise its respon-sibility. For those who regret the park as a profligate expenditure to blame private collaborators is no more logical than blaming the bond market when a city borrows beyond its means. And those who simply celebrate the private sector's acumen and generosity risk missing gov-ernment's crucial role in summoning and steering this capacity.

Mayor Daley made a few missteps, as was inevitable with any project of this scale and complexity. The mayor pushed for early com-

---

[35] Kelly Kleiman, "Who Owns Public Art?" *Christian Science Monitor*, March 30, 2005.

[36] Daley's control over all major, and many minor, decisions is discussed in Gilfoyle, *Millennium Park*, p. 351, and in Burqhart, "4 Years Late, Chicago Gets Millennium Park."

pletion, to justify the "millennium" label, long after it was clear that a rushed park would be a costly folly. And he publicly blamed delays on Frank Gehry without bothering to learn that Gehry, perhaps alone among celebrity architects, took pride in staying within budgets and schedules, and had actually delivered designs for his two Millennium Park projects earlier than he had promised. But for the most part Daley was sure-footed in his dealings with the private sector. He had an instinctive sense for when to pay, when to cajole, when to counsel, when to flatter, when to berate, when to sue, and when to trust. Frank Gehry, unusually humble for an architectural star, rose above the slight to declare Daley "the most extraordinary mayor in the world" at a dedication ceremony.[37] Dedication ceremonies, like funerals, tend to inspire hyperbole. But the mayor in any case was very much a leader for his time and place and mission, with a set of skills very different from those that had served his father so well in an earlier version of governance for a simpler and more pliant Chicago.

As we shift our focus upward, and adjust our moods downward, to return to health care as an example of collaboration, let's start by considering the contrast in leadership on the government's side. Mayor Daley was smart, savvy, and tough, neither cynical nor naive about the private players he was dealing with. His subordinates were chosen and shaped to take a similar stance. Nothing analogous shows up when you scan the horizon of health-policy leadership. A few members of Congress—those with appropriate training or long tenures on the relevant committees—are deeply expert in health policy, but most cast their votes on the basis of a casual familiarity with the issues, strong initial prejudices, and a deep solicitude for the interests, representative or not, of their constituents and donors. Perhaps what matters most of all, as we saw with the 2010 PPACA, is adherence to ideological orthodoxy.

In the executive branch, top federal officials, such as the secretary of Health and Human Services, or the administrator of the Centers for Medicare and Medicaid Services, are chosen on some mix of technical qualification and political reliability. Their views about dealing

---

[37] Gilfoyle, *Millennium Park*, p. 174.

with the private sector—to the extent that they have such views at all—
tend to be either instinctive suspicion or open-armed enthusiasm,
depending on the administration,[38] instead of the cold-eyed analytical stance effective collaboration requires. The governmental officials
who *are* specialized in managing the interface between public and
private actors in the health-care system on a day-to-day basis are usually investigators, contract officers, accountants, and a wide range of
other titles for various sorts of cops and clerks. Given how few they
are, and in light of the pay disparities that tend to drain top talent
away from government, and the constraints legislation and regulations place on their activities, these clerks and cops do a reasonably
good—though far from perfect—job of policing clear-cut fraud or
blatant self-dealing. But they are far less effective in stopping, or even
spotting, the perfectly legal but hugely expensive results of private
actors' exercise of payoff and preference discretion.

Similarly, arrangements with private providers are rarely structured to maximize the benefits of production discretion. We don't
blame or belittle government officials for behaving this way; they are
obliged to think like assembly-line workers fitting general rules to
each circumstance, rather than as craftsman applying their expertise
to each concrete situation in order to seize every opportunity to
create public value. We do not blame, but we lament, for American
health care is littered with the damage from poorly managed private
discretion.

Reams of empirical research show a weak link between governmental health-care spending and health outcomes. Indeed, Medicare
patients tend to get the *worst* care in those geographic areas where
government pays private providers the *most*.[39] Instinct calls out to
attribute such patterns to some combination of avarice and incompe-
tence, and we do not deny that troubling duo exists. But we submit
that failure to recognize and manage private discretion is a far larger
problem in American health care. Payoff discretion—shaping collabo-

---

[38] There is no corporate leader among President Obama's top cabinet officers or top officials.
A Republican administration would probably have many.

[39] For the summary of empirical research on Medicare spending cited in this paragraph, we
are indebted to Baicker and Chandra, "Myths and Misconceptions about Health Insurance."

rations to deliver more private and less public benefit—shows up, for example, in the unusually high levels of diagnostic and imaging services in these high-spending, low-results regions. Another manifestation of payoff discretion is "defensive medicine"—tests and procedures that do the patient no good but lower the physician's vulnerability to malpractice claims, and tend to pay doctors well for the effort required. Experts conservatively estimate that such stratagems account for 5.4 percent of total hospital spending.[40] Preference discretion— the imposition of agents' tastes—manifests itself pervasively as a tilt toward specialized services rather than general care in a system that patients find reassuring. And it shows up most poignantly in the surge of intensive, intrusive care that characterizes the final days for so many Americans, a pattern of heroic intervention that often does more to ease physicians' discomfort than that of patients or their families.[41]

But isn't it unfair, many may object, to juxtapose Chicago's joyous cultural showpiece with the notorious intransigence of the American health-care system? One is a walk in the park; the other is life and death. One is a single episode with a circumscribed cast of characters and (relatively speaking) a low-stakes goal. The other is a sprawling skein of tangled threads spanning the political, social, and economic landscape. One was put together as a concentrated effort in a few years. The other is the meandering product of multiple administrations and Congresses over decades.

We do not imply that Millennium Park and American health care pose comparably serious challenges. Nor do we anticipate that even in the improbable best of all possible worlds health-care policy will ever be resolved as elegantly or conclusively as Chicago's effort to do something useful with the old railroad yard. Health policy is a harder problem by many orders of magnitude.[42]

[40] Michelle M. Mello, Amitabh Chandra, Atul A. Gawande, and David M. Studdert, "National Costs of the Medical Liability System," *Health Affairs* 29, no. 9 (September 2010): 5.

[41] One-eighth of the Medicare budget is spent on individuals in the last thirty days of life. See Peter H. Schuck and Richard J. Zeckhauser, *Targeting in Social Programs* (Brookings Institution Press, 2006), p. 61.

[42] It is not just that government, private actors, and the public—in the aggregate, and as individual patients—each have a role to play. As we have seen, this intricate interplay of the three

Pairing these disparate examples as our book approaches its close is nonetheless illuminating. As Millennium Park took shape, government officials understood their roles as the clever application of the lessons of this book—orchestrating, but not fully controlling, the actions of private collaborators wielding substantial discretion. They understood this to be their job, the political environment authorized them to carry it out, and they did it well.

Government officials responsible for health care, by contrast, are objectively challenged to employ such strategies. But their training and enculturation, their political and organizational context, all urge them to believe and to behave as if they are doing something different, and simpler—enforcing contracts, empowering philanthropy, steering clear of the complexity of shared discretion. The tools we permit them are a poor match for the task: pliers, not stethoscopes; hammers, not scalpels. Careful diagnosis and artful trimming are not possible. We threaten these officials with the loss of reputations, positions, and sometimes even liberty if shared discretion leads to honest error, as it frequently does. And we tolerate the mediocre performance and ruinous expense that result from the pretense that health-care policy is a matter of contracts and charity rather than collaboration. We can do better. And we will, once we recognize the nature of the job.

Toward a Better Era of Governance

In every era of its history, America has surprised its skeptics by inventing new ways to solve its problems. America surprises itself, too, fixing its flaws and facing down threats with creativity and flexibility and resourcefulness that it never knew it possessed. Nobody imag-

---

sorts of actors applies to every instance of leverage, successful or not. One reason that health care is especially hard is the requirement that the individual play her role well. Health care involves complexity, uncertainty, and consequences that play out over time, three factors that notoriously bedevil people's efforts to make good choices in their purchase of insurance or their consumption of health care. Jeffrey Liebman and Richard Zeckhauser, "Simple Humans, Complex Insurance, Subtle Subsidies," in *Using Taxes to Reform Health Insurance: Pitfalls and Promises*, ed. Henry J. Aaron and Leonard E. Burman, (Brookings Institution Press, 2008), pp. 230–252.

ined in the 1780s that a squabbling handful of breakaway British colonies could forge a new form of government that would bind them together—and inspire reformers around the globe—for centuries. Nobody imagined, as the 1940s dawned, that an isolated, adolescent nation would make such a decisive difference in winning a global war, still less that it would reshape the world by the way it led the peace. Nobody imagined in the 1960s that a country so long divided by race would purge discrimination from its law books in a few tumultuous years, or make such progress scrubbing racism from its heart and soul in just a generation or two. Surprising solutions are America's strong suit.

We cannot count on governmental institutions to possess the knowledge and the resources needed to get the public's work done. And we cannot simply wait for citizens and businesses and nonprofits to take up the burdens that government shrugs off. Neither can we just turn the public's business and the public's money over to private contractors with the hope that they decide to do the right thing.

Fortunately, the solutions of the past don't exhaust the options for the future. In statehouses and city halls, board rooms and living rooms throughout the country, new forms of collaboration are taking shape. Echoing time-honored American instincts of pragmatism and partnership, the kinds of innovation described in this book point the way forward. Collaborative governance harnesses all of America's capacity—public and private, for-profit and nonprofit, employee and volunteer—to the pursuit of the common good. And it unleashes the unpredictable resourcefulness of an entrepreneurial people to improvise fresh, flexible solutions. It encourages private engagement in public missions, and is optimistic—but not naive—about the potential for sharing responsibility while ensuring accountability. Unlike calls to cede public missions entirely to nonprofits, or to count on socially responsible corporations to attend to our common interests, it maintains a key role for public institutions that must answer to the electorate. Within this framework, it also recognizes that private institutions, both for-profit and nonprofit, will and should have significant degrees of discretion as they operate in areas that have been traditional preserves of government.

Collaborative governance has spread across the American land-scape. It is employed to produce public value at every level, from small tasks for small communities to major undertakings for the largest federal agencies. Successful collaboration requires that its methods and motivations be understood both by government officials and by their private counterparts. Understanding alone, though, will not be enough. Good governance, when discretion is divided, will require a substantial shift in the skills and capacities needed within govern-ment itself. It is a shift, not merely a supplement. Managing bureau-cracy will fall in the hierarchy of key governance skills. Knowing how to pick the right collaborators and orchestrate the creation of public value from diverse kinds of actors will become much more impor-tant. This kind of public management will require a sophisticated un-derstanding in areas such as contracting, negotiation, finance, arm's-length motivation, and the monitoring and assessment of results. If public officials are to efficiently and accountably represent the interests of the citizenry within networks of collaboration, they must assimi-late a skill set that empowers them to:

- Determine when delegation to the private sector of a particu-lar function has the potential to enhance value. That determi-nation must start with a realistic assessment of government capabilities.

- Discriminate among potential collaborators according to how they are likely to employ any discretion granted, and how pro-ductive they will be in producing public value.

- Estimate the balance between value gained and value lost as discretion is relinquished to the private sector for a particular task.

- Appreciate the objectives, constraints, and internal dynamics of potential collaborators in sufficient detail to predict the gains from production discretion and the degree and nature of risks associated with payoff and preference discretion.

- Structure, implement, and uphold a relationship that loosely constrains productive discretion and tightly constrains payoff and preference discretion.

- Evaluate the net public benefits from conducting different levels and variants of an undertaking.

- Manage the collaboration effectively even when, as will frequently be the case, the private parties in the collaboration outmatch the public parties in terms of resources, political influence, and popular esteem.

- Revise and reform arrangements when, as is inevitable, even thoughtfully conceived structures fall short of their potential.

We do not mean to imply that government officials must be confident of performing all of these tasks perfectly before contemplating a collaborative arrangement. It is relative performance that counts, and the parallel requirements of public management for direct governmental action, after all, are seldom realized in full. Early efforts should be valued in part for the skills learned, not merely their immediate outcome. We expect agencies to improve their results as their experience grows, and to learn from one another.

Orchestrating collaborative arrangements calls upon skills that are frequently found among corporate executives, venture capitalists, and senior consultants, but much less commonly among frontline public managers. Governments are not currently accustomed to selecting, compensating, or evaluating their employees on the basis of such competencies. The requisite skill set is predominantly conceptual, having relatively little to do with classic public administration and a great deal to do with economics, institutional analysis, game theory, decision analysis, and other relatively advanced tools for predicting and influencing outcomes.

The need for conceptual sophistication, moreover, applies at the level of implementation (not just policy making), and continuously (not just at the outset of an initiative). When the menu of implementation models was short and simple, government could get by with a small pool of analytical talent near the top. Specialized thinkers in policy shops or academia would reveal the right answer to top decision-makers, who would accept the solon's guidance, insofar as political realities allowed, and the faceless minions below would put the policy it into effect. A growing role for collaborative governance —while a promising prospect on many dimensions—undeniably confronts the public sector with the need for analytical capacity that is fine-grained, durable, and widely and deeply distributed through government.

It would be foolish to underestimate the magnitude of the recruiting, training, and retention challenge the widespread use of collaboration poses for government. Yet a reform model that challenges us most on the scales of creativity and talent is one that plays, ultimately, to this nation's historical strong suit. As Americans organize themselves to create value in new ways—without preconceptions about public and private roles, with open minds about what might work and open eyes to the evidence—they will be once again, as they have always been, inventing the future.

◇◇◇

ACKNOWLEDGMENTS

◇◇◇

Many colleagues offered insightful comments on the draft manuscript or its precursor essays and cases. Robert Behn, David Ellwood, Archon Fung, Tony Gomez-Ibanez, John Haigh, Steve Kelman, Mark Moore, Malcolm Sparrow, and Julie Wilson deserve particular mention. We have also benefited from innumerable interactions with participants in various seminar series and other forums at Harvard and well beyond, including the University of Pennsylvania, Real Colegio Madrid, Bocconi Business School, the Dubai School of Government, the Knowledge Forum in Korea, and Tsinghua University. The University of Barcelona, and in particular Germa Bel, provided a congenial sabbatical locale that accelerated work on several chapters. Stephen Breyer not only taught us much—in person and in print—about the relationship between the public and private sectors, but he graciously offered his thoughtful foreword.

We acknowledge the invaluable contributions of many able research assistants who chased down studies, data, and cases and prepared figures and tables that enrich our book, including Eric Driggs, Jason Elliot, Vicky Ge, Esther Krofah, Ben Reno-Weber, Ashin Shah, Semil Shah, Jon Swan, and Nils Wernerfelt. Peter Zhang gets the "Where's Waldo?" award for his resourceful pursuit, from a remote location outside Shanghai, of the endless facts we needed checked out as the book neared completion. Patricia Garcia-Rios, Kirsten Lundberg, Susan Rosegrant, Esther Scott, and Pamela Varley contributed to case studies that inform several of the book's examples.

Douglas Sease skillfully helped shape prior drafts to sharpen the message and overcome our academic inclinations toward complexity and abstraction. Peter Dougherty performed splendidly as our on-call editor, despite the occasional distractions of his job running Princeton University Press. Lauren Lepow copyedited the manuscript with a deft and steady hand, and Lorraine Doneker produced our arresting cover image. Wendy Wyatt and Erica Jaffe-Redner, our longtime assistants, kept the entire enterprise from going off the rails many a time. We thank our families for cheerfully enduring and lovingly supporting our long-standing collaboration on collaborative governance. While this book was in progress, each of our families saw rather more of the coauthor and less of their own spouse and father than in normal times, but neither seems worse for the swap.

Our greatest debt is to Frank Weil, who (with his razor-sharp spouse and collaborator Denie) launched this project and supported it over many years with his ideas, his philanthropy, and his boundless energy and enthusiasm. We hope this product helps in some small way to realize his dreams for the potential for collaborative governance to promote the common good.

John D. Donahue
Richard J. Zeckhauser

Cambridge, 2010

INDEX